PROUST'S ENGLISH

The 'jolies yachtswomen': manuscript addition to the corrected proofs of *À l'ombre des jeunes filles en fleurs* (Bibliothèque Nationale, Rés. M. Y2 824, fo. 381). See pp. 152–3.

Proust's
English

DANIEL KARLIN

OXFORD

UNIVERSITY PRESS

OXFORD
UNIVERSITY PRESS

Great Clarendon Street, Oxford OX2 6DP

Oxford University Press is a department of the University of Oxford.
It furthers the University's objective of excellence in research, scholarship,
and education by publishing worldwide in

Oxford New York

Auckland Cape Town Dar es Salaam Hong Kong Karachi
Kuala Lumpur Madrid Melbourne Mexico City Nairobi
New Delhi Shanghai Taipei Toronto

With offices in

Argentina Austria Brazil Chile Czech Republic France Greece
Guatemala Hungary Italy Japan Poland Portugal Singapore
South Korea Switzerland Thailand Turkey Ukraine Vietnam

Oxford is a registered trade mark of Oxford University Press
in the UK and in certain other countries

Published in the United States
by Oxford University Press Inc., New York

© Daniel Karlin 2005

The moral rights of the author have been asserted
Database right Oxford University Press (maker)

First published 2005

British Library Cataloguing in Publication Data

Data available

Library of Congress Cataloging in Publication Data

Karlin, Daniel, 1953–
Proust's English/Daniel Karlin.
p. cm.
Text is in English and French.
Includes index.
ISBN 0–19–925688–8 (alk. paper)

1. Proust, Marcel, 1871–1922—Language.   2. French language—Foreign
words and phrases—English.   3. England—In literature.   I. Title.
PQ2631.R63Z64745 2005   843′.912—dc22   2005019763

Typeset by Newgen Imaging Systems (P) Ltd., Chennai, India
Printed in Great Britain
on acid-free paper by
Biddles Ltd., King's Lynn, Norfolk

ISBN 0–19–925688–8   978–0–19–925688–4

In memory of my mother

Miriam Stahl
Miriam Karlin
Miriam Henderson

2 October 1931–9 October 2003

Acknowledgements

A paper given to the graduate seminar at the English Department of the University of Sheffield helped me start the writing of this book. Emily Eells, of the University of Paris, Nanterre, made several helpful suggestions for my research and identified the manuscript which forms the front-ispiece; I greatly benefited from reading her book, *Proust's Cup of Tea*. Dr Angus Wrenn, then at King's College London, gave me valuable advice about literary *anglomanie*.

I first read Proust twenty-five years ago, in the summer before starting my academic career as a lecturer in the Department of English at University College London—thinking, perhaps, that I would never get another chance. I was fortunately mistaken in that, and more fortunate still in the intellectual companionship, good will, and affection of my colleagues and students. 'Que ce qui vient de l'enseignement, à bon droit y retourne'; 'May that which comes from teaching, return to it as of right': the words are Mallarmé's, in *Les Mots anglais*, and express my hope for this book as for all my work.

One word more, for Samantha Matthews: 'Where the heart lies, let the brain lie also.'

Contents

List of Illustrations

The publisher and the author apologize for any errors or omissions in the above list. If contacted, they will be pleased to rectify these at the earliest opportunity.

Note on Texts and Translations

The text of *À la recherche du temps perdu* is that of the most recent Gallimard/*NRF* edition in the Bibliothèque de la Pléiade, published in four volumes in 1987–9; for details see the List of Works Cited. The text of the translation is that of C. K. Scott Moncrieff and Terence Kilmartin, revised by D. J. Enright, *In Search of Lost Time*, in six volumes (Penguin, 1992, now published by Vintage).

I refer to the sixth volume of *À la recherche du temps perdu* as *Albertine disparue*, following the *Pléiade* edition; the English version uses the alternative title, *The Fugitive* (*La Fugitive*).

Quotations from *A la recherche* are followed by the translation in square brackets; reference is then given to the volume and page number of both texts, separated by a semicolon, as in: 'Longtemps, je me couchais de bonne heure' [For a long time, I used to go to bed early] (I, 3; I, 3). Occasionally I have left a brief phrase untranslated where it seemed overly fussy to translate it; most readers won't need to be told that 'la majesté shakespearienne d'un roi Lear' means 'the Shakespearean majesty of a King Lear' (IV, 438; VI, 208) or that 'chevalier de la Légion d'honneur' means 'Chevalier of the Legion of Honour' (III, 111; IV, 130). Even so, I have erred on the side of fussiness.

My choice of translation does not constitute a judgement of value, though I have not had time fully to compare the Scott Moncrieff–Kilmartin–Enright version with the new Penguin translation which appeared in six volumes in 2002 (general editor Christopher Prendergast). Any translation, for a book such as this which is concerned with the interaction of English and French in Proust's French text, is going to pose problems. *Vintage* is not consistent in 'marking' English words, even when they are marked in French ('magazine' for example, is in quotation marks in the French text at II, 746, but unmarked in *Vintage* at III, 524; many unmarked words which nevertheless stand out as English in the French text become indistinguishable in English (*bluff, bridge, clown*, etc.); others, such as *wagon*, disappear entirely, since this word is only used in French in railway terminology, and is therefore always translated as 'carriage' or 'compartment'. But though the more modern version might be more accurate, my first impressions of it are that it also strives to be more colloquial, to give more English equivalents of French idioms, and that would raise difficulties in another direction. I might have done the translations myself; but it seemed right to use a published translation so that English readers would have a standard text for reference. The Scott Moncrieff–Kilmartin–Enright version has the advantage of having been longer in the field: it is still, probably, the version which most English readers know, and which many of them own, and I have chosen it on that basis.

Unless otherwise specified, all other translations, whether from Proust's other works or from other French texts, are my own. I have not avoided a felicitous phrase when I stumbled across one, but my principal aim has been accuracy and clarity. Failure is inevitable on both counts; all the translator can hope for is that it occurs in a low ratio to adequacy. I would make a special plea for tolerance in my attempts at Mallarmé.

References

Abbreviated titles used for editions of Proust's works, including his translations of Ruskin and correspondence, are listed in the Abbreviations; for fuller publication details in each case, see the List of Works Cited. For books or articles which are only cited once, I give publication details and page references in the notes; page references to frequently cited works are given in the main text, and publication details in the List of Works Cited. Such works are identifiable by author's name, with the exception of Harrap and Le Robert, two dictionaries which are cited by the name of their publisher. The short title 'Tadié' refers to Tadié's biography of Proust, not to his general editorship of the Pléiade edition of *A la Recherche*, for which the short title Pléiade is used.

Spelling and punctuation

French uses lower case for aristocratic titles ('duchesse de Guermantes', 'princesse de Parme') and for street names ('rue La Pérouse', 'faubourg Saint-Germain'); I have followed this convention in my own references, though I have respected the use of upper case in translated passages. At the risk of offending those who know, may I point out that the holders of aristocratic titles in France are also referred to as 'M. de——' or 'Mme de——', so that the 'duchesse de Guermantes' is often 'Mme de Guermantes', etc.

Book titles are also given in their French form: *À la recherche du temps perdu*, not *À la Recherche du Temps Perdu*.

Names

I refer to Marcel Proust, the author, as 'Proust', and to the character who narrates *A la recherche* as 'Marcel'; I believe this is a workable distinction, but where it is problematic I have said so.

For Proust, as for many French people then as now, 'l'Angleterre' was a generic term, covering 'Britain' as much as 'England'; characters during the Great War refer to the actions or national character of 'l'Angleterre', for example (IV, 321, 355). The same goes for the proper noun 'Anglais, Anglaise' (English/British person) and the adjective 'anglais, anglaise'. Proust only uses 'Grande Bretagne once (IV, 211), and 'britannique' a few times (I, 218, II, 232, III, 747). In my own writing I have used 'England' and 'English' throughout.

The term *faubourg Saint-Germain*, in Proust's time, referred by metonymy to the most exclusive aristocratic society in Paris. The literal faubourg Saint-Germain, on the left bank of the Seine, was a centre of aristocratic society in Paris in the seventeenth and eighteenth centuries, and again in the first decades of the nineteenth century when the aristocrats who had gone into exile after the Revolution returned (*Oxford Companion to French Literature*, ed. Sir Paul Harvey and J. E. Heseltine, corr. edn. 1969).

Abbreviations

A la recherche	*À la recherche du temps perdu*
BA	*La Bible d'Amiens*
Bonnaffé	*Dictionnaire étymologique et historique des anglicismes*
Corr.	*Correspondance*
CSB	*Contre Sainte-Beuve* (Pléiade edition)
Écrits	*Écrits sur l'art*
Harrap	J. E. Mansion (gen. ed.), *Harrap's Standard French and English Dictionary*
JS	*Jean Santeuil* (Pléiade edition)
Le Robert	Alain Rey (gen. ed.), *Dictionnaire historique de la langue française*
Pléiade	*A la recherche du temps perdu* (Pléiade edition)
SL	*Sésame et les lys*
Vintage	*In Search of Lost Time* (Vintage edition)

Introduction

On seeing the title 'Proust's English', readers may be tempted to respond, as one of my colleagues did, by remarking: 'No, he's not.' And of course he isn't. And yet . . . At the seaside resort of Cabourg, in Normandy, in the summer of 1911, Proust wrote to his friend, the art dealer and collector René Gimpel:

Je vous verrai quand mon livre sera fini mais quand le sera-t-il? Je meurs d'asthme ici cette année. Je me lève un jour sur quatre et descends ce jour-là dicter quelques pages à une dactylographe. Comme elle ne sait pas le français et moi pas l'anglais mon roman se trouve écrit dans une langue intermédiaire à laquelle je compte que vous trouverez de la saveur quand vous recevrez le volume. (*Corr.* X, 320–1)[1]

[I shall see you when my book is finished but when will that be? I'm dying of asthma here this year. I get up one day in four, and on that day come downstairs to dictate a few pages to a stenographer. As she doesn't know French and I don't know English, my novel is being written in an intermediate language which I trust you will savour when you receive the volume.]

Proust exaggerates, of course; he wasn't really dying, and *À la recherche du temps perdu* isn't written in Franglais. Nevertheless his joke about the novel's *langue intermédiaire* suggests a profound truth—as, indeed, does the joke about his illness. This book is about the 'intermediate language' of *A la recherche*: the presence in it of English words and phrases, the 'Englishness' of its social and artistic worlds, and the larger theme of mixed or impure language—the language which Proust is confident that his friend will 'savour'.

I trace the origin of my own book to one such savoury moment—a small one in the novel, but which still gives me intense pleasure. It occurs

---

[1] The stenographer's name was Cecilia Hayward; she was retained by the Grand Hotel. Painter (II, 172) accepts the dictation story; Tadié (p. 557) says that in fact Proust dictated most of the pages to his secretary Albert Nahmias in his room, and that Miss Hayward then typed them. She certainly typed the first 700 or so pages of the novel, first at Cabourg and later in Paris. See also Philip Kolb's introduction to vol. X of *Correspondance*, pp. xxix–xxx. It is entirely in keeping with the 'Englishness' of the Grand Hotel at Cabourg that Proust should have come across Miss Hayward there, as I explain in Chapter 3. She annoyed Proust, to her immortal English credit, by refusing to work at weekends.

at the end of a grand dinner Marcel attends, where among other aristocratic figures he has been introduced to the princesse de Parme. Marcel is on his way out:

Dans le vestibule où je demandai à un valet de pied mes snow-boots que j'avais pris par précaution contre la neige, dont il était tombé quelques flocons vite changés en boue, ne me rendant pas compte que c'était peu élégant, j'éprouvai, du sourire dédaigneux de tous, une honte qui atteignit son plus haut degré quand je vis que Mme de Parme n'était pas partie et me voyait chaussant mes caoutchoucs américains. La princesse revint vers moi. "Oh! quelle bonne idée, s'écria-t-elle, comme c'est pratique! voilà un homme intelligent. Madame, il faudra que nous achetions cela", dit-elle à sa dame d'honneur, tandis que l'ironie des valets se changeait en respect et que les invités s'empressaient autour de moi pour s'enquérir où j'avais pu trouver ces merveilles.

[In the hall where I asked a footman for my snowboots, which I had brought, not realising how unfashionable they were, as a precaution against the snow, a few flakes of which had already fallen, to be converted rapidly into slush, I felt, in the contemptuous smiles on all sides, a shame which rose to its highest pitch when I saw that Mme de Parme had not yet gone and was watching me put on my American "rubbers." The Princess came towards me. "Oh! what a good idea," she exclaimed, "it's so practical! There's a sensible man for you. Madame, we shall have to get a pair of those," she said to her lady-in-waiting, while the mockery of the footmen turned to respect and the other guests crowded round me to inquire where I had managed to find these marvels.]

(II, 835; III, 632)[2]

What is it about the word *snow-boots* which makes it stand out here, and which gives the passage its 'savour'? The word was very recent in French (first recorded in 1893) and belongs to a large group of English words which the French language borrowed for the new products, technologies, and social practices of the nineteenth century. Many more of these occur in *A la recherche*, from *les films* to *les cocktails*, from *le revolver* to *le golf.* Yet, as we shall see, Proust's use of such words was almost never dictated by necessity; if he had wanted to avoid the word *snow-boots* here he could easily have done so, as the phrase 'caoutchoucs américains' demonstrates. He

---

[2] *Vintage* has 'I asked the footmen'. Further on, 'American rubbers' is perfectly correct, and is found also in Mark Treharne's recent version (*The Guermantes Way* (Penguin, 2002), 546), but the modern American slang sense of 'rubber' as a contraceptive sheath is hard to put aside, and I would suggest 'galoshes'. Translation really is the devil, and the devil has a coarse sense of humour.

chose it, I think, because it made a small but distinct contribution to the theme of snobbery and social embarrassment which is being developed in this episode. The shame that Marcel feels at his footwear *faux pas* is transposed to the word itself; is it an accident that it contains within it the word *snob*, itself one of the English keywords of *A la recherche*?[3] Proust's scrutiny of individual words, both French and English, was detailed and passionate enough to make this *sous-entendu* possible. At any rate, this is not the first time that an English word pops up in a context of social awkwardness.

I think it was the pleasure I took in Marcel's *snow-boots* which prompted me, some ten or fifteen years ago, to start collecting the English words and phrases in *A la recherche*. Long after I had made my own list, I came across Étienne Brunet's *Le Vocabulaire de Proust*, a concordance and detailed bibliometric study which analyses Proust's vocabulary in the context of other literary works in the electronic corpus held at Nancy, the 'TLF' (*Trésor de la langue française*). Fascinating though Brunet's work is, however, it has some gaps in its coverage of foreign words. Few single words slip through the net, though even here Brunet misses *babys, darling, fast, liftman, patronizing, pianola, pushing, season, waters*, and *yes*; but phrases and hyphenated words are not recorded at all, so that, for example, *a cup of tea, cold cream, fair play, fishing for compliments, five o'clock tea, garden-party, hansom cab, good morning, good evening*, and *good bye* are all missing, not to mention *my dear, my love*, and *the right man in the right place*.[4] One of the aims of this book is therefore to present a fuller list and location map of identifiable English words and phrases in *A la recherche*, all of which, whether discussed in the main text or not, are given in the Appendix.

---

[3] I owe this observation to Samantha Matthews, who added that the effect would be accentuated by pronouncing both *snob* and *snow-boots* like Inspector Clouseau. For *snob* and *snobisme*, see Ch.1.

[4] Brunet's errors of omission are compounded by misleading inclusions, where a word whose orthography is the same in French and English is recorded as French even though its actual meaning in the text is English. Thus, although the phrase 'fishing for compliments' is not recorded, two of its words, 'for' and 'compliments', are recorded individually as though they were French words, alongside real occurrences such as 'dans mon for intérieur' 'in my heart of hearts', I, 586 (II, 198). The same goes for 'place' in 'the right man in the right place', 'parties' (imperfect tense, feminine plural, of the verb *partir*) in 'garden-parties', and 'chairs' (plural of 'chair', flesh) in 'rocking-chairs'. Such errors are evidently the result of not checking the computer-generated lists against the text as a semantic field; it is less easy to account for the fact that, in the phrase 'cold cream', the second word should be recorded individually but not the first.

I say 'fuller', and not 'comprehensive', both because my own list may well be incomplete, and because there is a difficulty in actually deciding what constitutes an 'English' word in the first place. Take the word 'redingote' (a frock-coat), which sounds perfectly French, and indeed is French—I'm confident that no modern French reader coming across it in a nineteenth-century French novel would think twice about it. Yet *redingote* is a corruption of the English 'riding-coat', first recorded in its francisized form in 1725. When it first appeared it elicited howls of protest, as did another word for a similar garment, *frac*, from 'frock-coat', which later came to designate what we now call 'tails'. The English word 'frock' itself derives from an older French word, *froc*, meaning a monk's habit, hence the priestly function itself; this sense survives in English where we still speak of an 'unfrocked' clergyman. Defenders of the French language especially resented such 'reimportations', which are one aspect of the continuing traffic between French and English which makes the origin and 'nationality' of many words so hard to determine. Volume I of Fraser Mackenzie's historical survey, *Les Relations de l'Angleterre et de la France d'après le vocabulaire* (1939), combatively subtitled *Les Infiltrations de la langue et de l'esprit anglais*, make clear that English (in the form of Anglo-Saxon) had been 'infiltrating' French from before the Norman Conquest, and that the current of fashion which many English readers believe sets so strongly in the direction of Paris feels very different on the other side of the Channel. A host of words which look and sound French, which are in fact naturalized to the point of invisibility, turn out to have English antecedents, sometimes relatively recent ones—among them, for example, the word *train* (in the railway sense) which dates to the 1840s. No one, surely, would expect to see this word in a list of 'English' words in *A la recherche*; but what about *album, clown, hall, jury, stock*, and *tennis*?

The problem in the specific case of *A la recherche* is compounded by historical change. Like the scarlet threads in an old tapestry, the colour of some of Proust's English words has faded with time. What stood out as unusual, or at any rate 'marked', for a French reader of *Du côté de chez Swann* when it was first published in 1913, might not do so today—sporting terms especially, perhaps (*football, golf, match, record, skating*), but also terms from social life (*lunch, sandwich, pudding, toast*). Contemporary reference works such as Édouard Bonnaffé's *Dictionnaire étymologique et historique des anglicismes*, published during Proust's lifetime, in 1920, offer some help here; I have used Bonnaffé as a guide—though not an infallible one—as to the degree of 'Englishness' which attaches to Proust's use of words such as *interview*, *meeting*, or *speech*.

My judgement in this area has been influenced by the relatively high number of unequivocal English words and phrases in *A la recherche*. English is, beyond question, the 'second language' of the novel; it outstrips all the other ancient and modern languages combined (principally Latin, Italian, and German, in that order); Proust's linguistic, like his literary countenance, was turned towards England.[5] My first chapter explores the paradox by which this writer who never travelled to England, never learned English, and confessed his inability either to speak the language or understand it when it was spoken, nevertheless not only translated two books by Ruskin but filled his novel with English words. Proust's strange intimacy with English is the product of a personal history, but also of a wider social history whose keyword is *anglomanie*, the craze for Englishness in politics, social life, and the arts, which has affected (or afflicted) France since the mid-eighteenth century, and which was in a particularly virulent phase in Proust's lifetime. The fashion for English manners, dress, furniture—for everything we now call by the term 'lifestyle'—included a fashion for English words—for *le gentleman*, who might suffer the agonies of *spleen* in *le Jockey-Club*, or even in his comfortable *home*; for the *lady-like* duchess who might return from *une garden-party* at the height of *la season*, rueing the presence of so many *snobs* and wishing that her husband didn't look so ungainly in his *smoking*, before going upstairs for a relaxing *tub*. *Good-night, my love!*[6]

The connection of *anglomanie* to 'high society'—or the aspiration to belong to it—will be evident from these examples; it forces itself on the attention of readers of *A la recherche* through the figure of Odette de Crécy, the mistress and later the wife of Charles Swann—Odette with her proliferation of English phrases (most of the ones in the list on p. 3 are hers—*a cup of tea*, *fair play*, *fishing for compliments*, etc.)—and her love of English social rituals such as *le five o'clock tea* and *le lunch*, to the point where the French Noël has been replaced in her house by the English *Christmas*. But the relationship between Odette and Swann, the focus of

[5] See Ch. 1, p. 27, for his letter to Robert de Billy expressing a preference for English literature over every other, even on occasion French.

[6] All these words and phrases are in *A la recherche*, though I have used some of them in slightly different contexts. *Smoking* is an abbreviation of *smoking-jacket*, incorrectly used to denote evening dress.

the second chapter, is inflected by Englishness in a far deeper and more significant way, one which begins to suggest the architectonic power of this theme in the novel, and which is as much to do with the exquisitely polished, artistically minded Swann, with his membership of *le Jockey* and his friendship with the Prince of Wales, as with the vulgar, ignorant Odette. Through Odette's love for orchids, particularly the cattleya, and through Swann's sexual identification of her with this flower, we can begin to grasp the complex network in which English words mediate both desire and loss in the novel; the significance of this theme becomes clear when we realize that both Swann and Odette, in different ways, trace their nature to an *origine anglaise*.

The 'sign' of Englishness, like so much else in the novel, is a double one, its Janus face turned towards vanity and spiritual death, but also towards the salvation of art. My third chapter explores this doubleness in the setting of Normandy, where, at the seaside resort of Balbec, Marcel will meet the great painter Elstir, one of the presiding artistic geniuses of the novel; but he will also learn that Elstir was one of the familiar faces in the Verdurins' salon where Swann and Odette's liaison first flourished, where he was known as 'M. Biche' and played the role of a dissolute buffoon. Elstir's magnificent portrait of Odette as 'Miss Sacripant' links the 'English' world of the *demi-monde* to that of Balbec; for the whole resort, and especially its main attraction, the Grand Hotel, is suffused with Englishness, from the chatter of *le lift* to the appearance of Robert de Saint-Loup, whose allure is that of a supremely elegant *sportsman*. Balbec is based on Cabourg, which Proust knew well; he himself had stayed at its Grand Hotel, had accompanied friends around a golf course and been taken to a polo match. At Balbec, English sports and amusements fill the days of the *jeunes filles en fleurs*, the young girls in flower among whom Marcel will find his great love, Albertine; he has come to Balbec in search of Gothic churches and tempestuous seas, but finds *le tennis* and *le yachting*; yet these very emblems of vulgar modernity, which he despises on aesthetic grounds, are, it turns out, the material of Elstir's transcendent canvases. Elstir shows Marcel that *le yachting* is a source of poetry, not vulgarity; and in redeeming the thing, he goes some way also towards redeeming the word. As for Albertine herself, her first appearance in the novel, before Marcel actually meets her in Balbec, is signalled by an English word, delivered by Odette's anglophile daughter, Gilberte Swann, who says of her: 'Elle sera sûrement très "fast", mais en attendant elle a une drôle de touche' [She's certain to be dreadfully "fast" when she's older, but meanwhile she's an odd fish] (I, 503; II, 98). The Pléiade editors note that *fast* in this context implies a *fashionable* freedom of behaviour; Gilberte is predicting not simply that Albertine will be loose-living, but that she will be so in a smart set. The use of an English slang term is entirely apt for Odette's daughter; yet as so often in *A la recherche* a character is made to speak more than they know. Gilberte might not intend the meaning of *fast* as 'rapid, swift', but Proust does. The vulgar word prefigures, in its earlier sense, Albertine's association with speed, fleeing along the roads around Balbec on her bicycle, eluding Marcel's desire, finally eluding him in death. By the end, this 'être de fuite' [creature of flight], as Marcel calls her, emblem of the passage of time, has fulfilled Gilberte's unconscious oracle.[7]

The example of *fast* suggests that the presence of the English language in *A la recherche* has more than a thematic significance; it is also a reflexive sign of the novel's preoccupation with language itself. *Anglomanie* has never had things all its own way in France, whether in Proust's day or ours; it stimulated fierce hostility, nowhere more so than in the linguistic domain, where resistance to the 'invasion' of English words was conducted with nationalistic fervour. Defenders of the 'purity' of the French language found themselves confronted, however, not just by the inexorability of change, the tide of popular usage which makes a mockery of prescriptive regulation, but by a fundamental paradox in their own position. Historical philology suggested that the concept of a 'pure' language was profoundly flawed; all languages are mixed; words such as 'degeneration', 'corruption', and 'deformation' lose their moral force when applied to the process of linguistic change, becoming modes of creation and renewal. Proust's novel could not be written in an 'unmixed' language; purity is associated in the novel not with creation but with sterility, in the beautiful old French, for example, spoken by the childless Mme de Guermantes. My fourth chapter stages a kind of debate between writers and critics such as Remy de Gourmont, who protested against English and all its works, and others such as the poet (and teacher of English) Stéphane Mallarmé, whose treatise *Les Mots anglais* (1877) has a powerful affinity with Proust's aesthetic. Mallarmé makes the philologist's, but also the poet's, case for

---

[7] For these 'êtres de fuite' to whose class Albertine belongs, see III, 600; *Vintage* renders the phrase as 'fugitive beings' (V, 98).

language as necessarily mixed and cross-bred; his analysis of English as an 'idiome composite' speaks directly to *A la recherche*; more important even than this, he suggests a potent reason for Marcel's fascination with etymology, which occupies whole swathes of the novel's later volumes and seems, at first sight, such an odd distraction from the business of social comedy or sexual tragedy. The connection between etymology and 'involuntary' memory, the mainspring of the novel's creative impulse, forms the culminating point of the argument and the book.

When all is said and done, however, I come back to the 'savour' of words such as *snow-boots* and *yachtswomen*, *great event* and *revolving door*. When I think of the English words of *A la recherche*, it is these I see in my mind's eye, along with the flying angels in Giotto's frescos in the Arena Chapel in Padua, like aeroplane pilots 'executant des *loopings*'. I hope the reader, too, will share this pleasure, for the 'savour' of Proust's words is as vital to the novel as the little patch of yellow wall which Bergotte sees, before his death, in Vermeer's *View of Delft*.

1

Proust's English World

Anglomanie

Poor Odette! She is in a muddle about the titles of the French royal family.

Si quelqu'un disait: "le prince" en parlant du duc de Chartres, elle rectifiait: "Le duc, il est duc de Chartres et non prince." Pour le duc d'Orléans, fils du comte de Paris: "C'est drôle, le fils est plus que le père", tout en ajoutant comme elle était anglomane: "On s'y embrouille dans ces 'Royalties' . . ."

[Were anyone to say "the Prince," in speaking of the Duc de Chartres, she would put him right: "The Duke, you mean; he's Duc de Chartres, not Prince." As for the Duc d'Orléans, son of the Comte de Paris: "That's funny; the son is higher than the father!" she would remark, adding, for she was afflicted with Anglomania, "Those *Royalties* are so dreadfully confusing!"]

(I, 510; II, 106)[1]

Readers of Proust can call on the *Pléiade* editors for help. Briefly (!) the duc de Chartres has the right to be called 'prince' because he is a member of the French royal family; he is the younger brother of the exiled pretender to the French throne, who uses the courtesy title of 'comte de Paris' (as Queen Victoria, not in exile but on holiday in the Riviera, called herself Countess of Balmoral). The son of the comte de Paris has the title of

---

[1] Odette transposes the word into French when she introduces Marcel to the princesse Mathilde (see.n. 3): ' "Vous devriez aller écrire votre nom chez elle, un jour de cette semaine, me dit Mme Swann; on ne corne pas de bristol à toutes ces *royautés*, comme disent les Anglais, mais elle vous invitera si vous vous faites inscrire" ' ["You should go and write your name in her book one day this week," Mme Swann counselled me. "One doesn't leave cards upon these 'Royalties,' as the English call them, but she will invite you to her house if you put your name down"] (I, 534; II 136). 'Corner le bristol' is a vulgarism for leaving one's visiting card (with one edge turned down); 'le bristol' comes from the English 'Bristol-board', a smooth pasteboard used in the manufacture of such cards; Bonnaffé dates it to 1836.

duc d'Orléans, but his 'real' rank is of course below that of his father. But why should Odette interest herself in 'ces "Royalties" ' in the first place, and what has her being *anglomane* to do with it?

The answer to the first question springs from the social position of Odette's husband, Charles Swann. Odette is a former courtesan—a high-class one, a *grande cocotte*—who has married one of the most admired men of Parisian high society, the *faubourg Saint-Germain*; and Swann's circle is intimate with both the French and the English royal families. Almost the first thing we are told about Swann in the novel (long before we meet Odette) is that he is an 'ami préféré du comte de Paris et du prince de Galles' [a particular friend of the Comte de Paris and of the Prince of Wales] (I, 15; I, 16); Swann himself cherishes the thought that if he were suddenly to be taken ill, one of the people whom his manservant would summon to his side would be the duc de Chartres (I, 305; I, 374). Swann's closest friends in the *faubourg Saint-Germain* belong to the aristocratic Guermantes family, and they, too, know the Prince of Wales, both before and after his accession as Edward VII; Mme de Guermantes has occasion to defend the King's character, and by extension the political alliance between France and England, in a dinner-table argument with a German prince (II, 816–17; III, 610–11).

The answer to the second question has a wider focus. Soon after the mention of Swann's friendship with the comte de Paris, there is an allusion to his having 'une lettre de Twickenham' (I, 18; I, 19). What seems odd today would have been clear to Proust's original readers: England in general, and Twickenham in particular, had been associated, since 1800, with the comings and goings of the Orléans branch of the French royal family. Louis-Philippe, duc d'Orléans and future king, lived there from 1800 to 1807, and again from 1815 to 1817.[2] He came to the throne after the revolution of 1830, which overthrew the last 'legitimate' Bourbon monarch, Charles X, and was himself overthrown in the revolution of 1848, which resulted in the formation of the Second Republic. From 1848 there were, therefore, two exiled, competing branches of the French royal family; the 'legitimist' Bourbons, whose court was at Frohsdorf in Austria, and the 'constitutional' Orléans, who settled in England. The

---

[2] For dates and details of the houses occupied by the Orléans family during their various residences in Twickenham, see T. H. R. Cashmore, *The Orléans Family in Twickenham 1800–1932* (Twickenham Local Historical Society, 1982).

Second Republic did not last long; it became, in 1852, the Second Empire, under the rule of Napoleon III, which lasted until the disastrous Franco-Prussian War of 1870 and the establishment of the Third Republic.[3] After his abdication, it was Napoleon III's turn to seek refuge in England; Louis Philippe Albert, comte de Paris, the grandson of Louis-Philippe, returned to France, and in 1873 came to terms with his Bourbon rival, the comte de Chambord, grandson of Charles X (still ensconced at Frohsdorf). When the comte de Chambord died without issue in 1883, the comte de Paris became, for all but a handful of legitimist diehards, the single pretender to the French throne. His enjoyment of this position in his native land was brief. The Republic became suspicious of his political manoeuvring; he was exiled once more in 1886, and returned to England, not this time to Twickenham but across the Thames to East Sheen. Proust's chronology and topography may be a little out of sync (Swann would probably have been carrying 'une lettre de Sheen House' in his pocket at the time of his visits to Marcel's parents at Combray) but the main point is not affected. Paris was indeed to be found on the banks of the Thames; that was where you went to pay court to the pretender to the French throne. You might meet the Prince and Princess of Wales at his dinner-table; you might meet his uncle, the duc d'Aumale, at the annual dinner of the Twickenham Rowing Club, of which he was president. The fact that England was the headquarters of a French royalist party that still clung to the delusion of Restoration gave a social cachet to a tendency that was already strong in France, that of *anglomanie*.

The terms *anglomanie* and *anglomane* originate in the mid-eighteenth century, and are intrinsically terms of abuse: they describe an excessive admiration for Englishness, whether in politics, social behaviour, philosophy, or literature. Already, in 1757, a book was published with the warning title *Préservatif contre l'anglomanie* [Remedy against Anglomania]; in 1764 Palissot's poem *La Dunciade* (its title borrowed from Pope) attacked the literary

> anglomanes jaloux
> Sifflés à Londres, applaudis chez nous
>
> . . . .
>
> Et qui, tous fiers du nom de novateurs,
> Détruisez l'art en corrompant nos mœurs.

---

[3] It is to this imperial family that the princesse Mathilde, the niece of Napoleon I, belongs; see.n. 1.

[jealous Anglomaniacs, hissed in London and applauded at home . . . and who, all proud of the name of innovators, destroy art while corrupting our morals.]

An article in *L'Observateur français à Londres* published in 1769 traced the malady to the end of the Seven Years War and the Peace of Paris: 'Après la paix de 1762, des *fracs*, des voitures à l'angloise, des chevaux anglois, des courses à l'imitation de celles de Newmarket, des paris, du ponche, du robif, du pouding . . . envahissent la France' [After the peace treaty of 1762, *fracs*, English carriages, English horses, races in imitation of those at Newmarket, bets, punch, roast beef, pudding . . . invade France].[4]

That this *invasion* takes place after a *peace treaty* is not surprising: resistance to *anglomanie* is an embattled business. English political economy gifted the French the word *budget*, which entered the language around the same period of the mid-eighteenth century, but was only acknowledged by the Académie Française in 1835; to the conservative statesman and poet Viennet it represented, metonymically, a fiscal system both alien in origin and destructive in its effects: 'pour le mot *budget* importé d'Angleterre, | J'ai vu gronder trente ans une effroyable guerre' [because of the word *budget*, imported from England, I have seen a frightful war rage for thirty years] he says, referring to the fierce debates in the Assembly; from this war of words only the word *budget* itself has emerged victorious:

Ce mot victorieux
Seul de tant de combats est sorti glorieux;
Laissant sur le carreau rois et chartes royales,
Gorgeant de millions ses colonnes fiscales,
Grossi de règne en règne, et toujours affamé . . .

[Only this victorious word has emerged with glory from all these combats; leaving kings and royal charters prostrate, gorging its fiscal columns on millions, swollen from reign to reign, and always hungry . . .][5]

---

[4] These examples are all taken from Mackenzie, I, 108. *Frac* comes from 'frock(-coat)'; by Proust's day it signified formal wear ('tails'). The spellings 'angloise' and 'anglois' conform to French usage of the period for words that would now be spelt 'ais'; 'robif' is a less usual form of 'rosbif'. For the different ways in which the English word 'pudding' can be transcribed and pronounced in French, see Ch. 3, p. 131.

[5] *Épître à Boileau sur les mots nouveaux*, 121–31. The poem was delivered at a public session of the Académie Française in 1855. Jean-Pons-Guillaume Viennet (1777–1868)

Again, an English import is associated with violence and disorder, and with something unnatural or un-French. In Paul Bourget's novel *Un cœur de femme* (1890), a hostess of the *faubourg Saint-Germain* is happy to have English silverware and English china on her dinner-table, without thinking of her noble ancestor's 'haine implacable contre le peuple britannique' [implacable hatred for the British people] (p. 270).[6] A contemporaneous attack on 'l'anglomanie française' begins with a militant reminder of the traditional hostilities between England and France: 'au dessus des modes, mœurs ou costumes, il n'est pas un cœur français où l'anglais ne soit resté en bataille avec Jeanne d'Arc, aussi bien en son rôle de vaincu, qu'en celui de bourreau' [leaving aside fashions, whether in manners or dress, there isn't a French heart in which the Englishman is not pitted against Joan of Arc, both in his role as defeated enemy and as executioner].[7] Nevertheless 'modes, mœurs [et] costumes' play a large part in the picture, and it does sometimes seem to the unbiased observer as though an *anglomane* such as Odette in *A la recherche* might have forgotten about Joan of Arc, if only for a moment.

Even the most summary history of *anglomanie* is beyond the remit of this book; I have space only to sketch the broad framework it provides for Proust's novel. Take, for example, the diplomat, M. de Norpois. He admires England, and supports the Anglo-French alliance; his outlook belongs to the century of peace between England and France that followed the end of the Napoleonic wars in 1815, the first such century since the Middle Ages. The political accommodation between these ancient enemies had many causes, but one of them derives from the English influence on French political thought, beginning in the eighteenth century with the admiration professed by Enlightenment *philosophes* for the English constitution, in opposition to French monarchical and absolutist

---

began his career as a naval artillery officer (he spent eight months as a prisoner of war in Plymouth in 1797); he was a supporter of Louis-Philippe and was elected to the Académie Française in 1830. To add insult to injury, *budget* is one of those words that English first took from old French (*bougette*, a small leather bag), then gave back in anglicized form.

[6] Later in the novel an older man decries 'l'anglomanie de la jeunesse moderne' [the Anglomania of modern youth]: 'tout leur vient de Londres, aujourd'hui, leurs vices comme leur toilette' [they get everything from London these days, their vices as much as their dress] (p. 374). For more on Bourget, see below, pp. 23–5.

[7] The author of this patriotic outburst was a blue-blooded noblewoman with an English name, the duchesse de Fitz-James: see below, pp. 31–6.

traditions.[8] Ideas of constitutional monarchy and of a representative legislature, together with their vocabulary (including *le budget*) were taken up in the nineteenth century by French politicians and political philosophers on both the left and right. M. de Norpois sees his political vision realized in the alliance between France and England during the Great War; this political current mingles with that of social fashion, so that Odette's *anglomanie* finds a new outlet in her incessant use of 'l'expression de *fair play*' and her admiration for 'les braves *tommies*', including those who come 'des plus lointains *dominions*' [from the most distant dominions] (IV, 368; VI, 123).

Another form of *anglomanie* concerns sexual mores. In *Proust's Cup of Tea*, Emily Eells cites a letter by André Gide in which crossing the Channel, 'aller outre-Manche', means 'passer outre' [going beyond], which involves 'une embardée du côté du Diable' [a lurch in the Devil's direction]—the direction being that of homosexual freedom (p. 4 and n. 11).[9] Readers of English literature are used to the John Bull view of French effeminacy; we are less familiar with its counterpart, the 'queer theory' that the French held (and hold) of England as the homeland of sodomy, often associated with flagellation, 'le vice anglais'. The culture of the public schools did not escape French notice; nor did the provocative strictness of the English lady's riding-habit. Indeed it might be said that what attracted the English to France was looseness, and what attracted the French to England was strictness; but this dualism is far from absolute. England also offered France a spectacle of sexual ambiguity, of blurred gender, of cross-dressing and erotic disguise. (This spectacle was, literally, theatrical, in

---

[8] Zeldin, I, 101–2. Proust has a joke about the prolonged peace between England and France, in the shape of the absurd but ineradicable opinion held by Françoise's niece that England had attacked France in 1870 alongside Prussia; she looks forward to a coming war with England after which English visitors to France will be charged an entrance fee of 300 francs (III, 124–5; IV, 146–7).

[9] Eells's title derives in part from the fact that 'prendre le thé' [to take tea] was slang for gay sex; 'tasse' [cup] and 'théière' [teapot] could both mean a urinal. Jarrod Hayes, in an article called 'Proust in the Tearoom' (*PMLA* 110 (1995), 992–1005) makes this pun the basis for a rereading of practically all the tea-drinking episodes in *A la recherche*, starting of course with the most famous, that of the *petite madeleine* dunked in a cup of herbal tea (I, 44–7; I, 51–5); it's surprising how different the sensuous orality of that moment looks if you take it as a disguised allusion to sex in a public toilet. However, it should be said that the earliest dating of the slang usage, to the 1910s and (more definitely) the 1920s, is a bit late for Proust, and there is no evidence that he knew it; after all, as Freud might have put it, sometimes a cup of tea is just a cup of tea.

Shakespearian comedies such as *Twelfth Night* and *As You Like It*, which became immensely popular in late nineteenth century France, and both of which Proust knew.) In Victorian literature and painting, and in the aesthetic criticism that accompanied them, the French found an imaginative energy focused on what Eells calls 'Anglosexuality', a constant current of thought and source of imagery in Proust's work.

In literature, Englishness constitutes an incalculably extensive network of allusion. Les *fashionables*, le *dandy*, le *gentleman*, les *milords* et *miladies*, la *miss* (either as young lady or governess), the victim of le *spleen*, and, of course, le *snob*—variously figure in the work of almost every major French writer of the nineteenth century, including those most important to Proust—Chateaubriand, Balzac, Hugo, Baudelaire, Mallarmé, besides a host of minor figures. These writers both responded to, and helped to create, the fashion for English manners, dress, attitudes; English vocabulary was disseminated in novels and on the stage, and in newspapers and journals from the immensely respectable *Revue des Deux Mondes* to society papers such as *Le Gaulois* or *Le Tout-Paris*. An article in an illustrated monthly magazine, *Paris Illustré*, published in June 1883, happily combines the outmoded and the up-to-date in its depiction of an 'Englishness' which is all the rage:

Hurrah! pour les *Garden-parties* et les plaisirs de la vieille Angleterre! Hurrah! hurrah! Courses de chevaux, réunions dans les jardins, *Crocket, Polo, Champaign-cup, Gainsborough, Reynolds* et *Kitty-Bell, Jerseys* et *Petty coats,* tout cela est anglais à rendre des points à un *Cockney*. Nous nous moquons de John Bull et des *Snobs* et nous copions, avec fureur, leurs usages, leurs fêtes, et leurs modes. Oui, leurs modes, malgré l'orgeuil français, il faut en convenir. England *for ever*! Nos *Babies* ont l'air de personnages de Miss Greenaway et nos jolies femmes avec leurs chapeaux à longs panaches et leurs cuirasses collantes, d'héroïnes de *Keepsake*.

[Hurrah for *garden parties* and the pleasures of old England! Hurrah! Hurrah! Horse races, garden parties, *Croquet, Polo, Champagne-cup, Gainsborough, Reynolds* and *Kitty-Bell, Jerseys* and *Petticoats*—it's all English enough to knock spots off a *Cockney*. We make fun of John Bull and of *les Snobs* and we fall over ourselves to copy their customs, their parties, and their fashions. Yes, their fashions, despite French pride, we have to admit as much. England *for ever*! Our *Babies* look like characters out of Miss Greenaway, and our pretty women, with their hats with long ribbons and their clinging bodices, like heroines out of the *Keepsake*.]

I have interpreted 'Crocket' as croquet rather than cricket, but the indeterminate spelling is charcteristic of popular *anglomanie*, as many of its

THÉODORE DE BANVILLE.

LES
PARISIENNES
L'ETE

Hurrah¹ pour les
Garden-parties
et les plaisirs
de la vieille
Angleterre! Hur-
rah! hurrah! Courses de chevaux, réunions dans les jardins,
Crocket, Polo, Champaign-
cup, Gainsborough, Reyn-
olds et *Killy-Bell, Jerseys*
et *Petty coats,* tout cela est
anglais à rendre des points à un *Cockney.*

Nous nous moquons de John Bull et des *Snobs* et nous copions, avec fureur, leurs usages, leurs fêtes et leurs modes.
Oui, leurs modes, malgré l'orgueil français, il faut en convenir. England *for ever!* Nos *Babies* ont l'air de
personnages de Miss Greenaway et nos jolies femmes avec leurs chapeaux à longs panaches et leurs cuirasses collantes, d'héroïnes de *Keepsake.*

1. A young lady with the fashionable 'English' look, in an equally fashionable
rowing boat on the river; the accompanying text acknowledges the influence of
Englishness on the look, and the vocabulary, of leisure and fashion; from *Paris
Illustré,* June 1883.

critics pointed out; so is the carefree mingling of periods and styles in the
service of fashion. Reynolds and Gainsborough are visual resources for
the 'England look', of no higher value than Kate Greenaway's contemporary illustrations for children's books, or the pseudo-Romantic imagery of

the *Keepsake*, the ladies' annual whose hey-day in England belongs to the 1830s (it ceased publication in 1857). Along with illustrated magazines such as *Paris Illustré*, fashion magazines were influential in propagating this 'look' and the vocabulary which accompanied it. One of them, *La Dernière Mode*, was edited by Mallarmé for four months in 1874, and included a 'Gazette de la Fashion' signed 'Miss Satin'. Mallarmé wrote for the magazine as well as editing it; in the issue of 18 October he imagines the statue of Diana in the Tuileries descending from her pedestal 'pour aller . . . chez un des tailleurs ou l'une des couturières en renom et de chasseresse devenir sportwoman' [in order to visit . . . a fashionable tailor or dressmaker and metamorphose from a huntress to a *sportwoman*]; on 1 November he discusses 'l'emploi de ces Toilettes à la campagne ou à la Ville reglé par le High-Life' [the way in which *le High-Life* dictates that these dresses should be worn in the country or in town].[10]

Journalism was not one-sided, of course; the same newspaper could both attack *anglomanie* and exemplify it, sometimes on the same page. In June 1885 *Le Figaro* published an article on its front page about the excesses of *anglomanie*, thoroughly typical of its kind; it begins with the observation that a society has just been founded to promote the use of French in other countries, supported by the Chief Rabbi and Cardinal Lavigerie, as well as by fierce republicans and diehard royalists. But this picture of social harmony did not reassure the author: 'avant de porter notre langue au loin, ne faudrait-il pas commencer par la bien parler chez nous, et ne conviendrait-il pas d'assurer sa correction à Paris avant d'en exporter l'usage au Congo?' [before we carry our language to distant parts, shouldn't we begin by speaking it well at home, and wouldn't it be as well to make sure of its correctness in Paris before exporting it to the Congo?].[11] There followed a series of satirical sketches of modern conversation, featuring *le five o'clock*, *le private-meeting*, *les garden-parties*, with special attention to racing jargon—*les performances*, *dead-heat*, *le winning-post*, etc. But on the same page there was a report on the Grand-Prix de Paris which had been run the day before, in which it is said that the winning horse had been visited 'dans son box' by a number of distinguished French admirers. He was an English horse, and his name was Paradox.

---

[10] Stéphane Mallarmé, *La Dernière Mode*, ed. S. A. Rhodes (New York: Institute of French Studies, 1933), 39, 41. For the vocabulary of sport which produced *sportwoman*, see Ch. 3.   [11] Ph. de Grandlieu, 'La Langue', *Le Figaro*, 14 June 1885, p. 1.

For what fault have you most toleration?

Proust's upbringing exposed him both to literary and social forms of *anglomanie*, though it did not, as we shall see, enable him to learn English. A childhood photograph shows him and his younger brother Robert in fanciful and fashionable 'Scottish' costume. One of the earliest examples we have of his writing comes in an English 'confession album' belonging to his friend Antoinette Faure, a small red volume embossed with the words 'An Album of Confessions to record Thoughts and Feelings' in gold tracery on the cover, thoroughly characteristic of the English fancy-goods that were so fashionable in the period; Antoinette had bought it at Galignani's famous bookshop in the Rivoli Arcades, the first port of call for English and American books and newspapers in Paris throughout the nineteenth century.[12] Proust was about 13 or 14 when he replied (or in some cases avoided replying), in French, to a set of standard questions such as 'Your favourite virtue', 'Your idea of happiness', 'Your favourite painters and composers', and 'Your pet aversion'; the answer to 'Your idea of misery' has become famous: 'Être séparé de maman' [being separated from Mummy].[13] This episode could easily have found its way into the passages of *A la recherche* that describe Marcel's adolescent passion for Gilberte Swann. It would have taken its place alongside other manifestations of *anglomanie* in the Swann household, such as Gilberte's writing paper, 'orné d'un caniche bleu en relief surmontant une légende humoristique écrite en anglais et suivie d'un point d'exclamation' [adorned with a poodle embossed in blue, above a humorous inscription in English with an exclamation mark after it] (I, 495; II, 88).[14] The fact that the 'confession album' was not just an object of English manufacture, but one that used the English language, would also have been apt. I envisage it as a Christmas present—not a 'cadeau de Noël', because both Mme Swann and her daughter have banished the old French word, and 'ne parlaient que du pudding de Christmas, et de ce qu'on leur avait donné pour leur

---

[12] Valérie Duponchelle, 'Le questionnaire de Proust aux enchères', *Le Figaro*, 21 May 2003; I am grateful to Emily Eells for drawing this article to my attention, and for subsequently informing me that the album fetched 120,227 euros; the buyer was the dress designer Gérard Darel.

[13] *CSB* 335–6. His reply to the question on toleration was: 'Pour la vie privée des génies' [For the private life of geniuses].

[14] Admittedly Gilberte has several other designs of writing paper; English doesn't have a monopoly of teenage kitsch.

2. Proust and his younger brother, Robert, in 'Scottish' costume.

Christmas' [would speak of nothing but 'Christmas pudding', what people had given them as 'Christmas presents']. Marcel, of course, is enchanted: 'Même à la maison, je me serais cru déshonoré en parlant de Noël et je ne disais plus que Christmas, ce que mon père trouvait extrêmement ridicule' [Even at home I should have thought it degrading to use the word "Noël," and always said "Christmas," which my father considered extremely silly] (I, 517; II, 115). The infatuated young booby squirms with embarrassment at being accompanied, on his outings to the Champs-Élysées, by the unfashionable figure of the old family servant (the significantly named Françoise)—until she, too, is magically

> **Maison fondée en 1690**
> ————
> **PAPIERS ANGLAIS**
> **GROSVENOR, CHATER & Cᵒ˙**
> **Magasins, 68, Cannon Street, à Londres**
> ————
> **PARIS**   **PARIS**
> ⁎ **HENRY COLLET** ⁎
> **6, RUE DE PARADIS-POISSONNIÈRE, 6**

3. Advertisement for English writing paper, from *Paris Illustré*, May 1883.

anglicized by Mme Swann, who sings the praises of his 'vieille "nurse"'
(I, 499; II, 93).[15]

Even Marcel's family, however, is not immune from the infiltration of
English words, one of which, 'un pudding à la Nesselrode', makes its
appearance at the (relatively) grand dinner offered to M. de Norpois (I,
457; II, 43), an occasion for which Françoise has also insisted on the very
best York ham—itself the subject of an elaborate linguistic joke, since not
only does she think it is 'New York' ham, but mispronounces it 'Nev'York'
(I, 437; II, 18). It turns out, too, that the only restaurant in Paris for
which Françoise has a good word is, strangely enough for this fierce local
patriot, the Café Anglais, the restaurant of choice for rich tourists (I, 477;
II, 67; see also *Pléiade* note, I, 1355).

Marcel makes fun of Gilberte's taste in writing paper, yet Proust's own
writing paper was hand-made in London—or so at least his stationer
swore—and when it ran out on one occasion he offered an elaborate
comic apology to Madame de Clermont-Tonnerre for writing to her on

---

[15] The younger Marcel did not know English when he met 'la dame en rose' (see Ch. 2,
pp. 75–7); here again, on hearing the word *nurse* he comments: 'Je ne savais pas l'anglais,
je compris bientôt pourtant que ce mot désignait Françoise' [I did not know any English;
I soon gathered, however, that the word was intended to denote Françoise]. Le Robert dates
the word, in the sense of a nanny or governess, to 1896.

4. Proust wearing one of his 'drawerful' of Liberty ties.

what he called 'ce papier pseudo-anglais' (*Corr* X, 103). When the middle-aged Marcel revisits the Bois in the famous concluding pages of *Du côté de chez Swann*, he notes with scorn the women's fashions that have replaced those of his youth and which include 'des chiffons liberty semés de fleurs comme un papier peint' [Liberty chiffons sprinkled with flowers like wallpaper] (I, 417; I, 510); perhaps he has forgotten his sympathetic reaction to the 'tentures de liberty' [Liberty hangings] in Robert de Saint-Loup's quarters at Doncières (II, 373; III, 78).[16] As for the author, he had a drawerful of Liberty cravats 'de toutes nuances' [of every hue], as he boasted to Robert de Billy in 1892, one of which he can be seen wearing

---

[16] Marcel's visit to Doncières takes place later in the book but earlier in his life.

in a photograph from the same period. When Céleste Albaret knew him he no longer wore these Liberty ties, which she remembers seeing put away in a box; but his tailor was still English and his boots came from a shop called Old England.[17]

Anglomanie influenced many of the rituals of upper-class social behaviour in Proust's Paris, both the one he lived in and the one that appears in *A la recherche*. Imitation of *le high-life* generated both long-lasting fashions, such as 'le *five o'clock tea*' to which Odette is constant (I, 584; II, 196), and transient absurdities, to which she is equally susceptible, such as having lunch invitations printed with the phrase '*to meet* un personnage plus ou moins important' [*To meet*, followed by the name of some more or less important personage], or having visiting cards for her husband 'où le nom de Charles Swann était précédé de "Mr."' [on which the name Charles Swann was preceded by 'Mr.'] (I, 536; II, 138).[18] Yet it would be a mistake to associate every such aspect of *anglomanie* in the novel with Odette; one of the highlights of the social calendar in *A la recherche* is Mme de Sainte-Euverte's *garden-party* (III, 69; IV, 80)[19] and the most English of all French imports was *le club*. This term supplemented the French word 'cercle' from the late eighteenth century, but acquired political notoriety during the Revolution when it was used to designate radical groupings such as the *Club des Jacobins*, the *Club des Cordeliers*, and the *Club des Femmes*; as a result the word was banned, and no club could officially call itself a club until the law was repealed in 1895. The most important club in *A la recherche*, *le Jockey-Club*, was founded in 1834 in direct imitation of the English Jockey Club (founded in Newmarket in 1750), but its official title was 'Cercle de la Société d'Encouragement' (the encouragement

---

[17] Céleste Albaret, *Monsieur Proust*, p. 84; references are to the English translation unless otherwise specified. Proust also had a duvet made specially at Liberty, whose Paris store was located on the boulevard des Capucines, but this, too, was no longer in use when Céleste entered his service. For 'Old England' see below, pp. 33–4. Proust's letter to Robert de Billy is in *Corr.* I, 183.

[18] Marcel, still in his impressionable adolescent phase, pleads with his father to order visiting cards in the same fashion; but his father is remorseless, and after a few despairing days Marcel decides that he might be right after all. The effect of Odette's whim is to complete the anglicising of Swann's name, whose 'origine anglaise' I discuss in Ch. 2 (pp. 109–10).

[19] Bonnaffé dates *garden-party* to 1885. In Normandy the marquise de Cambremer gives weekly *garden-parties* which are evidently less exclusive than those of the *faubourg Saint-Germain* but are none the less desperately sought after by the local snobs (II, 42–3; II, 301).

being that of better breeds).[20] The fact that the most prestigious masculine association in Paris should be (even nominally) linked to horse-racing draws attention to another feature of *anglomanie*, the fashion for aristocratic English sports that began in the eighteenth century, and which was given a further boost by the émigrés who returned from exile in England after 1815.

All these aspects of *anglomanie*—its social prestige, its attachment to forms of behaviour as well as of dress, manner, and language—are summed up in the early fiction and travel-writing of Paul Bourget (1852–1935). Bourget's novel *Un cœur de femme* has already been cited in connection with *anglomanie*; he was a frequent traveller to England in the 1880s, and his *Études anglaises* include 'Lettres de Londres' and 'Croquis d'Outre-Manche'. The work by Bourget most often cited in relation to *A la recherche* is the short story 'Gladys Harvey', whose half-English heroine is based on the courtesan Laure Hayman, who in turn was one of the models for Odette. Like Odette, Gladys speaks 'avec un léger accent anglais' [with a slight English accent] and her speech is peppered with English phrases: '*You are a very jolly fellow*,' she says to an old lecher who is playing footsie with her under the dinner table (p. 25). The young Proust cultivated Bourget's acquaintance, and Bourget wrote to Laure Hayman, who was fond of collecting Dresden china: 'Votre saxe psychologique, le petit Marcel, comme vous l'appelez, est tout simplement exquis' [Little Marcel, your porcelain psychologist, as you call him, is quite simply delightful];[21] Laure herself gave Proust a separately printed copy of 'Gladys Harvey' bound in silk from one of her petticoats, with an inscription: 'N'aimez pas une Gladys Harvey' [You mustn't love someone like Gladys Harvey].

Even more Proustian, in my view, is the novella with which Bourget made his name, *Cruelle Énigme* (1885), which concerns the affair between a young man of good family and a married woman, from whom his family

---

[20] See Louis de Beauchamp, *Marcel Proust et le Jockey Club* (Paris: Éditions Émile-Paul, 1973); the introduction, by the duc de Lévis Mirepoix, is a masterpiece of snobbery in itself, condescending to Proust for writing about the clubs to which he did not belong, yet claiming his endorsement of them as places 'où le snobisme est pourchassé, honni, interdit' [from where snobbery is expelled, put to shame, forbidden] (p. 11). And then you wake up, as George Orwell said . . .

[21] Tadié, 83. Proust didn't forget this detail, either: Odette, after she marries Swann, surrounds herself with 'Saxe', 'dont elle prononçait le nom avec un accent anglais' [which she pronounced with an English accent] (I, 605; II, 222).

and friends attempt to separate him.[22] The young man, Hubert Liauran, lives in Paris with his devoted, unworldly mother and grandmother, who have set him up in a bachelor flat in the grounds of their own *hôtel* so that they can keep an eye on him.[23] Hubert's male friends, who all belong to the *faubourg Saint-Germain,* visit him in an environment that is steeped in Englishness and has, indeed, been directly inspired by *anglomanie.* All the bedroom furniture comes from England, based on models that the ladies have seen at the house of one of their relations who is 'anglomane forcené' [a raving Anglomaniac]; the whole effect is of 'ce *home* d'une commodité raffinée que chaque Anglais riche aime à se procurer' [that refined, comfortable *home* that each wealthy Englishman likes to secure for himself] (p. 14). Hubert's affair with Thérèse de Sauve takes him, not to Dijon or Poitiers or even Nice, but to Folkestone. Mme de Sauve herself is dressed in the height of fashion, which means that her dress is of English material (p. 32).[24] At Folkestone she has chosen to stay at the Star Hotel, 'à cause de ce nom de *Star,* qui veut dire étoile', as Bourget helpfully explains (p. 44). When Hubert arrives he finds that, although it is his first visit to England, his spoken English is correct and intelligible, something he attributes to his Yorkshire governess and his mother's insistence

---

[22] *Cruelle Énigme* is dedicated to Henry James in memory of 'nos conversations de l'été dernier, en Angleterre, prolongées tantôt à une des tables de l'hospitalier *Athenæum-club,* tantôt sous les ombrages des arbres de quelque vaste parc' [our conversations of last summer, in England, sometimes conducted at one of the tables of the hospitable *Athenaeum* club, at other times beneath the shade of the trees in some vast park].

[23] Hubert has his mother's looks, the fragile, melancholy countenance of an exhausted aristocratic line which itself bears an English imprint: he is compared to 'ces portraits de jeunes princes, peints par Van Dyck, où la finesse presque morbide d'une race vieillie se mélange à la persistante fierté d'un sang héroïque' [those portraits of young princes painted by Van Dyck, in which the almost morbid refinement of an ancient race is blended with the continuing pride of a heroic lineage] (p. 20), an image that may have influenced Proust's description of his English friend Willie Heath: see below, p. 25, and Ch 3, p. 150 and n. 54.

[24] There are resemblances between Thérèse and Odette, in some respects even more suggestive than those between Odette and Gladys Harvey; for example in the way in which each is compared to an Italian portrait: Mme de Sauve reminds Hubert of portraits by Luini and his followers, whether of Salomé or the Madonna (p. 31); Proust may have remembered this passage when he described Swann's assimilation of Odette to paintings by Botticelli (I, 220); he may also, as Tadié suggests, have been influenced by another of Bourget's novels, *Mensonges* (1887), where an actress is said to have the melancholy, sensual mouth of Botticelli's madonnas and angels (p. 235). Thérèse's Italianate looks come, we are told, from her mother's adulterous liaison with an Italian count—a fact unknown to the innocent Hubert, but common knowledge in 'la chronique des clubs'. When Thérèse betrays Hubert, he discovers that his rival lives in the rue La Pérouse, Odette's street (p. 110).

on making him practise his English every day (p. 45). If the romantic beginning of Hubert's liaison with Thérèse is marked by Englishness, so is its bitter outcome. Mme de Sauve is a good deal less pure in her appetites than her lover. Back in France, and separated from Hubert, she finds herself at the Normandy seaside resort of Trouville, exposed to temptation in the company of old friends, 'ces femmes et leurs attentifs, leurs *fancy men*,—comme disait une lady mêlée à ce cercle' [these women and their suitors, their *fancy men*,—in the words of a lady who belonged to this group] (p. 88). As Hubert finally faces up to his mistress's betrayal, memories of Folkestone flood back, of the Star Hotel, the waiter with his 'respectable British face' and his equally British politeness; he can hear him saying ' "*I beg your pardon*" ' (p. 104).

Both 'Gladys Harvey' and *Cruelle Énigme* allude to the salient features of *anglomanie*—its supposed affinity with the *faubourg Saint-Germain*, its preoccupation with the domestic arts, its ambivalent sexual mores—as well as parading Bourget's knowledge of England and the English language. Very little of this would have escaped Proust, either in Bourget's work, or in those by a host of other anglophile writers.[25] But Bourget was also a passionate admirer of English literature and art; we need to distinguish here between *anglomanie* as a social phenomenon and as an aesthetic movement. Proust came into contact with this movement when he moved beyond the circle of his childhood and early adolescence; its imprint is visible in several of his closest friendships, particularly with men. Such friendships included the young Englishman Willie Heath, to whose memory Proust dedicated *Les Plaisirs et les jours*, evoking the English Cavalier portraits by Van Dyck that he had seen in the Louvre;[26] later on he knew Robert d'Humières, the translator of Kipling, who helped him with his Ruskin translations, as did Douglas Ainslie (Grant Duff), with whom he argued about the relative merits of Ruskin and Pater. The man he most constantly loved, the composer and musician Reynaldo Hahn, and his would-be literary patron, Robert de Montesquiou, were both steeped in English culture; his close friendship and collaboration

---

[25] See on this subject Émilien Carassus, *Le Snobisme et les lettres françaises* (Paris: Librairie Armand Colin, 1966), 327–32. Jacques Boulenger's *Un professeur de snobisme* (Abbeville: Les Amis d'Édouard (No. 7), 1912) has a Thackerayan, shabby-genteel 'hero', Sir Richard Fawcett, living on his wits in *son flat* in Paris, who guides the narrator in the correct comportment of *un gentleman*, fortified by *les manhattan cocktails et les prairy oysters* (*sic*, p. 5).   [26] See above, n. 23.

5. Willie Heath, Proust's English friend who died in 1893, aged 20, and to whom Proust dedicated *Les Plaisirs et les jours* in 1896.

with Hahn's English cousin Marie Nordlinger was the most important of all as far as his Ruskin translations were concerned, and also provided a link to other English writers and artists. Towards the end of his life, devoted admirers such as Sydney and Violet Schiff kept him abreast of literary developments in England, including the progress of his own reputation.

The story of Proust's passion for Ruskin is well known, but his knowledge and love of English literature had a far wider scope. In 1910, while he was writing *Du côté de chez Swann*, he read Hardy's *The Well-Beloved* and discovered, with a mixture of chagrin and pleasure, its affinity with the design of his own novel; he wrote about this to Robert de Billy (another friend who knew English and had helped him with his translations), and added:

C'est curieux que dans tous les genres les plus différents, de George Eliot à Hardy, de Stevenson à Emerson, il n'y a pas de littérature qui ait sur moi un pouvoir comparable à la littérature anglaise et américaine. L'Allemagne, l'Italie, bien souvent la France me laissent indifférent. Mais deux pages du *Moulin sur la Floss* me font pleurer. Je sais que Ruskin exécrait ce roman-là mais je réconcilie tous ces dieux ennemis dans le Panthéon de mon admiration. (*Corr.* X, 55)

[It's odd that in all the different genres, from George Eliot to Hardy, from Stevenson to Emerson, no literature has a power over me comparable to English and American literature. Germany, Italy, quite often France leave me cold. But two pages of *The Mill on the Floss* make me cry. I know Ruskin detested that novel, but I reconcile all these opposed deities in the Pantheon of my admiration.]

The evidence of this worship is everywhere in *A la recherche*, where literary *anglomanie* is not mocked—with one very special exception which I will discuss in due course. But *anglomanie* as a social phenomenon is a different matter, and this includes its influence both in the domain of manners and of what has come to be called 'lifestyle'.

Marcel reports M. de Charlus's stated preference for 'les vieilles manières françaises, sans ombre de raideur britannique' [the old manners of France, without a hint of British stiffness] (III, 747; V, 273); admittedly this has the advantage of allowing him to greet his beloved Morel with a kiss on both cheeks, 'opposant au flegme britannique la tendresse d'un père sensible du XVIIIe siècle' [countering British phlegm with the affection of a warm-hearted eighteenth-century father]. Odette's handwriting has 'une affectation de raideur britannique' [an affectation of British stiffness] (I, 218; I, 266), and Albertine's speech, likewise, has 'une affectation juvénile de flegme britannique' [a juvenile affectation of British phlegm] (II, 232; II, 528). When Marcel meets his old friend Bloch at the 'bal des têtes' in *Le Temps retrouvé*, he barely recognizes him: 'Un chic anglais avait en effet complètement transformé sa figure' [an English chic had completely transformed his appearance] (IV, 530; VI, 326). Bloch's new look is largely attributable to his monocle, which, Marcel remarks, is so gross that it draws attention away from his face, 'comme devant ces objets anglais dont un garçon dit dans un magasin que "c'est le grand chic", après quoi on n'ose plus se demander si cela vous plaît' [just as, when a shop-assistant has told you that some object imported from England is "the last word in *chic*," you no longer dare to ask yourself whether you really like it] (IV, 531; VI, 327).

Proust's most intense resistance to *anglomanie* was prompted by what he saw as its attempt to mould domestic life according to an intellectual and aesthetic fallacy. In the preface to *Sésame et les lys*, entitled 'Sur la lecture' [On Reading] and subsequently reprinted in *Pastiches et mélanges* as 'Journées de lecture', he describes the bedroom in his great-aunt's house in Illiers where he spent hours reading as a child; it is a room whose inconsequential Frenchness rebukes the English school of moral-aesthetic design:

Les théories de William Morris, qui ont été si constamment appliquées par Maple et les décorateurs anglais, édictent qu'une chambre n'est belle qu'à la condition de contenir seulement des choses qui nous soient utiles et que toute chose utile, fût-ce un simple clou, soit non pas dissimulée, mais apparente. Au-dessus du lit à tringles de cuivre et entièrement découvert, aux murs nus de ces chambres hygiéniques, quelques reproductions de chefs-d'œuvre. À la juger d'après les principes de cette esthétique, ma chambre n'était nullement belle, car elle était pleine de choses qui ne pouvaient servir à rien et qui dissimulaient pudiquement, jusqu'à en rendre l'usage extrêmement difficile, celles qui servaient à quelque chose. Mais c'est justement de ces choses qui n'étaient pas là pour ma commodité, mais semblaient y être venues pour leur plaisir, que ma chambre tirait pour moi sa beauté.

[William Morris's theories, which have been so constantly applied by Maple and the English decorators, decree that a room is beautiful only on condition that it contain solely those things which may be useful to us and that any useful thing, even a simple nail, be not hidden but visible. Above the bed with copper curtain-rods and entirely uncovered, on the naked walls of those hygienic rooms, [only] a few reproductions of masterpieces. To judge it by the principles of this aesthetics, my room was not beautiful at all, for it was full of things that could not be of any use and that modestly hid, to the point of making their use extremely difficult, those which might serve some use. But it was precisely through these things which were not there for my convenience, but seemed to have come there for their own pleasure, that my room acquired for me its beauty.][27]

The London furniture shop Maple & Co. had a Paris branch in the square de l'Opéra; in April 1905 Proust asked his mother to obtain some 'detailed' catalogues for him, in one of which he presumably found this uncovered bed with the copper curtain-rods; he also asked her to get information about Morris's views on furnishing (*Corr.* V, 102–3). These views were to be found in Morris's lecture on 'The Beauty of Life' (1880), extracts from which had been published in French in 1896 under the suggestive title 'L'Art expliqué par les artistes: l'art et les maisons modernes' [Art explained by artists: art and modern houses].[28] Morris propounded a 'golden rule' of furnishing: 'Have nothing in your houses that you do not know to be useful, or believe to be beautiful'; the provincial vulgarity of Proust's Illiers bedroom, with its useless knick-knacks and absurd flourishes and flounces, violates this rule with relish. His description culminates in the evocation of a work of art about as distant from a 'chef d'œuvre' as you could hope to get:

Quant à la photographie par Brown du *Printemps* de Botticelli ou au moulage de la *Femme inconnue* du musée de Lille, qui, aux murs et sur la cheminée des chambres de Maple, sont la part concédée par William Morris à l'inutile beauté, je dois avouer qu'ils étaient remplacés dans ma chambre par une sorte de gravure représentant le prince Eugène, terrible et beau dans son dolman, et que je fus très étonné d'apercevoir une nuit, dans un grand fracas de locomotives et de grêle, toujours terrible et beau, à la porte d'un buffet de gare, où il servait de réclame à une spécialité de biscuits. Je soupçonne aujourd'hui mon grand-père de l'avoir autrefois reçu, comme prime, de la munificence d'un fabricant, avant de l'installer à jamais dans ma chambre. Mais alors je ne me souciais pas de son origine, qui me paraissait historique et mystérieuse et je ne m'imaginais pas qu'il pût y avoir plusieurs exemplaires de ce que je considérais comme une personne, comme un habitant permanent de la chambre que je ne faisais que partager avec lui et où je le retrouvais tous les ans, toujours pareil à lui-même.

---

[27] *SL* 45–6; *CSB* 164. The translation is by Jean Autret and William Burford, in *Marcel Proust: On Reading Ruskin* (New Haven and London: Yale University Press, 1987), 103. The next passage I quote is on pp. 106–7.

[28] The article appeared in *Le Bulletin de l'Union morale*, 15 Mar. 1896; I owe this reference to Eells, 19–20, from which the quotations in n. 29 are also taken. The association which Proust makes here between Morris and Maple ignores Morris's own Oxford Street shop, which was well known in France; it is mentioned in e.g. Bourget's *L'Esthéticisme anglais* where Morris is said to be putting Ruskin's theories into practice (pp. 500–1).

[As for the photograph by Brown of Botticelli's *Spring* or the cast of the *Unknown Woman* of the Lille Museum, which on the walls and mantelpieces of the rooms of Maple are the part conceded by William Morris to useless beauty, I must confess that they were replaced in my room by a sort of engraving representing Prince Eugene, terrible and beautiful in his dolman, and which I was astonished to see one night, in the midst of a great din of locomotives and hail, still terrible and beautiful, at the door of a railway-station buffet, where it was used as an advertisement for a brand of crackers. Today I suspect that my grandfather had once received it as a gift, thanks to the munificence of a manufacturer, before setting it up forever in my room. But at the time I did not care about its origin, which to me seemed historical and mysterious, and I did not imagine that there might have been several copies of what I thought of as a person, as a permanent inhabitant of the room I simply shared with him and where I found him every year always the same.][29]

This is one of the rare passages in his writing in which Proust alludes to the fact that his paternal grandfather had a grocer's shop in Illiers. The passage ironically juxtaposes the modest provincial family business with the grand cosmopolitan emporium, the marketing of high art to metropolitan snobs with the unassuming bargain of a small-town shopkeeper who gets his 'art' in the form of a sweetener from a biscuit manufacturer. There is more still. The works of art that carry, as it were, the 'William Morris' brand are themselves commercial products, not originals but copies, photographs of paintings or casts of statues, intended to disseminate universal principles of taste. By contrast—to the child's ignorant and imaginative eye—the engraving of Prince Eugene has the 'aura' of an original work of art, unique both in itself and in its determinate place.[30] It persists in time, like a person, not similar to other copies but 'toujours pareil à lui-même'.[31]

Aestheticism was, for Proust, one of the forms of idolatry to which Ruskin had fallen victim and from which his disciple had to free himself;

---

[29] *SL* 49–50; *CSB* 166. The references to bare walls and copies of masterpieces spring from a mistranslation. Morris recommended having 'pictures or engravings, such as you can afford, only not stopgaps, but real works of art on the wall; or else the wall itself must be ornamented with some beautiful or restful pattern'. This last phrase was rendered in French as 'quelque belle et intéressante copie'; as Emily Eells points out, 'Proust was therefore misled to believe that Morris counselled decorating the bedroom with reproductions of masterpieces'.

[30] The term 'aura' comes from Walter Benjamin's essay 'The Work of Art in the Age of Mechanical Reproduction', first published in 1936.

[31] The translation 'always the same' doesn't quite do justice to 'toujours pareil à lui-même', which has something of the force of 'always true to himself'.

'Sur la lecture' is one of the great documents of this liberation and one of the closest anticipations of the counter-aesthetic of *A la recherche*. Proust recognized the strength of the aesthetic movement in England, and the corresponding strength of its alliance with commerce; aestheticism in this passage has an English face; an English bedroom from the catalogue of a fashionable shop—impersonal and alienating—is conjured up as the antithesis of what is personal, familiar, and French. The fetishizing of interior design meant nothing to Proust—less than nothing, for it replaced the individual's memory and imagination with the hollowness of a received idea. The narrator of *A la recherche*, who lives with his parents for most of the novel, may be imagined as inhabiting a space filled with heavy, undistinguished, bourgeois furniture, mixed up with occasional 'precious' objects to which he is indifferent, the kind of interior that would strike an 'aesthetic' eye with horrified amusement.[32] It does so strike M. de Charlus: 'Comme c'est laid chez vous!' [What an ugly place you live in!] he remarks to Marcel (III, 888);[33] yet this French judgement also has (with apologies to the Irish) an 'English' origin; it was originally delivered, in the apartment of Proust's parents in the Boulevard Malesherbes, at a dinner party in 1891, by Oscar Wilde.

To conclude this discussion of *anglomanie* I want to look at a specific piece of writing that Proust is quite likely to have seen, and which, for all its narrowness of outlook and sourness of tone, offers a suggestive analogy with his own treatment of the topic. Its author has, at least by proxy, a place in *A la recherche*: she was the duchesse de Fitz-James, whose real aristocratic family is mentioned in connection with the fictional Guermantes, specifically because, though of English origin, they consider themselves to be 'de grands seigneurs français [a great French noble family]' and pronounce their name 'Fitt-jam' (III, 545).[34] In keeping with this prejudice, the duchesse de Fitz-James wrote an article in 1897 in which she inveighed

---

[32] One of the few fine things that we are told Marcel possesses is a Chinese porcelain vase (inherited from his great-aunt), whose value he does not appreciate; he sells it in order to buy flowers for Gilberte, and receives an undreamed-of 10,000 francs from the dealer (I, 612; II, 230). In one of the drafts for the first part of *A l'ombre des jeunes filles en fleurs* Gilberte tells Marcel that when she has her own house it will be like her father's before his marriage, filled with antiques. Safe in the knowledge that she won't ever visit him at home, Marcel pretends that his family, too, owns such things (Esquisse XVIII, *Pléiade*, I, 1025).

[33] My translation; *Vintage* turns the syntax a different way: 'he complained to me how ugly my rooms were' (V, 441).

[34] My translation; *Vintage* simply gives 'nobles' for 'grands seigneurs' (V, 31).

against *anglomanie* precisely because it represented the abandonment by the French aristocracy of its native traditions in favour of a shameful and ridiculous parody of English manners.[35]

Although Fitz-James's article is called 'L'Anglomanie française' it should really have been called 'L'Anglomanie de l'aristocratie française', since its focus is wholly on the social history of her own class. The duchesse traces the turn of the French aristocracy towards England in the aftermath of the Revolution, especially when contrasted with its treatment elsewhere:

chez les emigrés, l'admiration égalait la reconnaissance envers l'Angleterre qui avait respectueusement abrité leur malheur . . . En effet, bafoués en Allemagne, traqués dans les Pays-Bas, refoulés en Suisse, l'exil en Angleterre avait paru doux aux proscrits. (p. 596)

[the émigrés' admiration of England was equalled by their gratitude for her respectful sheltering of them in their misfortune . . . Indeed, scoffed at in Germany, hunted down in Holland, repulsed in Switzerland, exile in England seemed sweet to those who had been proscribed.]

England had provided a haven from the Revolution; it had defeated Napoleon; it had restored the Bourbon monarchy. Gratitude was certainly due; but even gratitude could be taken too far. The problem as Fitz-James sees it lies in the adoption by the French aristocracy of the costume or external features of its English counterpart, without understanding its spirit. This analysis is found repeatedly in French critiques of *anglomanie* in Proust's lifetime: there is a French national character, which is ill-suited to English ways; often these ways are linked to the weather, so that the gloomy, foggy, melancholic English temperament manifests itself in political, philosophical, and social forms inimical to the clear, sunny, light-hearted Gallic spirit.[36] The degree of crudity with which such stereotypes are deployed depends on the writer's intelligence, but they are rarely absent. In Fitz-James's article they shape her comments on subjects as diverse as steeple-chasing and the education of children: in both cases, the cold,

---

[35] 'L' Anglomanie française', *La Nouvelle Revue* (Sep.–Oct. 1897), 591–609.

[36] Notions of national character play a part in Proust studies, too. In an article published in 1957, the English are said to like Proust because they are more patient than the French, and therefore better at reading long, rambling works of literature. The English love for animals also features, though with a metaphorical twist: 'Se plaisant avec les animaux, ils aiment cette animalité du texte de Proust' [Enjoying the company of animals, they like this animality of Proust's text] (Claude Vallée, 'Proust et l'Angleterre', *Bulletin Marcel Proust*, 7 (1957), 411).

resolute, practical nature of the English is contrasted with the impulsive, carefree, tender attitude of the French, so that if they try to imitate the English they end up with broken bones and ungrateful offspring.

Fitz-James insists on the fitness of ancient French customs and manners to the national 'genius', which at least in one respect turns out to be a genius for maintaining the social hierarchy in place. The generation of French nobles born between the Revolution and the Restoration, Fitz-James declares, was the last to practise 'l'art difficile d'être poli, et même aimable, sans cesser de tenir à distance le plus familier des fâcheux' [the difficult art of being polite, and even friendly, without ceasing to keep the most pushy intruder at arm's length] (p. 605). Their predilection for England was kept within proper bounds; that of their children has degenerated into mindless imitation, whose effect has been to undermine their social position by allowing the promiscuous mingling of social classes. The stability of the social system depends on the clarity with which a person's position within it can be determined, and this clarity, Fitz-James notes, is linked to image, to how people dress and look. The fashion for English dress—she is referring here specifically to male costume—and for English manners, gives the *parvenu* 'un habit matériel et moral que chacun est apte à porter' [a material and moral dress that everyone is able to wear], contrary to the distinctions apparent 'dans l'ordre français' of dress and demeanour: 's'il est donné à tous de s'habiller en "gentleman" chez un Old England quelconque, il appartient à peu de voir à travers l'étoffe si c'est un galant homme ou un manant qu'elle couvre ou qu'elle cache' [though anyone can dress like a "gentleman" at any Old England, few can see through the cloth to determine if it covers a man of honour or hides a boor] (p. 593).

The uniformity of the gentleman's costume was often noted in the period, though not always with this negative accent. 'Le *gentleman* est ici légion,' Bourget remarked in *Lettres de Londres*; 'il est vraiment prodigieux de constater le nombre de personnes qui se soumettent à cette discipline mondaine' [The *gentleman* is legion here; it is really astonishing to see the number of people who submit to this social discipline] (p. 456). But for Bourget this proliferation is a sign not just of the solidarity of a class but of its moral quality, 'la grande vertu anglaise: cette capacité d'exiger beaucoup de soi-même qui fait qu'un *gentleman*, ici, vit et meurt en tenue, comme un soldat' [the great English virtue: that ability to be exacting with oneself, which means that a gentleman, here, lives and dies in uniform, like a soldier'] (p. 457). The word *ici* (twice used in this passage) is the rub: what is authentic in London turns to pastiche in Paris. Fitz-James's reference to 'Old England' as a place where you could buy the look of a *gentleman* ingeniously conflates the literal and the emblematic; this shop on the corner of the rue Scribe and the boulevard des Capucines was described in an article in *Le Gaulois* in 1885 as one of a number of English firms that were content with 'une clientèle de second ordre' [a clientele of the second rank].[37] It was, we recall, the shop where Proust bought his boots.

Along with the levelling effects of English fashion, Fitz-James drew attention to those of English social institutions, notably gentlemen's clubs and horse-racing. During the reign of Louis-Philippe, even an exclusive club such as the Cercle de l'Union might admit a government minister or a financier, so that 'le nouveau venu se trouvait de plein-pied le partner au whist d'un adversaire politique ou d'un indifférent qu'il n'aurait certes pas fréquenté ailleurs' [the newcomer found himself partnering at whist, on terms of equality, a political opponent or casual acquaintance whom he would certainly not have frequented elsewhere] (p. 602).[38] Even so, the clubs of the July Monarchy set bounds to their social promiscuity: 'Pour rien au monde un grand seigneur n'aurait reçu chez sa femme une relation de club qui n'eut pas appartenu, comme lui-même, à l'élite de la gentil-hommerie française' [Not for the world would a great nobleman have brought home to his wife a club acquaintance who did not belong, like him, to the elite of the French nobility].

For Fitz-James, the rot sets in with the foundation of *le Jockey-Club* in 1834; she shares with other conservative social critics a particular animus against the fashion for English horse-racing, seen as fostering a degrading social intimacy between the château and the stable. The very word *jockey*, enshrined in the name of *le Jockey-Club*, epitomizes the malady. 'Ce n'est certes pas sous nos vieux rois,' thundered Francis Wey in 1845, 'ce n'est pas sous Louis XIV que l'on eût renié jusqu'à la langue de sa patrie, pour se ranger sous la bannière des Anglais! Jamais les seigneurs de Versailles ne se fussent glorifiés, eux, de faire partie d'une société *des postillons*, ou *des*

---

[37] 'Fermé pour cause de grève' [Closed because of a strike], *Le Gaulois*, 8 Mar. 1885, a survey of tailoring in Paris prompted by a strike by the lowest rank of employees in the trade, the journeymen known as 'pompiers'. For Proust's dealings with Liberty and Old England, see above, pp. 21–2.

[38] *Le whist* (often *whisk* or *wisk*) is an early 18th-cent. import; *partner* dates from 1767 (Le Robert).

jockeys' [It would certainly not have been under our kings of old, it would not have been under Louis XIV that one would have renounced the very language of one's homeland, to side with the English! The nobles of Versailles would not have prided themselves in forming part of a club *of postillions*, or *of jockeys*].[39] Fitz-James, for her part, quotes with approval the prince de Ligne's denunciation of 'les façons d'être des seigneurs anglais . . . leurs courses, leurs paris, leurs orgies subséquentes et surtout leur tenue de "palfreniers" ' [the behaviour of English noblemen . . . their races, their bets, the orgies that follow, and above all their 'stable-boy' outfits] (p. 595). She has nothing but scorn for the effete descendants of French chivalry whose mastery of horsemanship consists in an early initiation into 'les mystères du "ring" '.[40]

Fitz-James's analysis of the historical origins of *anglomanie* is, as I have indicated, extremely partial. It makes excuses for the behaviour of the French royal family and nobility in the eighteenth century and none for their conduct in the nineteenth; she is especially bitter about Charles X, whom she accuses of patronizing Anglomania in its most frivolous form, and of spending more time restoring the fortunes of horse-racing than safeguarding his throne. Moreover, Fitz-James is not interested in the literary or cultural aspect of the social changes she describes. She does not mention the cult of the dandy, or the Byronism with which it overlapped in post-Revolutionary France; she does not mention Chateaubriand, let alone Mallarmé; her account of the evolution in France of that strange figure, *le gentleman*, is radically incomplete. Nor is she interested in the extent to which the *anglomanie* of her own day—which is also that of *A la recherche*—had penetrated beyond the aristocracy, shaping the behaviour, the opinions, and the vocabulary of other social classes. Lastly, Fitz-James takes no account of the circulation of Englishness in French social culture through the medium of journalism.

Nevertheless Fitz-James has grasped something essential about *anglomanie*, though she takes a very different view of it from Proust: namely its quality of play-acting, of mimicry, of social performance. For Fitz-James this is simply a bad thing, 'la très déraisonnable visée de jouer à l'anglo-saxon alors qu'on a l'honneur d'être latin et gaulois' [the very unreasonable aim of playing at being Anglo-Saxon when one has the honour of

---

[39] *Remarques sur la langue française au dix-neuvième siècle*, II, 60. 'Société' can mean 'group' or 'company', so the allusion is probably to the Jockey Club.

[40] The term in the sense of 'betting ring' dates from 1850 (Le Robert).

being Latin and Gallic] (p. 592). Proust, although he ridicules the affectation of Englishness many times in *A la recherche*, is by no means so unequivocal about the impulse towards social performance from which it springs. There is a profound critique of inauthenticity in the novel, and *anglomanie* is certainly implicated in many kinds of fakery; but there is an equally profound scepticism about authenticity, particularly when it is located in such concepts as 'latin et gaulois', with their intransigent assertions of racial or national purity. *Le gentleman*, in *A la recherche*, summed up in the tragic figure of Charles Swann, may prove to be a hollow idol, signifying intellectual frivolity and emotional desiccation, but the authentic French *gentilshommes* of the novel fare no better. Robert de Saint-Loup, the incarnation of nobility and 'beauté de race', spends his wartime leave in Jupien's male brothel and loses his military cross there. On a visit to Marcel, in perhaps the meanest moment of the entire novel, he is overheard giving poisonous advice to a servant on how to secure the dismissal of a rival (IV, 53; V, 537–8). The effect on Marcel of 'ces paroles machiavéliques et cruelles' is as though Saint-Loup 'récitait un rôle de Satan' [had been rehearsing the role of Satan for a play]; but he has to acknowledge that this isn't the case, that Saint-Loup is speaking, not in a make-believe devil's name, but in his own.[41]

'Je ne prétends pas savoir l'anglais'

'I don't claim to know English': Proust's disclaimer is followed by an emphatic claim: 'Je prétends savoir Ruskin' [I do claim to know Ruskin]. Claim and disclaimer come in a letter to his friend Constantin de Brancovan, a touchy, injured letter prompted by Brancovan's having said to Proust, in public, that his forthcoming translation of Ruskin was bound to be flawed: 'Au fond vous ne savez pas l'anglais, et cela doit être plein de contresens' [When it comes down to it you don't know English, and the thing must be full of misreadings].[42] The greater the truth, the greater the libel; if Brancovan's thoughtless remark gained currency, Proust said, his translation would be discredited and the time he had spent on it wasted: 'j'aurais aussi bien pu ne pas commencer une seule des

[41] *Vintage* mistakenly translates 'mais ce ne pouvait être en son nom qu'il parlait' to mean 'it could not be in his own name that he was speaking'; but 'son nom' refers to Satan, not Saint-Loup. The devil is the innocent party here.

[42] Letter dated to the second fortnight of January, 1903; *Corr.* III, 219–22. Proust mentions Brancovan's remark on p. 220; the riposte I quote is on p. 221.

mille heures de travail (et combien plus!) que cet ouvrage m'a coûtées'
[I might as well not have begun a single one of the thousand hours (and
how much more!) that this work has cost me] (*Corr.* III, 220).

This book is not about Proust's knowledge of English literature, or his
Ruskin translations. I am interested in his defence of these translations
solely for what it reveals about his actual knowledge of the English
language. In his letter Proust makes a distinction between three levels of
knowledge: the spoken language; the written language; and the language
of Ruskin:

Si vous saviez qu'il n'y a pas une expression ambigüe, pas une phrase obscure sur
laquelle je n'aie demandé des consultations à au moins dix écrivains anglais et sur
laquelle je n'aie un dossier de correspondance, vous ne prononceriez pas le mot de
"contresens". Et à force d'approfondir le sens de chaque mot, la portée de chaque
expression, le lien de toutes les idées, je suis arrivé à une connaissance si précise de
ce texte que chaque fois que j'ai consulté un Anglais—ou un Français sachant à fond
l'anglais—sur une difficulté quelconque—il était généralement une heure avant de
voir surgir la difficulté et me félicitait de savoir l'anglais mieux qu'un Anglais. En
quoi il se trompait. Je ne sais pas un mot d'anglais parlé et je ne lis pas bien l'anglais.
Mais depuis quatre ans que je travaille sur la *Bible d'Amiens* je le sais entièrement par
cœur et elle a pris pour moi ce degré d'assimilation complète, de transparence
absolue, où se voient seulement les nébuleuses qui tiennent non à l'insuffisance
de notre regard, mais à l'irréductible obscurité de la pensée contemplée. (*Corr.* III,
220–1)[43]

[If you knew that there isn't a single ambiguous expression, a single obscure phrase
on which I didn't seek advice from ten English writers and for which I don't have
a file of correspondence, you wouldn't use the word "misreading". And by dint of
going more deeply into the sense of each word, the bearing of each expression, the
connecting thread of all the ideas, I have gained so exact a knowledge of this text
that each time I consulted an Englishman—or a Frenchman with a thorough
knowledge of English—about some difficulty or other, it usually took him an
hour before he even grasped the difficulty, and he would congratulate me on
knowing English better than an Englishman. In which he was mistaken. I don't
know a word of spoken English and I don't read English well. But I've worked on
The Bible of Amiens for four years and know it by heart, and it has acquired for me

---

[43] Proust exaggerates somewhat. He began working on his translation in October 1899
(two and a quarter years earlier, not four), and the ten English 'writers' probably amount to
no more than two (Charles Newton Scott and Douglas Ainslie). Later in the letter Proust
mentions Robert d'Humières, the translator of Kipling, who was one of those French people
who knew English 'à fond'.

6. Marie Nordlinger, the English cousin of Reynaldo Hahn who helped Proust with his Ruskin translations. She was an artist and sculptor who had studied at the Manchester School of Art. This portrait was made by another cousin of Hahn's, and friend of Proust's, Federico ('Coco') de Madrazo.

that degree of assimilation, of absolute transparency, in which the only cloudy passages one sees are due not to the inadequacy of one's scrutiny but the irreducible obscurity of the thought that one is contemplating.]

The verb *approfondir*— the master-word of Proust's technical vocabulary as an artist—answers Brancovan's casual idiom, '*Au fond* vous ne savez pas l'anglais'. On the contrary—as far as Ruskin is concerned, Proust claims to have gone as deep as anyone can go, as those who know English 'à fond' will testify. Anything that is still obscure is Ruskin's fault, not his.[44]

[44] However touchy he was at the time, Proust was able to make fun of himself later, in the unpublished pastiche of Ruskin which he drafted in 1909, in which he imagines an

Proust's method of translation is well known. He worked from literal versions supplied first by his mother and later by his English friend Marie Nordlinger. He pored over Ruskin's text using these versions, reworking them, as he says, in the light of an ascending order of meaning—'le sens de chaque mot, la portée de chaque expression, le lien de toutes les idées'—and, he might have added, using his knowledge of other Ruskin works. He inhabited Ruskin's text in a way which enabled him to scrutinize words and phrases, to absorb them, to understand them from the inside. He recreated Ruskin in French; but he did not learn English in the process.

The evidence as to Proust's ability to read English is mixed. 'Je lis l'anglais difficilement [I read English with difficulty],' he wrote to Violet Schiff in November 1919, acknowledging receipt of an issue of *Arts and Letters* with a critical article on him, and a copy of *Richard Kurt*, a novel by Violet's husband Sydney Schiff, who wrote under the pseudonym 'Stephen Hudson' (*Corr.* XVIII, 475–6); in September 1920 he apologized to Sydney himself for his 'lecture peu approfondie' [superficial reading], saying 'je ne sais plus un mot d'anglais' [I no longer know a word of English] (XIX, 436). A letter to Antoine Bibesco of November 1920 seems to confirm that he could read critical articles on his work (he mentions the *Athenaeum* and the *TLS*; *Corr.* XIX, 599); on the other hand he wrote to Paul Morand in March 1921 of 'une amnésie de l'anglais ayant suivi mes traductions de Ruskin' [an amnesia with respect to English following my Ruskin translations] (XX, 115), and in January 1922 he asked Gaston Gallimard: 'Avez-vous des collaborateurs qui sachent l'anglais? Il y a deux ou trois articles dont je voudrais bien savoir le sens' [Do you have any contributors who know English? There are two or three

editor commenting on his 'translation' of an imaginary work by Ruskin: 'La traduction que nous suivons ici est celle de l'Édition des Voyageurs, due à M. Marcel Proust . . . traduction où d'adroits contresens ne font qu'ajouter un charme d'obscurité à la pénombre et au mystère du texte. M. Proust toutefois ne paraît pas avoir eu conscience de ces contresens, car à plusieurs reprises, dans des notes extrêmement fréquentes, il remercie avec effusion un directeur de théâtre, une demoiselle du téléphone et deux membres du comité de la Société des Steeple-Chase, d'avoir bien voulu lui éclaircir les passages qu'il n'avait pas compris' [The translation we follow here is that of the Travellers' Edition, which we owe to M. Marcel Proust . . . a translation in which adroit misreadings only add a further charm of obscurity to the penumbra and mysteriousness of the text. M. Proust however does not seem to have been aware of these misreadings, for several times, in his all-too frequent footnotes, he effusively thanks a theatre manager, a telephone operator, and two members of the committee of the Steeple-Chase Club for having been so good as to clarify for him the passages which he had not understood] ('La Bénédiction du Sanglier', *CSB* 201–2).

articles I'd like to know the meaning of] (XXI, 40). Aside from the equivocal case of *Richard Kurt*, and with the unequivocal exception of Ruskin, he seems never to have read literary works in the original—he quotes from, or alludes to, many English writers, from Shakespeare to Kipling, but almost always in French. On several occasions he showed himself unable to grasp quite simple grammatical points, for example in his telling Scott Moncrieff that 'To Swann's Way' would have been more accurate than 'Swann's Way' as a translation of *Du côté de chez Swann*.[45]

Proust's inability to speak English is easier to verify. In his letter to Constantin de Brancovan he does refer to learning English, but in a vague way that is intended to account for his inability to speak it:

si vous me demandiez à boire en anglais, je ne saurais pas ce que vous me demandez parce que j'ai appris l'anglais quand j'avais de l'asthme et ne pouvais parler, que je l'ai appris des yeux et ne sais ni prononcer les mots, ni les reconnaître quand on les prononce.

[if you asked me for a drink in English, I wouldn't know what you were asking because I learned English when I had asthma and couldn't speak, I learned it by sight and can neither pronounce words, or recognize them when pronounced.]

The period at which this 'learning' took place is hard to establish, and I believe it may simply refer to the time Proust spent after he became interested in Ruskin. He did not study English at school, but German—in which he received mediocre grades and which has left practically no traces in his work, though he was able to write a schoolboy note in German to his grandmother Mme Nathé Weil, and twenty years later review a German book on Ruskin.[46] There was no *anglaise*, or English governess, in the Proust household, no English tutor, and (whether because of his health, or from family prejudice) no holiday trips to England.[47] The most

---

[45] 'Quant à *Swann's Way* cela peut signifier *Du côté de chez Swann*, mais tout aussi bien la manière de Swann. En ajoutant *to* vous auriez tout sauvé' [As for *Swann's Way* that can mean *Du côté de chez Swann*, but it can equally well mean Swann's manner. If you had added *to* you would have made all right] (*Corr.* XXI, 499). I hesitate to accuse Proust of perpetrating a macaronic pun (*to . . . tout*) in order to trump Scott Moncrieff's ambiguity, but in any case the suggested phrase is bad English.

[46] For the letter in German, dated 5 Feb. 1881, see *Corr.* XXI, 540; the review of *John Ruskin, sein Leben und sein Werken*, by Marie von Bunsen, was published in *La Chronique des arts et de la curiosité*, 7 Mar. 1903; repr. *Écrits*, 143–4.

[47] Proust's father, Dr Adrien Proust, had no reason to love the English; his views on hygiene and infectious disease, especially cholera, brought him into conflict with English medical opinion and imperial policy: see Tadié, 29, and *Corr.* III, xviii–xix.

we can say is that his younger brother Robert's family nickname, for reasons that remain obscure, was 'Dick'. However, as we have seen, Proust's social world included many English and English-speaking friends; he was exposed to the *anglomanie* both of his 'native' bourgeoisie and of the *faubourg Saint-Germain* when he penetrated it; and he would have encountered English words in the literature of the nineteenth century from Chateaubriand to Bourget. The English vocabulary of *A la recherche* didn't spring from nowhere; it was the product of choices which Proust made from the English words and phrases he knew. The limits of this knowledge, and the nature of the choices, are discernible from his use of English elsewhere in his work.

With the exception of the words *snob* and *snobisme*, a special case which I discuss in a separate section of this chapter, Proust's use of English words in his fiction and journalism is sparse. In his correspondence it is virtually non-existent, apart from the use of the word *poney* as his private nickname in his letters to Reynaldo Hahn.[48] I have found only one example in which Proust uses an English word that had not been naturalized or adopted in French, and which is not part of a quotation; in a letter to Reynaldo Hahn from 1910, he refers to some drawings he had made of Hahn: 'N'ai pas eu le temps de faire *beaux* dessins mais regardez inside il y en a *petits*' [Didn't have time to make *beautiful* drawings but look inside there are some small ones]; on the facing page he wrote '*Dessins inside / Engraving en dedans*'; the four drawings are on the verso of this page (*Corr.* X, 62). The motive for this macaronic note is mysterious, and there is nothing else like it. Whatever impulses swayed people at the time to mix English and French in their conversation or correspondence evidently had no effect on Proust. But that does not mean that he did not take an interest in English words; indeed, it may imply the reverse.

What of the Ruskin translations? Here a number of English words appear either untranslated or as explanatory additions, for example 'le moderne voyageur fashionable', [le] dernier leader Conservateur', 'My Lords', 'Flèche—arrow' [of a church spire], 'l'historien cockney', 'Free Lord', ' "Nageurs" (Swimmers) . . . "Saulteurs" (Leapers)', 'des "kickshaws" ', 'notre home insulaire', 'un penny', 'un vieux gentleman

---

[48] *Poney* had been in use since the 1820s and was accepted by the Académie in 1878 (Bonnaffé); the added 'e' indicates the French pronunciation, 'po-nai'. It occurs in the opening scene of 'La Mort de Baldassare Silvande' in *Les Plaisirs et les jours* (*JS*, 9).

sacré'.[49] The examples of *leader*, *home*, and *gentleman* belong to a class of words that might be considered at least semi-naturalized in French at the turn of the century; for the propriety of using such terms we have Proust's own rationale, with reference not to his own case but to that of his friend Antoine Bibesco, who in 1913 was working on a translation of Galsworthy's novel *The Country House*. Bibesco asked for advice on translating the word 'squire' (in the sense of country gentleman); Proust suggested 'gentilhomme de comté' or 'seigneur', but noted that in André Chevrillon's critical work, *La Pensée de Ruskin*, the word was left in English; in Robert de la Sizeranne's Ruskin translations he had come across an untranslated *gentleman*, not to mention the fact that la Sizeranne also used the term *bar maid* in his own prose. '[U]n traducteur n'a pas de raison de ne pas employer le terme anglais qu'un prosateur français non traducteur emploierait en anglais' [a translator has no reason not to use the English term that a French prose writer would use, in English, in a work that was not a translation], Proust stated; and again, this time with a suggestive link to *A la recherche*:

Sans aller jusqu'à approuver Guiche qui dit: "allez-vous au petit *meeting* de Mᵉ de Ganay" au lieu de réunion et appelle Saint-Marc *baronnet* au lieu de baron etc., en revanche je trouve légitime les écrivains qui disent *squire*, *home* etc. Et puisque le français qui n'est pas une traduction le comporte, pourquoi le français qui est une traduction ne le comporterait-il pas?

[Without going so far as to approve of Guiche who says: "are you going to Mᵉ de Ganay's little *meeting*" instead of *réunion* and calls Saint-Marc *baronet* instead of baron, etc., on the other hand I think it's legitimate for writers to say *squire*, *home* etc. And since that goes for French that is not a translation, why shouldn't it go for French that is a translation?][50]

When he wrote these words Proust was expecting the proofs of *Un amour de Swann*, in which Odette's vulgar anglicisms are prominent; in *A l'ombre*

[49] These examples come from *BA* 101, 105 n. 2, 111, 125, 165, 169, 193 n. 1, 195, 196, 235. In the unpublished pastiche of Ruskin I mention above (n. 44), Proust repeatedly deploys the word 'cockney': 'votre pitoyable mentalité de lecteur cockney', 'peintre cockney de Pentonville', 'votre cervelle darwinienne de lecteur cockney' (*CSB* 204–5).

[50] These comments are found in three letters to Bibesco, 16, 17, and 19 Apr. 1913, *Corr.* XII, 137, 141, and 148. The word *baronnet* in the third letter is Proust's misspelling; this title does not exist in France. Bibesco's translation was delayed by the war and did not appear until 1922, under the title *Le Domaine* (p. 149 n. 9, where Kolb however wrongly identifies *The Country House* as the second volume of *The Forsyte Saga*, to which it does not belong).

des jeunes filles en fleurs she uses the phrase Proust singles out here, *un petit meeting.*[51] He is distinguishing between the vulgarity of using English words in conversation and the propriety of doing so in a written work; the use of identifiable English words by the narrator of *A la recherche* does not always connote vulgarity or affectation, though the matter is complicated by the deployment of English words as part of a larger design than the denotation of 'character'. At any rate, Proust himself does use such words in writing outside *A la recherche*: 'les halls vitrés' [glazed hallways], 'les grands express', 'couvert de plaids' [covered with travelling-rugs], 'les clergymens de George Eliot', 'hay fever', 'il demeura [he stayed] *at home*', all these in non-fiction pieces;[52] besides the already-mentioned 'poney', we find 'un revolver', 'un jockey', 'un stock de gens [a collection of people]', 'une garden party', 'la commission du budget', 'le steamer à l'horizon', 'en coupé et en victoria', 'le turf' in published and unpublished fiction.[53] Of these, only the phrase *at home* is marked as English; there is no compelling reason why it shouldn't be 'chez soi'. Some instances belong to a category of words that are hard to spot as English, such as *hall*, though this word was a relatively recent import, whose appearance in 'Choses normandes' has a light but discernible English 'accent'.[54] It is one of the hardest tasks of historical philology to pin down the moment at which a word like 'budget' lost its last tinge of Englishness and became fully naturalized; certainly the sense in which Proust uses it in *Jean Santeuil* (it is Jean's father who is a member of the budget commission) was for a long time associated with English political economy, to the mingled political and linguistic chagrin, as we have seen, of conservative purists;[55] but when Marcel's grandmother uses it in *A l'ombre des jeunes filles en fleurs*, I have other reasons for arguing that Proust was conscious of the word's English origin.[56] The same is true of words like *stock* and *steamer*, and to an even

---

[51] See *Corr.* XII, 147 n. 4; for Odette's use of the word *meeting*, see I, 516; II, 114.

[52] 'Choses normandes' (1891); 'John Ruskin (Deuxième et dernier article)' (1900); 'Le salon de la princesse Edmond de Polignac' (1903); *BA* (1904), p. 131 n. 2; 'Sur la lecture' (1905). 'Les clergymens' is a common solecism in the period; in a footnote to a passage in *BA* which includes a translation from another Ruskin text, *The Queen of the Air*, Proust has the phrase 'la plupart de nos gentlemens' [the majority of our . . .] (p. 241 n. 1). But in other places the correct form of the plural occurs, e.g. the translation of 'illiterate clergymen' as 'des clergymen illettrés' in *SL* 146 (sec. 18).

[53] The first four are from pieces in *Les Plaisirs et les jours* (1896), the rest from *Jean Santeuil* (written between 1895 and 1900); neither list is complete.

[54] See p. 117, n. 4.   [55] See above, n. 5.   [56] See Ch. 3, p. 129.

greater extent of words like *jockey* and *garden party*, which are tightly linked to the social manifestations of *anglomanie*.

With some caution, I would suggest that Proust was aware of, and played on, the nuances of certain English words as they would appear to French readers, well before he began work on *A la recherche*. Take, for example, the word *home*, deployed in *A la recherche* as a specific mark of Odette's affected Englishness;[57] it occurs in Ruskin's *Sesame and Lilies* in a quotation from a newspaper which Ruskin uses to illustrate the condition of the working poor, and when Proust has to translate the pitiable sentiment of a man reduced to near-starvation, but who cannot bear the idea of the workhouse—'We wanted the comforts of our little home'— he gives: 'Nous avions besoin des conforts de notre petit chez nous'.[58] He recognized, I think, that the word *home* in French has a certain unctuous quality which would grate in this context; but he is quite content to use it later in *Sésame et les lys*, in a passage where Ruskin is talking about the duties of men and women in their respective spheres: 'A man has a personal work or duty, relating to his own home . . . So a woman has a personal work or duty, relating to her own home'; here Proust uses the phrase 'son propre home', either because the particular inflection of the word in French doesn't matter, or because it actually enhances the savour of Ruskin's banality.[59] Another such example concerns the word *gentleman*; whenever Ruskin uses the term to indicate superior refinement, Proust uses it too: 'a well-educated gentleman' is 'un gentleman instruit'; 'in nothing is a gentleman better to be discerned from a vulgar person' comes out as 'rien ne peut mieux distinguer un gentleman d'un homme vulgaire'; but when Ruskin uses the term politically, to designate the class which has the money and the power, Proust reacts differently: 'the gentlemanly mind of England' is rendered as 'l'esprit conservateur anglais', and 'we live, we gentlemen, on delicatest prey, after the manner of weasels' as 'nous nous nourrissons, nous les gentilshommes, à la façon des belettes, de la proie la plus délicate'.[60]

---

[57] See Ch. 2, pp. 79–80.

[58] Sec. 36 (*SL* 204). The newspaper extract also has the phrase 'so as to keep the home together', translated as 'de manière à vivre en famille à la maison', again avoiding the term.

[59] Sec. 86 (*SL* 297).

[60] Secs. 15, 30, 37, and the endnote to sec. 30 (*SL* 139, 180, 211, 243). The case for Proust's attentiveness to such shades of meaning is strengthened by the occasional footnotes in which he discusses the translation of particular words or phrases, for example 'lady' in sec. 88 of *Sesame and Lilies*.

Proust would have found a justification in Ruskin's own writing for taking such close interest in the shades of meaning of selected words. In the first part of *Sesame and Lilies*, 'Of Kings' Treasuries', in his discussion of the right way of reading, Ruskin enjoins 'the habit of looking intensely at words, and assuring yourself of their meaning, syllable by syllable—nay, letter by letter' (section 15). Part of this scrutiny of words concerns etymology, a topic I will discuss in more detail in Chapter 4; what matters here is Ruskin's distinction between knowledge of *words* and knowledge of *language*. 'Nearly every word in your language', Ruskin tells his English readers, 'has been first a word of some other language—of Saxon, German, French, Latin, or Greek'; the reader should 'get good dictionaries of all these languages, and whenever you are in doubt about a word, hunt it down patiently' (section 19). But, Ruskin goes on,

this does not imply knowing, or trying to know, Greek or Latin, or French. It takes a whole life to learn any language perfectly. But you can easily ascertain the meanings through which the English word has passed; and those which in a good writer's work it must still bear.

This emphasis on the word is crucial to understanding Proust's use of English in *A la recherche*. If (as is possible) he knew Mallarmé's extraordinary work, part pedagogic manual part aesthetic treatise, *Les Mots anglais* (1877), he would have discerned its profound affinity with the principle which Ruskin formulates here; for Mallarmé, too, the word is sovereign, and the significance—better say the resonance—of English words can be conveyed, to a French reader, with a bare minimum of grammar and with no syntax at all.[61] Leaving aside the special knowledge of Ruskin which Proust claimed to possess, his (at best) fluctuating ability to read other English writers, and his confessed inability to understand the spoken language or speak it himself, what remains is the single word or phrase, to which Proust brought the passionate, exacting scrutiny which Ruskin demands, even if *le maître de Coniston* would have thrown up his hands in horror at the result.

'I do not speak french'

The only complete English sentence uttered in *A la recherche* expresses the inability to speak the language in which the novel is written. It comes in

---

[61] I refer to Mallarmé's work in more detail in Ch. 4 (see esp. pp. 185–93).

Sodome et Gomorrhe when the young duc de Châtellerault arrives at the princesse de Guermantes's house for an evening party. As it happens he has not been to the house before, and so the usher has never had occasion to announce him. Yet he and the usher are already acquainted, as Marcel explains:

quelques jours auparavant, l'huissier de la princesse avait rencontré dans les Champs-Élysées un jeune homme qu'il avait trouvé charmant mais dont il n'avait pu arriver à établir l'identité. Non que le jeune homme ne se fût montré aussi aimable que généreux. Toutes les faveurs que l'huissier s'était figuré avoir à accorder à un monsieur si jeune, il les avait au contraire reçues. Mais M. de Châtellerault était aussi froussard qu'imprudent; il était d'autant plus décidé à ne pas dévoiler son incognito qu'il ignorait à qui il avait à faire; il aurait eu une peur bien plus grande—quoique mal fondée—s'il l'avait su. Il s'était borné à se faire passer pour un Anglais, et à toutes les questions passionnées de l'huissier désireux de retrouver quelqu'un à qui il devait tant de plaisir et de largesses, le duc s'était borné à répondre, tout le long de l'avenue Gabriel: "*I do not speak french.*"

[a few days earlier, the Princess's usher had met in the Champs-Elysées a young man whom he had found charming but whose identity he had been unable to establish. Not that the young man had not shown himself as obliging as he had been generous. All the favours that the usher had supposed that he would have to bestow upon so young a gentleman, he had on the contrary received. But M. de Châtellerault was as cowardly as he was rash; he was all the more determined not to unveil his incognito since he did not know with whom he was dealing; his fear would have been far greater, although ill-founded, if he had known. He had confined himself to posing as an Englishman, and to all the passionate questions with which he was plied by the usher, desirous to meet again a person to whom he was indebted for so much pleasure and largesse, the Duke had confined himself to replying, from one end of the Avenue Gabriel to the other: '*I do not speak french.*']
(III, 35; IV, 40)[62]

Needless to say, the Duke is appalled when he sees the usher waiting to announce him at the door of the salon—the one fatal conjunction of

---

[62] The spelling 'french' corresponds to the French practice of using lower-case for the name of a language as opposed to a person of that nationality (so that the Duke passes himself off as 'un Anglais' but would have spoken 'en anglais'). I have altered *Vintage* to retain this necessary detail. See also next note. The *Pléiade* editors note the germ of this episode in a notebook entry from 1908, in which the younger man is not a fake but a real Englishman: 'Jeune hussard anglais et vieux domestique dans le brouillard d'une allée du bois mettant un sceau d'obscurité sur la nature' [Young English hussar and old servant in the fog of an alley of the park placing a seal of darkness on Nature] (III, 1353).

circumstances in which he cannot conceal his identity. For his part the usher realizes that not only is he about to learn the real name of his generous and accommodating young 'Englishman', he is about to bawl it out to the assembled company. The Genius of Comedy has ensured that the smooth functioning of the social machine—the hierarchy in which the hapless Duke is so afraid of losing his place—will of itself engineer his downfall. But this is a benign farce, and the Duke is let off. The usher behaves with exemplary professional decorum—at most, Marcel remarks with malicious relish, the energy of his diction, as he proclaims the Duke's full name and title, 'se veloutait d'une tendresse intime' [softened with intimate tenderness] (III, 37; IV, 43).

In the anecdote of the Duke and the usher, English appears as a form of disguise—appropriate, as we have seen, for a French gay man in the period. By claiming to be English, the Duke avows his homosexuality as 'natural', or at least normative; but because the claim is a lie, he is also denying that his homosexuality has anything to do with his real self. The sentence *I do not speak french* perfectly encapsulates this doubleness; to appreciate its force we should imagine it spoken with a light but unmistakable French accent, the aural equivalent of the tiny orthographic flaw that reveals, in writing, its French origin.

The Duke's false statement has a further implication if we think of it as expressing a truth—not about the character, but about his author. Proust has found an ingenious, witty, and characteristically oblique way of declaring his ignorance of English—by inversion, so to speak (his preferred term for homosexuality). That he should confine himself to one English sentence in *A la recherche*, and to this sentence in particular, seems to me not accidental but perfectly deliberate. This self-restriction is represented by the idiom which twice describes the Duke's behaviour: 'Il s'était borné à se faire passer pour un Anglais . . . le duc s'était borné à répondre'.[63] Proust will confine himself to this one, grammatically correct but limited utterance. Although Odette speaks in English to Gilberte, we are not given a sample of this conversation; the English we actually hear Odette speak consists of words and phrases incorporated into French sentences, and this is true of every other user of English in the novel, the narrator included.

---

[63] *Vintage* disguises this effect by replacing the second occurrence with 'the Duke had merely replied'.

We have seen that Ruskin himself would have drawn Proust's attention to the significance of the word, as opposed to the sentence; as far as English is concerned, this is the direction that Proust's imaginative energy followed. English is fragmented into shards and specks, which glint in the novel's soil, some more eye-catchingly than others. Only one of these, the word *snob*, has what may be called a key or constitutive role in *A la recherche*, and I discuss it in the final section of this chapter. As against this exceptional instance, what patterns can be discerned in the novel's general or 'average' deployment of English words and phrases?

Some English words in *A la recherche* are generated by circumstances— railway travel, for example—in which English vocabulary could hardly be avoided.[64] Others pass without comment, being either already naturalized or in common use. Yet the distinction between such naturalized words (*bar, bifteck, budget, dandy, jury, puzzle, spleen*, etc.) and words whose English origin is self-consciously noted, whether by the character who uses them or by the narrator, is not as clear-cut as it seems.

It is easy to demonstrate that the use of 'marked' English words, and especially phrases, carries a pejorative implication, exposing the vanity, the pretentiousness, or the banality of the speaker. Almost all such phrases are recent; few date to beyond 1850. 'Vous savez que je ne suis pas *fishing for compliments*,' says Odette to Mme Verdurin, fishing for compliments [You know I'm not . . . (I, 188; I, 228). She flatters Marcel by referring to his influence over Gilberte: he is 'le grand favori, le grand crack, comme disent les Anglais' (I, 527; II, 127).[65] Boasting of her friendship with Bergotte, she says to Marcel: 'J'ai obtenu qu'il fasse désormais le *leader article* dans *Le Figaro*. Ce sera tout à fait *the right man in the right place*' [I've arranged that in future he's to do the *leaders* in the *Figaro*. He'll be distinctly . . .] (I, 571; II, 180).[66] Odette is predominant here, but not

---

[64] These words include *train* itself: see the chapter on 'The Terminology of the Railroad' in *French Terminologies in the Making* (New York: Columbia University Press, 1918) by (it so happens) Harvey J. Swann. Marcel gets drunk on the way to Balbec in the *wagon-bar* (II, 12; I, 701).

[65] Le Robert records this sense of 'crack' from 1854, in an equestrian context; in the sense in which Odette uses it here, it dates from the 1880s.

[66] Bonnaffé gives the correct form of the first phrase, *leading article*, and its abbreviation *leader*, which he dates in journalistic usage to the 1850s; Le Robert is a decade earlier. The second phrase is found in Bourget's *Un cœur de femme* (see above, p. 13): 'Chaque homme traverse ainsi une époque où il est, dans sa vie privée ou publique, ce que les Anglais appellent énergiquement: *the right man in the right place*, celui qui convient à la place qui convient' [Thus each man traverses a period in which he is, in his private or public life, what

alone. English is not forgotten in the litany of pompous banalities uttered by M. de Norpois at dinner with Marcel and his parents: 'Pendant plus d'un mois les ennemis de Vaugoubert ont dansé autour de lui la danse du scalp, dit M. de Norpois, en détachant avec force ce dernier mot' [For a month and more Vaugoubert's enemies danced around him howling for his scalp (M. de Norpois detached the word with sharp emphasis)] (I, 453; II, 37).[67] And again, at Mme de Villeparisis's matinée: 'Comment! vous allez de nouveau à Balbec. Mais vous êtes un véritable globe-trotteur!' [What? Going to Balbec again? Why, you're a regular *globe-trotter*] (II, 522; III, 255).[68] Wishing to ingratiate himself with M.de Norpois, the prince von Faffenheim-Munsterburg-Weiningen alludes to the social exclusivity of his mistress, Mme de Villeparisis: 'je sais qu'elle vit très retirée, ne veut voir que peu de monde, *happy few*' [I know that she lives a most retired life, and sees only a very few people—*happy few*] (II, 558, III, 299); this is, incidentally, the only English phrase in *A la recherche* which has a literary origin, and it is spoken by a German.[69] The scholar Brichot has a pretentious habit of tagging historical figures with modern epithets: Maecenas appears as a Roman 'dandy' (III, 343; IV, 406), and the seventeenth-century Paul de Gondi, cardinal de Retz, as 'Ce *struggle for lifer* de Gondi' (III, 269; IV, 316).[70] Mme de Guermantes cruelly refuses Swann the one favour he craves, to be able to introduce his daughter to her; however, after Swann's death, Marcel remarks with fierce disdain, 'la décision de ne pas recevoir sa fille avait fini de donner à Mme de Guermantes toutes les satisfactions d'orgueil, d'indépendance, de *self government*, de

the English forcefully term . . .] (p. 376). Bourget often produces English phrases for no apparent reason: 'un *self made man*, comme disent les Anglais'; 'ce que les Anglais appellent les *drawbacks*,—les inconvénients à subir pour chaque avantage' (both from *Physiologie de l'amour moderne*, 357, 422).

67 Le Robert dates this phrase to 1845.

68 First cited in its English form 'globe-trotter' in 1873; the French form dates from 1880 (Le Robert).

69 The Pléiade editors (II, 1653) translate the phrase as 'quelques heureux' without apparently recognizing its source in *Henry V* (IV. iii. 65: 'We few, we happy few, we band of brothers'); on the other hand they note that Stendhal used it in a dedication to his readers, and this is probably where Proust found it.

70 Alphonse Daudet first used the term in the form *struggle-for-lifeur* in his play *La Lutte pour la vie* (1889); according to Remy de Gourmont, Daudet later confessed that in perpetrating this neologism 'il n'avait pas eu un sentiment vrai de la langue française' [he had not had a true feeling for the French language] (p. 54). For more on Brichot, and on Gourmont, see Ch. 4, pp. 172–85, 198–200.

persécution qu'elle était susceptible d'en tirer' [the decision not to receive his daughter had at last yielded Mme de Guermantes every ounce of pride, independence, *self government* and cruelty that she was capable of extracting from it] (IV, 157).[71]

In most of these examples the Englishness of the word or idiom is marked by italics, or by a comment by the speaker, and sometimes by both (Odette again, patronizingly: 'Ce que nos bons voisins de la Tamise appellent *patronizing*' [What our good neighbours by the Thames call . . .], I, 526).[72] A particular sub-set of such instances concerns *anglomanie*'s comedy of errors—words that are mistranslated or misapplied. Proust was alert to these linguistic ill-effects, which in *A la recherche* are themselves linked to moments of awkwardness, embarrassment, or incongruity. When Marcel has to accompany Françoise to the public toilet in the Champs-Élysées, he describes it as 'un petit pavillon . . . dans lequel étaient depuis peu installés ce qu'on appelle en Angleterre un lavabo, et en France, par une anglomanie mal informée, des water-closets' [a little pavilion . . . in which had recently been installed what in England they call a lavatory but in France, by an ill-informed piece of Anglomania, "water-closets"] (I, 483; II, 74).[73] When the duc de Guermantes accompanies his wife to a popular *café-concert*, where he is conspicuous by his size, his aristocratic demeanour, and his evening dress, Marcel remarks that the spectators perceive him as 'cet Hercule en "smoking" (puisqu'en France on donne à toute chose plus ou moins britannique le nom qu'elle ne porte pas en Angleterre)' [this Hercules in his "smoking" (for in France we give to everything that is more or less British the one name that it happens not to bear in England)] (II, 771; III, 555–6). The misapplication of the term *le smoking* (an abbreviation of *le smoking-jacket*) to mean a dinner-jacket, is noted here, though not on the fourteen other occasions

---

[71] My translation; *Vintage* (V, 661) has 'ceased to provide Mme de Guermantes with all the satisfactions', which is not quite right. Bonnaffé dates *self-government* to 1835 in its political sense, and to 1872 as applied to a person's own conduct, meaning 'autonomy' or 'independent-mindedness'.

[72] My translation; *Vintage* has 'our good friends on the Thames' (I, 576).

[73] It doesn't affect the point, but Proust himself is ill-informed here; the *OED* records 'lavabo' as a synonym for 'lavatory' from 1930, but it was rare even then and cannot have been current twenty years earlier; by contrast 'water-closet' is perfectly correct as a description of a flush toilet (the *OED* records it from the mid-18th cent.), and only the French use of the plural form is incorrect. Cottard later refers to the toilet on the little train in Normandy as 'les waters' (III, 268; IV, 316).

on which the word is used in the novel.[74] When Saint-Loup takes Marcel
out to dinner at a fashionable restaurant, he leaves him to make his entry on
his own, and Marcel's awkwardness takes both a social and linguistic form:

> Or, pour commencer, une fois engagé dans la porte tournante dont je n'avais pas
> l'habitude, je crus que je ne pourrais pas arriver à en sortir. (Disons en passant,
> pour les amateurs d'un vocabulaire plus précis, que cette porte tambour, malgré
> ses apparences pacifiques, s'appelle porte revolver, de l'anglais *revolving door*.)

> [Now, to begin with, once I had ventured into the turning door, a contrivance to
> which I was unaccustomed, I began to fear that I should never get out again. (Let
> me note here for the benefit of lovers of verbal accuracy that the contrivance in
> question, despite its peaceful appearance, is known as a "revolver", from the
> English "revolving door.")]

> (II, 695; III, 463)

Marcel here resembles those militant defenders of the French language
who, since the eighteenth century, campaigned against English on the
grounds that French had perfectly adequate terms for everything that
needed to be described. He finds not one but two native terms for a
revolving door, before producing the bastardized form *porte revolver*,
which carries ludicrous associations with *le revolver*, the firearm, a word
used on several occasions in *A la recherche*.[75] Ironically, the information
offered to 'les amateurs d'un vocabulaire plus précis' consists in pointing
out the imprecision with which French has adopted an English word. But
the irony cuts another way, since for Marcel the *porte revolver* is indeed a
hostile object; his comic inability to master it indicates his not being
accustomed to such fashionable places, and causes the proprietor of the
restaurant to treat him with disdain—until Saint-Loup comes indig-
nantly to the rescue. It is entirely within the spirit of the novel that the
gateway to such spaces should be marked by Englishness; the same is true,
as we shall see, of the Grand-Hotel at Balbec, where, on his first night,
Marcel ascends to his top-floor room in the awkward company of *le lift*,
noticing as they pass '[la] seule rangée verticale de verrières que faisait
l'unique water-closet de chaque étage' [a single vertical line of little

---

[74] Bonnaffé dates *smoking-jacket* to 1889 and gives the incorrect definition of formal
evening dress.

[75] *Porte revolver* seems to be Proust's invention; at any rate I have not found it in the
dictionaries I have consulted. *Le revolver* is found in French from 1848, and was accepted
by the Académie Française in 1878.

windows which were those of the solitary water-closet on each landing]
(II, 26; II, 280).[76]

Transmutations of English meanings into French words also catch
Proust's eye, and again they form a distinct cluster, in this case to do with
the hostilities of social existence: the irruption of English into French signals aggression or unease. Take, for example the use of 'couper' to mean
'cut' in the social sense, 'refuse to acknowledge someone's social existence'. Odette uses the word when correcting Marcel's mistaken impression that the Swanns are friendly with 'une personne que je "coupe" au
contraire aussi souvent que je peux, Mme Blatin! Je trouve très humiliant
pour nous qu'elle passe pour notre amie' [a person whom I cut as a
matter of fact whenever I possibly can, Mme Blatin. I think it's rather
humiliating for us that she should be taken for a friend of ours] (I, 525; II,
124).[77] Odette's own social insecurity makes her particularly sensitive to
such slights, and particularly prone to mask them in English. When
Marcel's relationship with her daughter comes to an end, she cannot resist
affirming her own position: 'Alors, me disait-elle, c'est fini? Vous ne vien-
drez plus jamais voir Gilberte? Je suis contente d'être exceptée et que vous
ne me "dropiez" pas tout à fait' ['Then it's all over?' she said. 'You aren't
ever coming to see Gilberte again? I'm glad you make an exception of me,
and are not going to *drop* me completely'] (I, 629; I, 689).[78] Her tone here
is light, but it changes in a later episode when Marcel asks her if she has
seen Mme de Guermantes at a matinée, and Odette has to feign indifference to the great lady who refuses to 'know' her: ' "Je ne sais pas, je n'ai pas
réalisé", me répondit-elle d'un air désagréable, en employant un terme
traduit de l'anglais' ['I don't know; I didn't *realise* she was here,' she replied
sourly, using an expression borrowed from English] (II, 569; III, 313).[79]

---

[76] For more on this episode, see Ch. 3, pp. 129–30.

[77] This sense of 'couper' has not become naturalized. It comes up again in *Le Côté de
Guermantes I*, higher on the social scale, applied to Mme Leroi's disdain for the marquise
de Villeparisis, who has lost her footing in the *faubourg Saint-Germain*; Marcel refers to
occasions on which 'Mme Leroi, selon une expression chère à Mme Swann, "coupait" la
marquise' [Mme Leroi was—to use an expression dear to Mme Swann—'cutting' the
Marquise] (II, 485; III, 212).

[78] Unlike *couper*, *droper* has become naturalized; Proust seems to have been the first
writer to use it.

[79] Had she been speaking proper French, Odette would have said 'je ne me suis pas ren-
due compte'; the sense of 'réaliser' as 'to be aware of' was in bad odour for many years after
A la recherche; my schoolboy dictionary, *Harrap* (in an entry which I would guess dates to
the original edition of 1934), picks it up with tongs: 'a hardly admissible Anglicism, frequent
in recent journalism of the more illiterate type'.

These French travesties of English words belong to a wider category of usage in *A la recherche*, in which English is associated with social malfunction. At a fashionable tea-shop, for example, Odette speaks in English to Marcel when she wants to say something to him that won't be understood by the people sitting at the neighbouring tables, or by the waiters; unfortunately everyone knows English except him, so that Odette takes the whole room into her confidence while he remains in the dark (I, 535; II, 136). The episode which precedes Marcel's break-up with Gilberte is less comic: Odette tries to force Gilberte to stay at home and keep Marcel company instead of going to a dance class, and in the course of the row switches to English: 'Aussitôt ce fut come si un mur m'avait caché une partie de la vie de Gilberte, comme si un génie malfaisant avait emmené loin de moi mon amie' [At once it was as though a wall had sprung up to hide from me a part of Gilberte's life, as though a wicked genie had spirited her far away] (I, 572; I, 627).[80] When, at Doncières, Marcel is summoned to the telephone to speak to his grandmother, it turns out to be a mistake; the 'wrong' grandmother speaks 'avec un fort accent anglais' [with a strong English accent] (II, 436; III, 152). Indeed, the more you consider the general use of English in *A la recherche*, the more dominant this note becomes. Whether done as satire or light comedy, English signals false consciousness, insincerity, and self-deception; at best it accompanies embarrassment and social blunders. The great writer Bergotte is capable of 'des ruses de gentleman voleur de fourchettes' [the tricks of the gentleman who pockets your spoons] in pursuit of his ambitions to become a member of the Academy (I, 548; II, 152). Even the gentle comedy of Marcel's *snow-boots*, with which this book began, has a context of potential humiliation, akin to his entanglement in the *porte revolver*; many other episodes have a less benign inflection.

Suppose we take a series of innocuous English imports—*buggy, skating, interview, clown*.[81] *Buggy* occurs twice in the novel, in *Du côté de chez Swann*. In the first passage, Marcel and his parents meet their friend, the

---

[80] *Vintage* has 'an evil genius', but Proust was surely thinking of the Arabian Nights here. This episode was added late to *A l'ombre des jeunes filles en fleurs*, and Proust was anxious and insistent about its inclusion: see his letter of 1 August 1918 to Madame Lemarié at the *Nouvelle Revue Française* (*Corr.* XVII, 337–8).

[81] Bonnaffé dates *buggy* to 1809, in the form *boguey*; the English spelling appeared in 1829. The Académie Française enjoined the spelling *boghei*, which Bonnaffé dismisses as 'inexplicable'. *Le skating* dates from 1876; *interview* from 1884; Bonnaffé dates *clown* to 1830, but Le Robert finds an occurrence of the phonetic spelling *claune* in 1817, and dates the English form to 1823.

musician M. Vinteuil, at Combray church on Sunday. Vinteuil is a widower, passionately devoted to his mannish-looking daughter. After the service they drive off in their buggy towards their home at Montjouvain; the daughter is driving (I, 112–13; I, 134–5).[82] Later, Marcel mentions that she is often seen on the roads around Méséglise, 'conduisant un buggy à toute allure' [driving a buggy at full tilt], and adds: 'À partir d'une certaine année on ne la rencontra plus seule, mais avec une amie plus agée, qui avait mauvaise réputation dans le pays et qui un jour s'installa définitivement à Montjouvain' [After a certain year we never saw her alone, but always accompanied by a friend, a girl older than herself with a bad reputation in the neighbourhood, who one day installed herself permanently at Montjouvain] (I, 145; I, 176).[83]

Skating: Robert de Saint-Loup, his mistress Rachel, and Marcel are at a little suburban station waiting for a train back to Paris; Saint-Loup has an elevated, ideal vision of Rachel, while Marcel knows her to have been a common prostitute, an identity she is about to assume, for one hallucinatory moment, in Saint-Loup's eyes, when she is greeted by two of her former comrades on the platform: ' "Tiens, Rachel, tu montes avec nous, Lucienne et Germaine sont dans le wagon et il y a justement encore de la place, viens, on ira ensemble au skating" ' ["Hello, Rachel, why don't you come with us? Lucienne and Germaine are in the train, and there's room for one more. Come on, we'll go to the rink together"] (II, 459; III, 180).

Interview: at Mme de Villeparisis's matinée, poor Bloch commits blunder upon blunder; offered the chance to meet M. de Norpois, he expresses loud satisfaction at the chance to grill him about the Dreyfus Affair: ' "Il y a là une mentalité que je connais mal et ce serait assez piquant de prendre une interview à ce diplomate considérable", dit-il d'un ton sarcastique pour ne pas avoir l'air de se juger inférieur à l'ambassadeur' ["There's a mentality at work there which I don't altogether understand, and it would be rather intriguing to have an interview with this eminent diplomat," he said in a sarcastic tone, so as not to appear to be rating himself below the Ambassador] (II, 516; III, 249).

Finally, and most painfully, *clown*: Marcel's grandmother, on the point of suffering her stroke, enters the public toilet in the Champs-Élysées

---

[82] *Vintage* renders *buggy* as 'dog-cart' (I, 135).

[83] The first phrase is my translation, because of the need to use 'buggy' rather than the term used in *Vintage*, 'dog-cart'.

presided over by the grotesque attendant, the so-called 'marquise', whose costume, like that of a character in a Fellini film, is a caricature of social pretension and a harbinger of death:

Au contrôle, comme dans ces cirques forains où le clown, prêt à entrer en scène et tout enfariné, reçoit lui-même à la porte le prix des places, la "marquise", percevant les entrées, était toujours là avec son museau énorme et irrégulier enduit de plâtre grossier, et son petit bonnet de fleurs rouges et de dentelle noire surmontant sa perruque rousse.

[At the entrance, as in those travelling circuses where the clown, dressed for the ring and smothered in flour, stands at the door and takes the money himself for the seats, the "Marquise," at the receipt of custom, was still in her place with her huge, irregular face smeared with coarse paint and her little bonnet of red flowers and black lace surmounting her auburn wig.]

(II, 605; II, 355)

In all these examples, it 'just so happens' that a word of English origin, more or less naturalized in French, makes its appearance. *Buggy* might just as easily have been 'cabriolet'; *skating* (as the purists repeatedly demanded) 'patinoir'; *prendre une interview* 'poser des questions'; *clown* 'bouffon' (especially as the allusion is to travelling circuses, smaller and more 'provincial'). For each example there is a rational explanation, but together they present an English face which is suffused with vulgarity, perversion, and suffering.[84]

There is not much to set on the other side of the ledger. I can think of only two examples where an English word carries positive connotations: the first comes in the beautiful meditation on sound in *Le Côté de Guermantes I*, in the course of which Marcel imagines a sick man lying in bed, his hearing completely blocked by balls of cotton wool, and then the sudden, miraculous rebirth of sound when these cotton wool balls are removed: 'on assiste, comme si elles étaient psalmodiées par des anges musiciens, à la résurrection des voix. Les rues vides sont remplies pour un instant par les ailes rapides et successives des tramways chanteurs' [we are present, as though it were the chanting of choirs of angels, at the resurrection of the voice. The empty streets are filled for a moment with the whirr of the swift and recurrent wings of the singing tram-cars] (II, 375;

---

[84] To the *buggy* we might add the *tilbury* (dated by Bonnaffé to 1820) in which Saint-Loup inexplicably drives right by Marcel in Doncières without stopping to return his greeting (II, 436; III, 153), and above all Swann's *victoria* (for which see Ch. 2, n. 39).

III, 80).[85] The second example, coincidentally, also involves angels, the ones Marcel admires in Giotto's frescos in the Arena Chapel at Padua, so lifelike and 'literal': 'on les voit s'élevant, décrivant des courbes, mettant la plus grande aisance à exécuter des loopings, fondant vers le sol la tête en bas . . .' [they can be seen soaring upwards, describing curves, "looping the loop," diving earthwards head-first . . .] (IV, 227; V, 744).[86] These are rare, privileged moments for English in the novel; even when English words appear elsewhere in the context of works of art (as they do with Elstir's paintings, for example) they do not have this free, untrammelled quality; they are words which, so to speak, have their hands dirty.[87]

The difference is striking between the use of English words in the novel, and that of English literature. Shakespearian allusion in *A la recherche*, for example, rarely follows the satirical bent of Prince von Faffenheim's 'happy few'; more often it connotes delight, as in Marcel's fantasia on the asparagus he sees in the kitchen at Combray, 'les délicieuses créatures qui s'étaient amusées à se métamorphoser en légumes' [exquisite creatures who had been pleased to assume vegetable form], and whose 'essence précieuse' he recognizes 'quand, toute la nuit qui suivait un dîner où j'en avais mangé, elles jouaient, dans leurs farces poétiques et grossières comme une féerie de Shakespeare, à changer mon pot de chambre en un vase de parfum' [when, all night long after a dinner at which I had partaken of them, they played (lyrical and coarse in their jesting like a fairy-play by Shakespeare) at transforming my chamber pot into a vase of aromatic perfume] (I, 119; I, 131).[88]

At the other end of the novel, the broken figure of M. de Charlus, with his wild white hair and beard, has 'la majesté shakespearienne d'un roi

---

[85] *Tramway* is not above reproach; it contributes to Marcel's first, disillusioning sight of the famous church at Balbec: 'il se dressait sur une place où était l'embranchement de deux lignes de tramways' [it stood on a square which was the junction of two tramway routes] (II, 19; II, 273).

[86] *Loopings* also occurs in a neutral context (though one which, for Proust himself, had profoundly painful associations, since it evoked the death in a flying accident of Alfred Agostinelli, his former chauffeur, and the model for the last stages of Marcel's relationship with Albertine); at an aerodrome, the keen spectator can follow 'les évolutions d'un pilote exécutant des loopings' [the gyrations of a pilot looping the loop] (II, 694; III, 462).

[87] For the 'English' aspect of Elstir's painting, see Ch. 3, pp. 148–58.

[88] *Vintage* has 'like one of Shakespeare's fairies'; the earlier version (i.e. the Scott Moncrieff–Kilmartin text before its revision by D. J. Enright) has 'as the fairies in Shakespeare's *Dream*'. The specific allusion is, indeed, probably to *A Midsummer Night's Dream*, though the term 'féerie' was also applied to *The Tempest*. Proust owned a *Théâtre complet* of Shakespeare *Pléiade* note, p. 1159. For 'happy few', see above, p. 49.

Lear' (IV, 438; VI, 208). An English literary reference corrects Marcel's first impression of Andrée as 'une maîtresse de coureur, enivrée de l'amour des sports' [the mistress of some racing cyclist, passionately interested in sport]; in fact 'ses meilleures heures étaient celles où elle traduisait un roman de George Eliot' [her happiest hours were those which she spent translating one of George Eliot's novels] (II, 295; II, 604–5).[89] The same is true, even more so perhaps, for painting, where Turner, Whistler, the Pre-Raphaelites appear with their presence and potency intact. Only one English literary reference is subjected to the kind of indignity visited on the English language, and it consists, appropriately enough, in a private joke which itself relies on a play on words. At the end of the great tragicomic episode of Marcel's visit to the male brothel in wartime Paris, Jupien, M. de Charlus's faithful companion, who is the brothel-keeper, ushers Marcel out of the building and bids him farewell. Marcel compares the scenes he has witnessed to tales from the *Arabian Nights*, and prompts Jupien to a parting shot:

"Vous parlez de bien des contes des *Mille et Une Nuits*, me dit-il. Mais j'en connais un qui n'est pas sans rapport avec le titre d'un livre que je crois avoir aperçu chez le baron" (il faisait allusion à une traduction de *Sésame et les lys* de Ruskin que j'avais envoyée à M. de Charlus). "Si jamais vous étiez curieux, un soir, de voir, je ne dis pas quarante, mais une dizaine de voleurs, vous n'avez qu'à venir ici; pour savoir si je suis là vous n'avez qu'à regarder la fenêtre de là-haut, je laisse une petite fente ouverte et éclairée, cela veut dire que je suis venu, qu'on peut entrer; c'est mon Sésame à moi. Je dis seulement Sésame. Car pour les lys, si c'est eux que vous voulez, je vous conseille d'aller les chercher ailleurs."

["You have mentioned one or two of the tales in the *Arabian Nights*," he said. "But there is another I know of, not unrelated to the title of a book which I think I have seen at the Baron's" (he was alluding to a translation of Ruskin's *Sesame and Lilies* which I had sent to M. de Charlus). "If ever you are curious, one evening, to see, I will not say forty but a dozen thieves, you have only to come here; to know whether I am in the house you have only to look up at that window; if I leave my little window open with a light visible it means that I am in the house and you may come in; it is my private Sesame. I say only Sesame. As for Lilies, if they are what you seek I advise you to go elsewhere."]

(IV, 411–12; VI, 175)

[89] Admittedly Marcel is disappointed to discover that Andrée is not, in fact, sports-mad and promiscuous. But that is because he already knows and loves George Eliot, and what he desires is what lies outside himself.

In this witty, impure, self-wounding joke, Proust pays homage to Ruskin's passionate scrutiny of the meanings and resonance of individual words by desecrating the title of the work in which that scrutiny is most devoutly enjoined, and which he had himself translated. It was Ruskin himself, in his conclusion to the first part of *Sesame and Lilies*, 'Of Kings' Treasuries', who had made the playful-yet-serious connection between books and the bread of life, 'bread made of that old enchanted Arabian grain, the Sesame, which opens doors;—doors not of robbers', but of Kings' Treasuries'. The final words are the same as those of the title, though with a different grammatical inflection, forming the kind of circular movement which would have appealed powerfully to Proust and which he adopted in the opening and closing sentences of *A la recherche* itself. In this literary allusion a whole aesthetic of language is caught up and travestied; it is Proust's own Shakespearian farce, 'poétique et grossière', only the magic operates in reverse, transforming a vase of perfume into a chamber-pot.

Le livre des snobs

The English words of *A la recherche* are dominated by *snob*, with forty-nine occurrences, and *snobisme*, with forty-one; together with one occurrence of *antisnobisme*, one of *snobinettes*, and two of the nonce-verb *snober*, these words constitute a distinctive cluster in the novel, certainly as far as its social world is concerned. The history of the words in French is complex, and their evolution had not finished when Proust started his writing career; their deployment in *A la recherche* is marked both by the senses that were current in his own time, and by the individual emphasis which he brought to their use.[90]

The word *snob* entered French in 1857 with Georges Guiffrey's translation of Thackeray's *Book of Snobs*, which had been published in 1848. *The Book of Snobs* gathered together the forty-four 'Snob Papers' Thackeray had contributed to *Punch* in 1846–7, under the rubric 'The Snobs of England, by One of Themselves' (the latter phrase was retained as the subtitle). The occasional nature of the work, and the long span of time over which it was produced, allowed Thackeray to play and experiment with a term which, though it already existed when he took it up, had no real

---

[90] For a detailed survey, see Goodell, 29–42.

currency, and which, by the time *The Book of Snobs* appeared, bore his indelible imprint.

The English etymology of the word *snob* does not concern us here; Proust almost certainly knew nothing of it, and he may never have read *Le Livre des snobs* either. What matters is, first, the concept of snobbery Thackeray presented, and, second, the transmutation of that concept into French usage.

Margaret Goodell points out that Thackeray's use of the words 'snob' and 'snobbishness' (the latter certainly his coinage) is loose and inconsistent; in particular, she identifies a sense which derives from earlier uses of the term, that of 'the swaggering, presumptuous vulgarian' (p. 11). Examples include the 'Great City Snobs', 'Military Snobs', and 'English Snobs on the Continent'—bullies, blustering ignoramuses, ill-mannered oafs, but not snobs as we now understand the term. This sense of the word has not survived in English; the core of Thackeray's analysis of snobbery, the social and psychological truth which became fused with the word, pertained to social class.

Goodell identifies, as a crucial feature of Thackeray's concept, its doubleness: snobbery faces both ways, designating both 'the person of superior social rank who is contemptuous of his social inferiors as well as the person who imitates or has an excessive admiration for his social superiors' (p. 8 n. 4). This is true, but it is equally true that the doubleness springs from a single cause, namely the concept of social rank itself. *The Book of Snobs* was published in the revolutionary year of 1848, and the brilliance of its comedy shouldn't disguise the savagery of its onslaught on British notions of gentility and what Thackeray called 'Lordolatry':

What Peerage-worship there is all through this free country! How we are all implicated in it, and more or less down on our knees.—And with regard to the great subject on hand, I think that the influence of the Peerage upon Snobbishness has been more remarkable than that of any other institution. (p. 11)

Though Thackeray broadens and diversifies his treatment, he never loses sight of this central premiss. The British social system ensures that an unjust share of national wealth, power, and honour is given to a 'privileged class': 'How can we help Snobbishness, with such a prodigious national institution erected for its worship?' It is this system of fundamental inequity that 'encourages the commoner to be snobbishly mean, and the noble to be snobbishly arrogant' (p. 12). Some of Thackeray's funniest, but also most angry outbursts are directed at the tokens of this 'national institution', such as the Court Circular:

As long as the *Court Circular* exists, how the deuce are people whose names are chronicled in it ever to believe themselves the equals of the cringing race which daily reads that abominable trash? . . . Down with the *Court Circular*—that engine and propagator of Snobbishness! I promise to subscribe for a year to any daily paper that shall come out without a *Court Circular*—were it the *Morning Herald* itself. When I read that trash, I rise in my wrath; I feel myself disloyal, a regicide, a member of the Calf's Head Club. The only *Court Circular* story which ever pleased me, was that of the King of Spain, who in great part was roasted, because there was not enough time for the Prime Minister to command the Lord Chamberlain to desire the Grand Gold Stick to order the first page in waiting to bid the chief of the flunkeys to request the Housemaid of Honour to bring up a pail of water to put his Majesty out.

I am like the Pasha of three tails, to whom the Sultan sends *his Court Circular*, the bowstring.

It *chokes* me. May its usage be abolished for ever. (pp. 16–17)

This is the heart of Thackeray's polemic: the worship of rank is corrupting to both the worshipper and the false god, and the mere existence of rank makes such degrading worship inevitable. Everyone, without exception, is a snob by this definition, including, as the subtitle acknowledges, the author, who continually offers proofs of his own susceptibility to the vice he attacks.

In its transmutation into French, the term *snob* retained its doubleness, a fact which is of profound importance to *A la recherche*, but it more or less completely lost its radical foundation. Georges Guiffrey's preface to his translation offers a woolly definition of the term, featuring 'un peu de tous les ridicules de l'humaine nature' [a little of all the absurdities of human nature] and 'absence totale de ce qui est beau, noble, et distingué' [the complete absence of that which is beautiful, noble, and distinguished]—terms which themselves reintroduce snobbery by the back door. *Le snobisme* might be ridiculed, but this ridicule did not aim at the principle of social hierarchy, only at the inappropriate behaviour of people occupying different places within it. Both the *grand seigneur* and the *bourgeois* could be snobs, but in an ideal world there would still be *grands seigneurs* and *bourgeois*, each behaving without affectation or false pride. Moreover, French usage clung to another meaning of the term, which is also found in Thackeray but which is not part of the core meaning as I have described it, namely the unreasoning admiration for whatever is fashionable; indeed, this is the main definition of *snobisme* given by

Bonnaffé as late as 1920: 'Affectation ridicule; admiration de commande pour tout ce qui est à la mode' [ridiculous affectation; enforced admiration for everything which is in fashion].[91]

Proust was not responsible for these shifts of meaning, just as he was not responsible for the distinctive form of the word *snob* itself. *Snob* is unusual in French, both because there are virtually no native words ending in 'ob', and because 'snob' did not acquire a feminine form, 'snobe', despite the attempts of some writers to introduce it. You can be *un snob* or *une snob*—Proust has both—and the noun is also the adjective, so that *un snob* can behave in a manner which is *extrêmement snob*. Something about the word resisted variation, something harsh which suits its unforgiving nature; in this respect *snob* resembles *flirt*, also unvarying in form through different grammatical aspects; as Paul Bourget says, lamenting the disappearance of the charming French word *fleureter*, 'le dur mot anglais triomphe' [the hard English word triumphs].[92]

The persistent connection of the word *snob*, in the first fifty years or so of its use, with Englishness, and indeed with *anglomanie*, may explain why it kept its original form. Strolling in Hyde Park on a beautiful summer's day and watching the procession of aristocratic carriages whose 'cochers . . . se tiennent droits sur les sièges à côté des "tigres" minuscules' [coachmen . . . sit upright on their seats next to miniscule "tigers"],[93] Bourget reflects:

C'est un des coins du monde où doit le plus souffrir un partisan de l'égalité, tandis que tout y réjouit un cœur atteint de snobisme.—Quel autre mot employer pour définir cette naïve maladie de la vanité qui se développe surtout ici et qui

---

[91] Bonnaffé's definition of *snob* is 'Homme sot et prétentieux; poseur' [foolish and pretentious man . . .], which stigmatizes manner rather than substance; but at least one of his examples, from an up-to-date article in the *Revue des Deux Mondes* of 1857, takes the opposite tack, correctly citing Thackeray even though Thackeray would have hotly disputed the assertion itself: 'Il [le Parlement Anglais] n'a pas le respect du rang, cette idolâtrie que M. Thackeray . . . a si vertement travaillée. Le Parlement n'est pas *snob*' [It lacks the respect for mere rank, that idolatry which Thackeray . . . has so sharply criticized. Parliament isn't snobbish]. Note also that this example uses *snob* adjectivally.

[92] *Physiologie de l'amour moderne*, 408. In *A l'ombre des jeunes filles en fleurs*, when Albertine is annoyed with Marcel for admiring Gisèle, she says: ' "Je ne crois pourtant pas qu'elle vous plairait. Elle n'est pas flirt du tout. Vous devez aimer les jeunes filles flirt, vous' [I don't believe you would care for her, though. She's not in the least a flirt. You like girls who flirt, I suspect] (II, 242; II, 541).

[93] 'Tigre' was a slang term for a groom. Proust transferred this scene to Paris, adding an anglophile reference to Balzac: see Ch. 2, p. 98 n. 40.

consiste dans une sorte de culte superstitieux pour toute supériorité sociale, de naissance, de fortune ou de renommée?

[It must be one of the corners of the globe where a partisan of social equality suffers most, while there is everything to rejoice a person whose heart is touched with snobbery.—What other word will do to define that naïve sickness of one's vanity which develops here above all other places, and which consists in a sort of superstitious worship of every social superiority, whether of birth, fortune, or fame?][94]

Note that Bourget refers to one side only of the double aspect of snobbery, that which relates to the worship of social superiority; he doesn't use the word to designate the attitude of the nobleman towards his inferiors. Although Bourget says here that snobbery is peculiarly prevalent in England, he does not mean that it was exclusively English—on the contrary.[95] But the word itself has an affinity with Englishness, especially when the snob is identified as a follower of fashion. Odette, for example, admires someone who 'ne va jamais que dans les endroits chics' [only goes to really smart places], and cites the example of a young man called Herbinger who has the authentic fashionable look: 'c'est un des hommes les plus lancés de Paris, ce grand jeune homme blond qui est tellement snob, il a toujours une fleur à la boutonnière . . .' [he's one of the best-known men in Paris, that tall blond young man who looks like such a snob, he's always got a flower in his buttonhole . . .] (I, 239).[96] *Snob*, here, signifies the elegance—or would-be elegance—of the man-about-town, a type for which French already had the word *gommeux*; it does not connote superiority of rank, but conformity to fashion.

The striking thing about this remark by Odette, however, is that it is unique in *A la recherche*. Nowhere else in the novel do the words *snob* and *snobisme* denote a preoccupation with what is *chic*; indeed, considering the frequency with which the terms are used, their range of meaning is extremely narrow. Proust fastened on *le snobisme* as the double face of

[94] *Lettres de Londres*, 452.

[95] He makes the point in *Physiologie de l'amour moderne*: 'Nos ancêtres, qui n'avaient pas le mot, avaient si bien la chose, que la liste des maris ou des amants trompés par les rois, et qui s'en sont réjouis, est à la liste de ceux qui s'en sont fâchés, dans les proportions de trois cents à un' [Our ancestors, who didn't have the word, had the thing itself to the point where the proportion of husbands or lovers who were happy to be cuckolded by royalty, as against those who were not, is about three hundred to one] (p. 478). See also n. 25 for Jacques Boulenger's English 'professeur de snobisme'.

[96] My translation; *Vintage* has 'that great big fair-haired boy who's such a toff' (I, 292).

social hierarchy, and stuck to it. Jealous of Marcel's friendship with Robert de Saint-Loup, the snob Bloch accuses him of snobbery: ' "Tu dois être en train de traverser une jolie crise de snobisme. Dis-moi, es-tu snob? Oui, n'est-ce pas?" ' ["You must be suffering from a severe attack of snobbery. Tell me, are you a snob? I think so, what?"] (II, 100; II, 370). Well, no, thinks Marcel: 'Quand Bloch me parla de la crise de snobisme que je devais traverser et me demanda de lui avouer que j'étais snob, j'aurais pu lui répondre: "Si je l'étais, je ne te fréquenterais pas." ' [When Bloch spoke to me of the attack of snobbery from which I must be suffering, and bade me confess that I was a snob, I might well have replied: "If I were, I shouldn't be going about with you"] (I, 103; II, 374).

But this very denial reveals that, though Marcel refrains from telling Bloch that he is his social superior, he does not refrain, so to speak, from knowing it. No one in the novel does refrain from this knowledge, except Marcel's grandmother; everyone's behaviour is more or less affected by it; it makes hypocrites of virtually every character we meet. M. de Bréauté, for example, an intimate friend of Mme de Guermantes, has the reputation of *not* being a snob, a reputation which he carefully cultivates:

Pour que sa réputation d'intellectuel survécût à sa mondanité . . . il partait avec des dames élégantes faire de longs voyages scientifiques à l'époque des bals, et quand une personne snob, par conséquent sans situation encore, commençait à aller partout, il mettait une obstination féroce à ne pas vouloir la connaître, à ne pas se laisser présenter. Sa haine des snobs découlait de son snobisme, mais faisait croire aux naïfs, c'est-à-dire à tout le monde, qu'il en était exempt.

[So that his reputation as an intellectual might survive his social activity . . . he would set out with ladies of fashion on long scientific expeditions at the height of the dancing season, and when a snobbish person, in other words a person not yet socially secure, began to be seen everywhere, he would be ferociously obstinate in his refusal to know that person, to allow himself to be introduced to him or her. His hatred of snobs derived from his snobbishness, but made the simple-minded (in other words, everyone) believe that he was immune from snobbishness.]

(II, 794; III, 582)

In one sense, this usage is thoroughly 'English'; Proust's clear-sighted concentration on the distortions of behaviour brought about by a social system based on rank brings us close to Thackeray's original vision.[97] But in

---

[97] Thackeray would have found the incident with which this book began, that of Marcel's *snow-boots*, a perfect test case; Marcel's shame at being unfashionable, the scorn of

another sense it represents the most concentrated attempt to naturalize the term within the specific conditions of French society, since Proust is careful to separate the principle of snobbery from that of *anglomanie*. His French snobs do not aspire to the company of *les milords*; his French nobles may themselves be *anglomanes*, but their own snobbery towards their social inferiors is not based on the fact that they know the Prince of Wales or are keen on blood sports. In fact, unlike Bourget (or Balzac, for that matter), Proust introduces no English aristocrats in person in *A la recherche*; references are always at second hand, as when Mme de Guermantes tells Marcel that her gold kid shoes came from a shopping trip in London with the Duchess of Manchester (III, 552; V, 41). Such English connections are taken for granted; Proust's analysis of French snobbery, Marcel's included, is rooted in native soil.

The first reference to *snobisme* in the novel comes in our introduction to the figure of Legrandin, a neighbour of Marcel's family at Combray:

Grand, avec une belle tournure, un visage pensif et fin aux longues moustaches blondes, au regard bleu et désenchanté, d'une politesse raffinée, causeur comme nous n'en avions jamais entendu, il était aux yeux de ma famille qui le citait toujours en exemple, le type de l'homme d'élite, prenant la vie de la façon la plus noble et la plus délicate. Ma grand-mère lui reprochait seulement de parler un peu trop bien, un peu trop comme un livre, de ne pas avoir dans son langage le naturel qu'il y avait dans ses cravates lavallière toujours flottantes, dans son veston droit presque d'écolier. Elle s'étonnait aussi des tirades enflammées qu'il entamait souvent contre l'aristocratie, la vie mondaine, le snobisme, "certainement le péché auquel pense saint Paul quand il parle du péché pour lequel il n'y a pas de rémission".

L'ambition mondaine était un sentiment que ma grand-mère était si incapable de ressentir et presque de comprendre qu'il lui paraissait bien inutile de mettre tant d'ardeur à la flétrir. De plus elle ne trouvait pas de très bon goût que M. Legrandin dont la sœur était mariée près de Balbec avec un gentilhomme bas-normand se livrât à des attaques aussi violentes contre les nobles, allant jusqu'à reprocher à la Révolution de ne les avoir pas tous guillotinés.

[Tall and handsome of bearing, with a fine, thoughtful face, drooping fair moustaches, blue eyes, an air of disenchantment, an almost exaggerated refinement of

the servants and the other guests, then their fawning change of tack when the princesse de Parme expresses her admiration—all this could have gone straight into *The Book of Snobs* as an illustration of the way in which snobbishness is not simply countenanced by the prevailing social system, but virtually enforced by it.

courtesy, a talker such as we had never heard, he was in the sight of my family, who never ceased to quote him as an example, the very pattern of distinction, who took life in the noblest and most delicate manner. The only fault my grandmother found with him was that of speaking a little too well, a little too much like a book, for not using a vocabulary as natural as his loosely knotted Lavallière neckties, his short, straight, almost schoolboyish coat. She was astonished, too, at the furious tirades which he was always launching at the aristocracy, at fashionable life, at snobbishness—"undoubtedly," he would say, "the sin of which St Paul is thinking when he speaks of the unforgivable sin against the Holy Ghost."

Worldly ambition was a thing which my grandmother was so little capable of feeling, or indeed of understanding, that it seemed to her futile to apply so much heat in its condemnation. Besides, she did not think it in very good taste for M. Legrandin, whose sister was married to a nobleman of Lower Normandy, near Balbec, to deliver himself of such violent attacks upon the nobility, going so far as to blame the Revolution for not having guillotined them all.]

(I, 67; I, 74–5)[98]

The violence of Legrandin's 'tirades' against snobbery resembles that of Thackeray's, but it is given an authentic French 'accent' not just by the reference to the Revolution but by Legrandin's own appearance and manner, which have a distinctively French elegance. His dress signals his attachment to older French fashions for men; the 'cravate lavallière', a loosely tied bow, was named after Louise de Lavallière, mistress of Louis XIV. Legrandin is spoken of as 'un homme d'élite', not *un gentleman*— not even by marriage, since his sister is married to 'un gentilhomme bas-normand'; it might be stated as an axiom that Proust never uses the word *gentilhomme* in *A la recherche* without the unwritten parenthesis '(et non pas *gentleman*)'.

Before we return to Legrandin, it is worth following up this *gentilhomme*, whom we will get to know at Balbec as M. de Cambremer, partly because Marcel's grandmother's incomprehension of 'l'ambition mondaine' is alluded to again in the context of his marriage to Legrandin's sister. M. de Cambremer may be an authentic French nobleman, but he also happens to be spectacularly ugly. When Marcel meets him at La Raspelière (the country house near Balbec in Normandy which the Verdurins have rented from the Cambremer family) he has fun

---

[98] *Vintage* has 'the very pattern of a gentleman', which is just what I take Legrandin not to be, and replaces the Lavallière neckties with 'bow-ties'; it has 'country gentleman' for his brother-in-law, and also 'My grandmother alone found fault with him', which is a straightforward misreading.

describing M. de Cambremer's heavy-lidded eyes, skewed nose, and coarse complexion, which seem to indicate (the nose especially) 'une bêtise vulgaire' [vulgar stupidity]; yet he has heard M. de Cambremer cited as 'un homme de haute distinction' [a man of supreme distinction], a judgement with which he believes his grandmother would have disagreed:

Il me sembla au contraire qu'il était des gens que ma grand-mère eût trouvés tout de suite "très mal" et comme elle ne comprenait pas le snobisme, elle eût sans doute été stupéfaite qu'il eût réussi à être épousé par Mlle Legrandin qui devait être difficile en fait de distinction, elle dont le frère était "si bien". Tout au plus pouvait-on dire de la laideur vulgaire de M. de Cambremer qu'elle était un peu du pays et avait quelque chose de très anciennement local; on pensait, devant ses traits fautifs et qu'on eût voulu rectifier, à ces noms de petites villes normandes sur l'étymologie desquels mon curé se trompait parce que les paysans, articulant mal ou ayant compris de travers le mot normand ou latin qui les désigne, ont fini par fixer dans un barbarisme qu'on trouve déjà dans les cartulaires, comme eût dit Brichot, un contresens et un vice de prononciation.

[It seemed to me on the contrary that he was one of those people whom my grandmother would at once have set down as "very common," and since she had no conception of snobbishness, she would no doubt have been stupefied that he could have succeeded in winning the hand of Mlle Legrandin, who must surely be difficult to please, having a brother who was "so well-bred." At best one might have said of M. de Cambremer's plebeian ugliness that it was to some extent redolent of the soil and had a hint of something very anciently local; one was reminded, on examining his faulty features, which one would have liked to correct, of those names of little Norman towns as to the etymology of which my friend the curé was mistaken because the peasants, mispronouncing or having misunderstood the Latin or Norman words that underlay them, have finally perpetuated, in a barbarism to be found already in the cartularies, as Brichot would have said, a misinterpretation and a faulty pronunciation.]

(III, 305; IV, 360)

These linguistic deformations have a larger significance in *A la recherche*, which I discuss in the final chapter of this book; what matters here is their use as a metaphor for M. de Cambremer's appearance. They indicate an authenticity which is not superficial, not 'skin-deep', but on the contrary draws its 'distinction' from the very twistedness of its roots.[99] For once

[99] Proust uses the same phrase, 'de travers', to describe the medieval peasants' ignorance and M. de Cambremer's modern nose, which is placed 'de travers au-dessus de sa bouche' [askew above his mouth] (III, 304; IV, 359).

Marcel's grandmother is wrong in her estimation of who is 'très mal' or 'si bien', and her incomprehension of *le snobisme*, which does her credit, is accompanied by a naïve propensity to take people at face value. M. de Cambremer is, in fact, devoid of snobbery, while Legrandin (not to mention his sister) is utterly penetrated and possessed by it. His exquisite conversation is a sham; the intensity of his fulminations against the aristocracy springs not from republican disdain but from repressed desire. He is not *un snob anglomane*: he is, so to speak, the authentic French variety.

Marcel and his family begin to suspect Legrandin's secret at Combray when they witness his fawning demeanour towards a local landowner and his wife, while at the same time he barely acknowledges their own existence. The matter is placed beyond doubt when Marcel dines with Legrandin and, without any intention to wound him, asks if he knows the Guermantes family. Legrandin's social ascent hasn't reached this level; his anguished reaction, and the futile effort he makes to conceal it, reveal the truth to Marcel: 'il était snob'. And more than that: they reveal Legrandin's double nature, the presence in him of 'un autre Legrandin qu'il cachait soigneusement au fond de lui, qu'il ne montrait pas, parce que ce Legrandin-là savait sur le nôtre, sur son snobisme, des histoires compromettantes . . .' [another Legrandin, whom he kept carefully hidden in his breast, whom he would never consciously exhibit, because this other could tell compromising stories about our own Legrandin and his snobbishness . . .] (I, 126–7; I, 153). This repressed self, though shameful, is at least authentic; it is not a social persona constructed for the benefit of others, but a self whose real desires are manifested by the very effort to keep them hidden.

This is not the end of the story as far as Legrandin's snobbery is concerned; later in the novel he will both fulfil his social ambition, and cease to care about it; but here, in the early part of *A la recherche*, it strikes the keynote of Proust's treatment of the theme. It gives rise, in this episode, to pitiless comedy; but snobbery is not just fertile in hypocrisy and self-delusion. Proust criticizes 'les romanciers mondains qui analysent cruellement du dehors les actes d'un snob ou prétendu tel, mais ne se placent jamais à l'intérieur de celui-ci, à l'époque où fleurit dans l'imagination tout un printemps social' [the social novelists who analyse mercilessly from the outside the actions of a snob or supposed snob, but never place themselves inside his skin, at the moment when a whole social springtime is bursting into blossom in the imagination] (III, 147; IV, 173). This beautiful last phrase opens an unexpected perspective on snobbery; it suggests that Proust's criticism of 'les romanciers mondains' is also a self-criticism, or at least a self-admonition; it should remind us, as readers, to take seriously Proust's objection to what he calls 'la littérature de notations' [the literature of observations] (IV, 473),[100] the kind of thing he satirizes in *Un amour de Swann* in the brilliant excursus on the monocles worn by the guests at Mme de Sainte-Euverte's soirée; one of these belongs to, again, 'un romancier mondain', for whom it seems 'son seul organe d'investigation psychologique et d'impitoyable analyse' [his sole instrument of psychological investigation and remorseless analysis], and who replies to an enquiry as to what he is doing: 'J'observe' (I, 321; I, 393–4). The attachment to the surface of life is a form of idolatry and a source of untruth.

The interiority which Proust demands is already present in 'À une snob', the last of four sketches with the collective title 'Snobs', in *Les Plaisirs et les jours*. Addressing the woman whose imagination is stimulated by her vice, Proust writes:

Les arbres généalogiques que vous cultivez avec tant de soin, dont vous cueillez chaque année les fruits avec tant de joie, plongent leurs racines dans la plus antique terre française. Votre rêve solidarise le présent au passé. L'âme des croisades anime pour vous de banales figures contemporaines et si vous relisez si fiévreusement vos carnets de visite, n'est-ce pas qu'à chaque nom vous sentez s'éveiller, frémir et presque chanter, comme une morte levée de sa dalle blasonnée, la fastueuse vieille France? (*JS*, 45)

[The genealogical trees which you cultivate with such care, whose fruits you pluck each year with such delight, plunge their roots in the most ancient soil of France. Your dream binds the present to the past. The soul of the Crusades animates banal contemporary figures for you, and if you read through your visitors' cards again and again, is it not because, at the sight of each name, you feel the France of old, in all her splendour, awake, tremble and almost sing aloud, like a dead person risen from her blazoned slab?]

We are close, here, to Marcel's own meditations in *À la recherche* on the evocative power for him of the name 'Guermantes', and of many other aristocratic names and titles; we are close, too, to the creative principle of the novel itself. Snobbery here is a form of imaginative life, which transforms a genealogical tree into an organic source of pleasure, and is allied to the power that matters most to Proust, that which abolishes time and

---

[100] *Vintage* (VI, 253) has 'the literature of description', but this is not quite right.

resurrects the past in the present. The snob's passionate contemplation of an aristocratic name restores its presence, raises its living meaning from a grave which until that moment bore only an empty sign, a 'blason'. And what this creative form of snobbery resurrects is, like involuntary memory, both ancient and authentic, rooted in 'la plus antique terre française'; like the memory of childhood, this historical, national, and racial memory has a quality of inevitability, of that which is necessary and essential, the precious guarantee of truth in the factitious, contingent modern world.[101]

Even the vice of snobbery, therefore, has a redemptive aspect; but this doesn't mean that every snob in *A la recherche* is let off the hook, or that Proust thought it was a matter of indifference whether a person were a snob or not. The last occurrence of either *snob* or *snobisme* in *A la recherche* performs an act of poetic justice which is also an act of social undoing; it concerns the eventual fate of the young, beautiful girl whom Marcel meets at the *bal des têtes* in *Le Temps retrouvé*, the daughter of Gilberte Swann and Robert de Saint-Loup, and the granddaughter of Swann and Odette:

Cette fille, dont le nom et la fortune pouvaient faire espérer à sa mère qu'elle épouserait un prince royal et couronnerait toute l'œuvre ascendante de Swann et de sa femme, choisit plus tard comme mari un homme de lettres obscur, car elle n'avait aucun snobisme, et fit redescendre cette famille plus bas que le niveau d'où elle était partie . . .

[Years later, this daughter, whose name and fortune gave her mother the right to hope that she would crown the whole work of social ascent of Swann and his wife by marrying a royal prince, chose for her husband an obscure man of letters, for she was devoid of snobbery, and sank the family once more, below even the level from which it started its ascent . . .]

(IV, 605–6; VI, 425–6)[102]

The grammar of this wonderful sentence ironically evokes a fantasy, only to deny it by the ruthless authority of the perfect tense; within the syntax of Mlle de Saint-Loup's decisive action ('choisit comme mari un homme

---

[101] In *A la recherche* the absolute, unquestioning value that is here placed on 'la fastueuse vieille France' itself comes under scrutiny; see the discussion of linguistic 'purity' in Chapter 4.

[102] *Vintage* turns the syntax a different way, making the single sentence into two: 'by marrying a royal prince, happening to be entirely without snobbery chose for her husband an obscure man of letters. Thus it came about that the family sunk once more . . .'

de lettres obscur . . . et fit redescendre cette famille') we are given its motive, represented by the imperfect tense, the tense that denotes not one's actions but one's nature: 'car elle n'avait aucun snobisme'. By this one brief clause the 'œuvre ascendante' of Swann and Odette is not crowned but demolished; their descendants will not have to worry about getting muddled 'dans ces "Royalties"'. Good luck to them, I think— especially the 'obscure man of letters' to whom the great writer gives the nod.

2

Swann and Odette

Enter Swann(s)

They know all about M. Charles Swann in Combray: he is 'le fils Swann' [young Swann], the son of a stockbroker; his fortune and social position are clear and fixed. He has, indeed, somewhat tarnished that social position by a dubious marriage; when he comes to see Marcel's parents after dinner, he comes alone; his wife cannot be received by respectable people. Swann is announced, first by the sound of the garden-gate bell—'le double tintement timide, ovale et doré de la clochette pour les étrangers' [the double tinkle, timid, oval, golden, of the visitors' bell] (I, 14; I, 14)—and then by his voice, as he makes his way through the garden to join the family seated under the big chestnut tree, virtually in darkness so as not to attract mosquitoes. 'On ne le reconnaissait en effet qu'à la voix, on distinguait mal son visage au nez busqué, aux yeux verts, sous un haut front entouré de cheveux blonds presque roux, coiffés à la Bressant . . .' [And indeed one could tell him only by his voice, for it was difficult to make out his face with its arched nose and green eyes, under a high forehead fringed with fair, almost red hair, done in the Bressant style . . .]. The 'tintement timide' is deceptive, and the difficulty of making Swann out as he emerges into Marcel's (and our) consciousness is emblematic of the novel's fascination with double or hidden selves. Swann's coiffure 'à la Bressant' is that of a celebrated actor;[1] but Swann's disguise is even more impenetrable. The modest, affable country neighbour conceals a second identity:

Pendant bien des années, où pourtant, surtout avant son mariage, M. Swann, le fils, vint souvent les voir à Combray, ma grand-tante et mes grands-parents ne soupçonnèrent pas qu'il ne vivait plus du tout dans la société qu'avait fréquentée

---

[1] Prosper Bressant (1815–86); he specialized in the role of the 'jeune premier' or juvenile lead. He is a figure from Swann's youth.

7. Charles Haas, the principal model for Charles Swann, taken in 1895 when Haas was 63 years old.

sa famille et que sous l'espèce d'incognito que lui faisait chez nous ce nom de Swann, ils hébergeaient—avec la parfaite innocence d'honnêtes hôteliers qui ont chez eux, sans le savoir, un célèbre brigand—un des membres les plus élégants du Jockey-Club, ami préféré du comte de Paris et du prince de Galles, un des hommes les plus choyés de la haute société du faubourg Saint-Germain.

[For many years, during the course of which—especially before his marriage—M. Swann the younger came often to see them at Combray, my great-aunt and my grandparents never suspected that he had entirely ceased to live in the society which his family had frequented, and that, under the sort of incognito which the name of Swann gave him among us, they were harbouring—with the complete innocence of a family of respectable innkeepers who have in their midst some celebrated high-wayman without knowing it—one of the most distinguished members of the Jockey Club, a particular friend of the Comte de Paris and the Prince of Wales, and one of the men most sought after in the aristocratic world of the Faubourg Saint-Germain.]
(I, 15; I, 16)

Marcel, the boy who sits with his parents and grandparents under the chest-nut tree in the garden, also has the perspective of many years from which he can penetrate Swann's 'incognito'; he too, though in a different and more fruitful sense, has a double self. What the writer knows will only be gradu-ally revealed to us, and will include much more about Swann. Still, the cream of the jest is served first. Swann has migrated from his caste to that of the aristocracy, the 'faubourg Saint-Germain'; he is indeed an outlaw, since he has broken the rigid rules of the social hierarchy on which 'Combray' rests—not just this particular town, but the French bourgeois respectability which it symbolizes, in all its narrow, oppressive, unbending integrity.

The high society which Swann frequents is denoted by a series of allusions—*Jockey-Club*, *comte de Paris*, *prince de Galles*, and *faubourg Saint-Germain*. All have English connotations, whether explicit or implicit. To these Swann adds a further mark of Englishness, that of reserve. He makes no parade of his social position, and leaves Marcel's family in their ignor-ance without a murmur. Marcel's great-aunt, in particular, treats Swann with vulgar familiarity; he is good for supplying recipes 'pour des grands dîners où on ne l'invitait pas' [for one of our big dinner-parties, to which he himself would not be invited] (I, 18; I, 19), and she mocks his choice of residence in Paris (the unfashionable quai d'Orléans; the sly clue to Swann's friendship with the Orléans branch of the French royal family escapes her). If the conversation turns to the 'princes of the French royal house', she assumes that Swann is as ignorant of them as she is: ' "des gens que nous ne connaîtrons jamais ni vous ni moi et nous nous en passons, n'est-ce pas", disait ma grand-tante à Swann qui avait peut-être dans sa poche une lettre de Twickenham . . .' ["people you and I will never know, and whom we can do without, isn't that so?" my great-aunt would say to Swann, who had, perhaps, a letter from Twickenham in his pocket . . .] (I, 18).[2] To this 'n'est-ce-pas' Swann makes no reply; it's not really a question, but an affirmation, and he simply lets it pass.

How should we read this reserve? Later on, at the beginning of the second volume of *A la recherche*, *A l'ombre des jeunes filles en fleurs*, we hear again of Swann's discretion, but in a different context. Swann has married the *cocotte* Odette de Crécy, and, as her husband, has made a precipitous descent down the social scale. His whole personality seems to have changed; far from being the elegant, reserved figure whom Marcel knew as a child, he has become, in the words of Marcel's father, 'un vulgaire esbroufeur' [a vulgar show-off]. Yet describing Swann in these terms is not quite accurate. Swann's personality has not altered, but expanded: 'il était arrivé qu'au "fils Swann" et aussi au Swann du Jockey, l'ancien ami de mes parents avait ajouté une personnalité nouvelle . . . celle de mari d'Odette' [what had happened was that, to the original "young Swann" and also to the Swann of the Jockey Club, our old friend had added a new personality . . . that of Odette's husband] (I, 423; II, 1). The incongruity to which this new personality gives rise is striking, even if it can be rationally explained:

on était étonné de l'entendre, lui qui autrefois et même encore aujourd'hui dissimulait si gracieusement une invitation de Twickenham ou de Buckingham Palace, faire sonner bien haut que la femme d'un sous-chef de cabinet était venue rendre sa visite à Mme Swann.

[it was still astonishing to hear him, who in the old days, and even still, would so gracefully refrain from mentioning an invitation to Twickenham or to Buckingham Palace, proclaim with quite unnecessary emphasis that the wife of some junior minister had returned Mme Swann's call.

(I, 424; II, 2)

The simple 'lettre de Twickenham' of the earlier passage has become a more positive invitation, its possible provenance richly enhanced by the addition of Buckingham Palace; Swann's merely having it in his pocket has become 'dissimulait si gracieusement', as though the force of his

---

[2] My trans.; *Vintage* (I, 19) has 'gentlemen' for 'gens' and 'would say tartly', where 'tartly' is a pure translator's interpolation.

discretion has grown to counter the vulgarity of his other social self. What connects the two passages is the verb 'sonner', here given as 'sonner tout haut', literally to 'ring out loud', a sound of noisy social display which contrasts with the sound of the garden bell at Combray, 'le double tintement timide, ovale et doré'. Yet it was always a double sound, capable of more than one interpretation. It announced the entry of more than one Swann into the garden and the novel.[3]

'La dame en rose'

In Paris, Marcel (older than in the garden at Combray, 12 or 13 perhaps) pays his great-uncle Adolphe a surprise visit. He is infatuated with the theatre, with the lives of actors and, above all, actresses—a category which shades into that of courtesans. Uncle Adolphe knows many of these fascinating, ambiguous women, and Marcel hopes that by going to see him on a day when he isn't expected he will make the acquaintance of one of them.

Outside his uncle's house an elegant carriage is waiting. Standing on the steps, Marcel hears a woman's laughing voice inside, then, after he rings the bell, silence and the sound of doors closing. The manservant has some doubts about letting him in, but the same voice can be heard pleading for a sight of him. Uncle Adolphe grudgingly agrees, and Marcel finds himself in the presence of a young woman in a pink silk dress, wearing a pearl necklace and eating a tangerine. As well as the fancy carriage, the pink silk dress and the pearls, she has exotic cigarettes, the gift of an unnamed 'Grand-Duc'. In fact everyone in the scene remains nameless, since Uncle Adolphe refuses formally to present his great-nephew to a *cocotte*, even one as *chic* as this. He is embarrassed and uneasy; as soon as he can, he tells Marcel it is time for him to go. In a rush of emotion the boy kisses the hand of 'la dame en rose', and elicits this response:

"Comme il est gentil! il est déjà galant, il a un petit œil pour les femmes: il tient de son oncle. Ce sera un parfait gentleman", ajouta-t-elle en serrant les dents pour

---

[3] In a later passage which also concerns Swann's new, vulgar persona, Marcel wonders whether he and his family might not have been mistaken in assuming that Swann's friendship with the comte de Paris meant that he was really launched in high society: 'Être l'ami du comte de Paris ne signifie rien. Combien y en a-t-il de ces "amis des princes" qui ne seraient pas reçus dans un salon un peu fermé?' [To be a friend of the Comte de Paris means nothing at all. Is not the world full of such "friends of princes," who would not be received in any house that was at all exclusive?] (I, 511; I, 561). But this is a transient doubt, never restated; and Swann's intimate friendship with the Guermantes is unarguable evidence of his 'real' social prestige.

8. Laure Hayman, the principal model for Odette de Crécy; she was half-English, half-Argentinian, a *grande cocotte* among whose patrons was Proust's great-uncle Louis Weil. She inspired Bourget's novella *Gladys Harvey*, itself a literary source for the anglophile Odette.

donner à la phrase un accent légèrement britannique. "Est-ce qu'il ne pourrait pas venir une fois prendre *a cup of tea*, comme disent nos voisins les Anglais; il n'aurait qu'à m'envoyer un "bleu" le matin."

["Isn't he delicious! Quite a ladies' man already; he takes after his uncle. He'll be a perfect 'gentleman,' " she added, clenching her teeth so as to give the word a kind of English accentuation. "Couldn't he come to me some day for a 'cup of tea,' as our friends across the Channel say? He need only send me a 'blue' in the morning?"]

(I, 77; I, 92)

Half of this is gibberish to Marcel,[4] and in any case his uncle brusquely refuses on his behalf. He leaves, still without learning the name of the 'dame en rose'.

Up to the point at which Marcel kisses her hand, the 'dame en rose' shows to advantage. Marcel can see little in her appearance to distinguish her from the pretty girls of good family whom he knows, except that she is better dressed; her manners are polished, indeed exquisite. This exquisiteness, however, evaporates when Marcel himself touches the lady, and is replaced by affectation, vulgarity, and ignorance, invisible to him but evident to the reader. As the boy leaves, his uncle maladroitly boasts of his prowess at school: ' "Il a tous les prix à son cours ... Qui sait, ce sera peut-être un petit Victor Hugo, une espèce de Vaulabelle, vous savez" ' ["He brings back all the prizes from his school ... Who knows? he may turn out a little Victor Hugo, a kind of Vaulabelle, don't you know"] (I, 78; I, 92).[5] It is always a bad sign in Proust when you can't tell the difference between genius and mediocrity. Uncle Adolphe shows himself up here, but the lady in pink meets him more than halfway: '— J'adore les artistes, répondit la dame en rose, il n'y a qu'eux qui comprennent les femmes ... Qu'eux et les êtres d'élite comme vous. Excusez mon ignorance, ami. Qui est Vaulabelle?' ["Oh, I love artistic people," replied the lady in pink. "There's no one like them for understanding women. Apart from a few superior people like yourself. But please forgive my ignorance. Who is Vaulabelle?"] (I, 78; I, 92).[6] The scene which began with such elegance and delicacy of touch ends with gross flattery and ignorance. The transformation hinges on a kiss and, proffered in return, a *cup of tea*.

---

[4] 'Je ne savais pas ce que c'était qu'un "bleu". Je ne comprenais pas la moitié des mots que disait la dame . . .' [I had not the least idea what a "blue" might be. I did not understand half the words which the lady used] (I, 78; I, 84). In one respect Proust exaggerates Marcel's ignorance here, as he often does in the early volumes of the novel; a schoolboy at a Paris *lycée* would certainly know that a 'bleu' (or 'petit bleu') was an express letter sent by pneumatic tube. On the other hand it is clear that Marcel, like Proust, has not learned English.

[5] Achille-Tenaille de Vaulabelle (1799–1879) was a journalist and historian, and briefly (in 1848) Minister of Education. Victor Hugo was Victor Hugo.

[6] *Vintage* has 'Who or what is Vaulabelle?', which is a bit too thick. Odette will later ask Swann if Vermeer is still living (I, 195; I, 237); Albertine makes the same error, but it passes unnoticed (III, 209; IV, 246–7).

We lose sight of the lady in pink for a hundred pages, and when she reappears she is not explicitly linked to her earlier incarnation. Nor does Marcel himself meet her on this occasion. We are in the second part of *Du côté de chez Swann*, 'Un amour de Swann', the only part of the novel to be recounted in the third person by Marcel as 'omniscient' narrator. At Mme Verdurin's salon, Odette de Crécy asks if she can bring along a man she has recently met, 'un homme charmant, M. Swann' (I, 188). Mme Verdurin is delighted:

—Mais voyons, est-ce qu'on peut refuser quelque chose à une petite perfection comme ça? Taisez-vous, on ne vous demande pas votre avis, je vous dis que vous êtes une perfection.
    —Puisque vous le voulez, répondit Odette sur un ton de marivaudage, et elle ajouta: vous savez que je ne suis pas *fishing for compliments*.

["Why, as if anybody could refuse anything to a little angel like that. Be quiet; no one asked your opinion. I tell you you're an angel."
    "Just as you like," replied Odette in an affected tone, and then added: "You know I'm not *fishing for compliments*."]

(I, 188; I, 208)

It can only be her; the lady in pink has reappeared. She is older now, but she has not yet become the person we heard of when we first met Swann— the woman with whom he contracted his disastrous marriage. Nor have we yet encountered Swann in his guise as Odette's husband, boasting of her pitiful social successes while maintaining his own impeccably discreet and refined place in the *faubourg Saint-Germain*. All that lies in the future, yet Swann's doom is sealed as soon as Odette opens her mouth.

Odette's smarts

Swann and Odette begin their affair in the bosom of the Verdurins' 'little clan', a wealthy, bourgeois, artistic milieu, tinged with Bohemianism, to which neither of them truly belong—Odette because she comes from the *demi-monde* and Swann because he comes from the *grand monde*. Proust goes to some lengths to differentiate not just their social positions but their social consciousness and scale of values. Like Marcel's great-aunt, Odette is ignorant of the real nature and extent of Swann's social connections, and for a long time these *relations mondaines* are unsuspected by the Verdurins too. Odette knows that Swann is rich and well connected, but her idea of what this last attribute, in particular, actually means, is limited by her own vague grasp of the social distinctions on which the *faubourg Saint-Germain* rests.

When we first meet Odette as the lady in pink in Uncle Adolphe's sitting room she makes, as we have seen, a brief impression of genuine poise and sophistication. Perhaps, on reflection, it is a bit flashy of her to show off the Grand-Duke's cigarettes; perhaps her pearl necklace is a bit too big; the fact that the horses of her carriage have carnations attached to their blinkers, and that the coachman wears the same flower in his buttonhole, may also convey something other than restrained elegance. Her speech, on the other hand—before Marcel kisses her hand—is a model of tact—when she mentions meeting Marcel's father she does so with 'un air modeste et sensible' [an air of warmth and modesty] (I, 77; I, 91). This Odette is never seen again, as though Marcel's kiss had really metamorphosed her into the vulgar, snobbish, narrow-minded, incurably ignorant *cocotte* who crumbles what is left of Swann's dusty heart.

Odette's initial judgement of Swann is beset by this ignorance. Again, like Marcel's great-aunt, she cannot understand why he lives in an unfashionable quarter of Paris, though she has her own way of expressing this prejudice: she can't hide her surprise 'qu'il habitât ce quartier qui devait être si triste et "qui était si peu *smart* pour lui qui l'était tant"' [that he should live in a neighbourhood which must be so depressing, and "was not nearly *smart* enough for such a very *smart* man"] (I, 193; I, 235). Swann is far from unconscious of his own elegance, but he would never use the term 'smart' to describe it, or that of any of his aristocratic friends. The thought of him calling Mme de Guermantes 'smart' to her face is inconceivable.[7] But to get the full force of Odette's misconception of her new lover we need to look at the sentence in which this misconception is embedded:

Quelque temps après cette présentation au théâtre, elle lui avait écrit pour lui demander à voir ses collections qui l'intéressaient tant, "elle, ignorante qui avait le goût des jolies choses", disant qu'il lui semblait qu'elle le connaîtrait mieux, quand elle l'aurait vu dans "son home" où elle l'imaginait "si confortable avec son

---

[7] Remy de Gourmont uses 'smart' to exemplify the way in which the importation of a word constricts the scope of its original meaning; he points out thirteen senses of the word in English, whereas in France it is reduced to one (p. 11 n. 1). Gourmont claims that it was only briefly fashionable in Paris, but Bonnaffé has examples from 1898 to 1906.

thé et ses livres", quoiqu'elle ne lui eût pas caché sa surprise qu'il habitât ce quartier qui devait être si triste et "qui était si peu *smart* pour lui qui l'était tant".

[Some time after this introduction at the theatre she had written to ask Swann whether she might see his collections, which would very much interest her, "an ignorant woman with a taste for beautiful things," adding that she felt she would know him better once she had seen him in his "*home*," where she imagined him to be "so comfortable with his tea and his books," though she had to admit that she was surprised that he should live in a neighbourhood which must be so depressing, and "was not nearly *smart* enough for such a very *smart* man."]

(I, 193; I, 234–5)

Le home is one of the most popular English jargon words of the period in France, representing a cluster of ideas about English domesticity and civilized comfort which were promoted on both sides of the Channel.[8] In France, however, it does not necessarily connote an ideal of bourgeois marriage; Swann is a bachelor and Odette is imagining him drinking tea on his own, surrounded by books and fine art. Still, if we rewrite Odette's sentence, using the plain French idiom—'il lui semblait qu'elle le connaîtrait mieux, quand elle l'aurait vu chez lui'—we can see that she means something different by using 'son home'. It is an imagined space marked by the word 'confortable', yet Odette is puzzled that Swann can feel comfortable living somewhere 'si peu *smart*'. She 'sees' Swann in English terms, and perhaps already sees herself with him—her letter, after all, is angling for an invitation—but Swann doesn't quite conform to the type she has in mind.

As we get to know more of Odette, this type acquires more colour, more 'body' so to speak, but doesn't change its fundamental aspect, the product of a vulgar affectation remorselessly exposed. '[E]lle avait soif de chic,' we are told, 'mais ne s'en faisait pas la même idée que les gens du monde' [she . . . thirsted to be in the fashion, though her idea of it was not altogether the same as that of society people] (I, 238; I; 291); the places she considers it 'chic' to be seen in at set times of the day are crowned by

---

[8] Needless to stay, it was stigmatized by Remy de Gourmont; indeed it is the first example given in the book. Gourmont begins by distinguishing three categories of word-formation: 'popular', 'learned', and 'foreign words brutally imported', and offers as an example of each *maison, habitation,* and *home* (pp. 1–2). Odette, after her marriage to Swann, advises Mme Cottard to enhance the doctor's 'consultation' days (when he received patients at home): 'vous devriez avoir un petit *home*, avec vos fleurs, vos livres, les choses que vous aimez' [you should make a point of having a little *home*, with your flowers and books and all your pretty things] (I, 588; II, 200).

'l'heure du thé, avec muffins et toasts, au "Thé de la Rue Royale" où elle croyait que l'assiduité était indispensable pour consacrer la réputation d'élégance d'une femme . . .' [tea-time, with muffins and toast, at the Rue Royale tea-rooms, where she believed that regular attendance was indispensable in order to set the seal upon a woman's certificate of elegance . . .] (I, 242; I, 295). Odette must be the only character in literature, whether French or English, to think it chic to be seen eating a muffin.[9] The 'Thé de la Rue Royale' may have been, as the *Pléiade* editors claim, one of the centres of Parisian *anglomanie* (I, 1213), but it is clear that no one with 'une lettre de Twickenham' in his pocket would be seen dead in it.[10] For Odette's *anglomanie* is a matter of appearance. When she first sees Swann adorned with a monocle, a fashion imported from England, but which Swann himself has adopted only because he finds it less disfiguring than spectacles, she cannot contain her delight: ' "Je trouve que pour un homme, il n'y a pas à dire, ça a beaucoup de chic! Comme tu es bien ainsi! tu as l'air d'un vrai gentleman. Il ne te manque qu'un titre!" ajouta-t-elle, avec une nuance de regret' ["I really do think— for a man, that is to say—it's tremendously smart! How nice you look with it! You have the look of a real gentleman. All you want now is a title!" she added with a tinge of regret] (I, 242; I, 296).[11] Odette can pay Swann no higher compliment than to say that he *looks like* 'un vrai gentleman'; the real thing is beyond her. Nor can she recognize distinction in women; it is all a matter of dress. When she sees the marquise de Villeparisis in the street wearing a black woollen dress, she exclaims: ' "Mais elle a l'air d'une ouvreuse, d'une vieille concierge, darling! Ça, une marquise! Je ne suis pas marquise, mais il faudrait me payer bien cher pour me faire sortir nippée comme ça!" ' ["But she looks like an usherette, like an old concierge,

---

[9] Le Robert dates 'muffin' to 1793; Bonnaffé's first citation is Balzac's feeble anglo-skit 'Peines de cœur d'une chatte anglaise' [Heartaches of an English (female) cat] (1842): 'attirée par de la crème contenue dans un bol, sur lequel un *muffing* [*sic*] était posé en travers' [attracted by some cream in a bowl, across which lay a muffin].Proust may have noticed the conjunction with 'toasts' in the society novelist Marcel Prévost's *Heureux ménage* (1901), also cited in Bonnaffé: 'Voici les toasts. Mais si vous le préférez, je vais vous beurrer un *muffin*' [Here are the toasts. But if you prefer I will butter you a muffin].

[10] The editors of the Garnier Flammarion edition of *Du côté de chez Swann* (Paris, 1987) acutely point out the near-yet-far affinity of the '*Thé* de la rue Royale', situated at n° 3, with the '*Cercle* de la rue Royale', at n° 4, one of the most exclusive clubs in Paris, to which the principal model for Swann, Charles Haas, belonged (p. 614 n. 226).

[11] *Vintage* has 'Every inch the gentleman!' which loses the emphasis on Swann's *appearance*.

darling! A marquise, her! Goodness knows I'm not a marquise, but you'd have to pay me a lot of money before you'd get me to go round Paris rigged out like that!"] (I, 240; I, 266). The word 'darling' is the aural expression of Odette's social blindness here, more so even than the vulgar French colloquialism 'nippée'.[12] We are to imagine Swann wincing, at least internally; yet when, much later, he enters the jealous, morbid phase of his love for Odette, he hears her utter an English endearment with profound misguided relief: ' "Ah! si vous connaissiez cet être-là autant que je le connais! n'est-ce pas, *my love*, il n'y a que moi qui vous connaisse bien?" ' ["Oh, if you only knew the creature as I know him! Isn't that so, my love, no one really knows you well except me?"] (I, 293; I, 359).[13] *My love* signifies, Swann believes, that Odette belongs to him, though the possessive form should tell him that it means the reverse: jealousy has bound him to Odette despite the fact that she is continuously and unscrupulously unfaithful to him. As it happens she calls him *my love* in front of his chief rival, the comte de Forcheville; the regret with which Odette viewed Swann's lack of a title was an omen. She introduces Forcheville to the Verdurins, as she had done Swann, and we are instantly told that he is 'grossièrement snob' [a colossal snob] (I, 246; I, 301); yet Forcheville will supplant Swann not despite his having less true distinction but because of it. He, too, is marked by the same coarseness of sensibility, shown up, as by a chemical test, in his English vocabulary. When the painter 'M. Biche' launches into a clowning, slangy tirade on a fellow artist, Forcheville expresses to Mme Verdurin 'son admiration pour ce qu'il avait appelé le petit "speech" du peintre' [his admiration for what he called the painter's "little speech"] (I, 253; I, 310).[14]

Odette's vulgarity has a moral as well as an aesthetic dimension. After Swann's first visit to Odette's house in the rue La Pérouse, he receives a note from her:

[il] reconnut tout de suite cette grande écriture dans laquelle une affectation de raideur britannique imposait une apparence de discipline à des caractères informes

---

[12] 'Darling' is first recorded by Bonnaffé in the same Balzac story which gave us the 'muffing' (see n.9), though there it is a substantive ('son ange, la joie de ses yeux, sa *darling*' [his angel, the delight of his eyes . . .], p. 37); Paul Bourget, that pillar of literary *anglomanie*, has it as a mode of address: 'Ah! darling, je ne vous aurais pas connue!' (*Outre-Mer*, 186).

[13] *Jean Santeuil* has an early version of this passage, without the English phrase (*JS* 749–50).

[14] Bonnaffé first records 'speech' in a letter by Lamartine of 1840; it entered Littré's dictionary in 1872. Proust's quotation marks suggest that Forcheville is using the term in a slang sense; the ordinary meaning would be represented by the French 'discours', but Forcheville implies something like 'saillie' or 'boutade'.

qui eussent signifié peut-être pour des yeux moins prévenus le désordre de la pensée, l'insuffisance de l'éducation, la manque de franchise et de volonté.

[he at once recognised that large handwriting in which an affectation of British stiffness imposed an apparent discipline upon ill-formed characters, suggestive, perhaps, to less biased eyes than his, of an untidiness of mind, a fragmentary education, a want of sincerity and will-power.]

(I, 218–19; I, 266–7)

The affectation of English rigour is especially pointed alongside the lack of *franchise*, a word which, as Proust knew from his translation of Ruskin, is linked to the etymology of the word 'franc' and therefore to the aboriginal character of the French race.[15] Odette's insincerity is a kind of transgression against Frenchness, and against the moral dimension of the French language. When a man she meets at dinner boasts of his unwordliness she is easily moved, but Swann's genuine disinterestedness leaves her cold, for what speaks to her imagination 'n'était pas la pratique du désintéressement, c'en était le vocabulaire' [was not the practice of disinterestedness, but its vocabulary] (I, 241; I, 295).

Odette orchidophile, Odette orchidée

Odette's taste, when Swann makes her acquaintance, is for the exotic and the ostentatious. The sitting room of her house in rue La Pérouse is stuffed with Chinese porcelain, screens covered with photographs, Japanese silk cushions and other evidences of the Orientalist vogue to which Odette has succumbed. It is a confected interior, which speaks of Odette's false taste, or rather her taste for artifice itself:

Elle trouvait à tous ses bibelots chinois des formes "amusantes", at aussi aux orchidées, aux catleyas surtout, qui étaient, avec les chrysanthèmes, ses fleurs préférées, parce qu'ils avaient le grand mérite de ne pas ressembler à des fleurs, mais d'être en soie, en satin. "Celle-là a l'air d'être découpée dans la doublure de mon manteau", dit-elle à Swann en lui montrant une orchidée, avec une nuance d'estime pour cette fleur si "chic" . . .

[She found something "quaint" in the shape of each of her Chinese ornaments, and also in her orchids, the cattleyas especially—these being, with chrysanthemums,

---

[15] Ruskin's (incorrect) etymology is politically motivated: he denies that 'franc' originally meant 'free' and claims it meant 'strong lordship'; in Proust's version: 'la qualité de franchise . . . signifie brave, fort, et honnête, au-dessus des autres hommes' (*BA* 165). For 'raideur britannique', see Ch. 1, p. 27.

her favourite flowers, because they had the supreme merit of not looking like flowers, but of being made, apparently, of silk or satin. "This one looks just as though it had been cut out of the lining of my cloak," she said to Swann, pointing to an orchid, with a shade of respect in her voice for so "chic" a flower . . .]

(I, 218; I, 265)

The orchid which Proust singles out here, the cattleya, was a relatively late addition to the descriptions of Odette; Proust was prompted by rereading his own early story 'L'Indifférent', whose heroine, Madeleine de Gouvres, wears this flower in her corsage at the Opera.[16] Proust may also have had in mind the dress worn by comtesse Greffuhle at a literary *fête* organized by Robert de Montesquiou in 1894, on which Proust reported for *Le Gaulois*; he describes it as 'de soie lilas rosé, semée d'orchidées, et recouverte de mousseline de soie de même nuance, le chapeau fleuri d'orchidées et tout entouré de gaze lilas' [of pink lilac silk, sprinkled with orchids, and covered with silk muslin of the same hue, the hat covered with orchids and surrounded by lilac-coloured gauze].[17] In 'L'Indifférent', the description of Madeleine's appearance (in a story many of whose elements prefigure the psychology of love in *A la recherche*) is marked by another English word:

Dans la salle les têtes s'étaient tournées vers elle; déjà des amis venaient la saluer et la complimenter. Cela ne lui était pas nouveau et pourtant, avec l'obscure clairvoyance d'un jockey pendant la course ou d'un acteur pendant la représentation, elle se sentait ce soir triompher plus aisément et plus pleinement que de coutume. Sans un bijou, son corsage de tulle jaune couvert de catléias, à sa chevelure noire aussi elle avait attaché quelques catléias qui suspendaient à cette tour d'ombre de pâles guirlandes de lumière.

[In the room heads had turned towards her; already friends were coming to greet and compliment her. This was not a new experience for her and yet, with the obscure clairvoyance of a jockey during a race or an actor on stage, she felt herself

---

[16] The five references to cattleyas in *Un amour de Swann* come in additions to the typescript made in 1910: see the *Pléiade* notes (I, 1205–6). 'L'Indifférent', written in 1893, was intended to form part of *Les Plaisirs et les jours* (1896), but was omitted to make way for 'La Mort de Baldassare Silvande'; it was separately published in *La Vie contemporaine*, 1 Mar. 1896.

[17] 'Une fête littéraire à Versailles' (*CSB* 360). Jérome Picon points out that Montesquiou himself described Mme Greffuhle as 'déguisée en cattleya, toute couverte du ton de cette mauve orchidée' [disguised as a cattleya, completely covered in the hue of this mauve orchid] (*Écrits*, 372). Montesquiou's comment was not published until 1923, in his memoirs, *Les Pas effacés*; but he may have made the remark at the time, and Proust remembered (and used) other unpublished anecdotes in *A la recherche*.

triumph more easily and more fully than usual. Without a jewel, her corsage of yellow tulle covered in cattleyas, in her black hair too she had fastened a few cattleyas which hung like pale garlands of light from this shady tower.][18]

The self-consciousness which Madeleine manifests here, linked to performance on the racecourse or the stage, belongs also to Odette, but the choice of cattleyas has further associations with the English network of *A la recherche*. The late nineteenth-century craze for orchids in France was imported from England, which had led the field in the (modern, Western) discovery, classification, and commercial exploitation of orchids. And according to Merle A. Reinikka's history of orchids, 'The most significant event influencing the orchid enthusiasm of English horticulturists was the first blooming of *Cattleya labiata* in cultivation. This occurrence heralded orchid growing as a highly fashionable pastime' (p. 23). In 1818, William Cattley, a merchant who lived in Barnet (now a north London suburb), and a passionate amateur horticulturalist, became interested in some 'strange-looking plants' which had been used as packing for a consignment of tropical flora from Brazil. 'He devised some method of growing them, and in November of that same year one of the plants bloomed. Cattley was extremely pleased, for the flowers were completely unlike anything seen before, the huge, trumpet-like labellum making this species the most attractive orchid thus far cultivated.'

At his death in 1832 Cattley was reputed to have 'the finest collection of Orchids then known', a collection which passed to the head of the Royal Exotic Nursery in Chelsea.[19] But his greatest contribution to botany was his patronage of the young John Lindley, who was to become Professor of Botany in the University of London, 1828–60, and one of the most renowned botanists of the nineteenth century, whose achievements included the first modern classification system of the orchid family. It was Lindley, in 1819, who described Cattley's plant and named the genus

---

[18] Marcel Proust, *Les Plaisirs et les jours, suivi de L'Indifférent*, ed. Thierry Laguet (Paris: Gallimard, 1993), 256.

[19] Émile V. Bretschneider, *History of European Botanical Discoveries in China* (London: Sampson Low, Marston & Co., 1898); facs. repr. with an introduction by Kerrie L. MacPherson (London: Ganesha Publishing, 2002), I, 256. Cattley's date of birth is not known. He earns a biographical sketch in Bretschneider's work because of his activities in the importation of orchids from China; Odette's flowers (chrysanthemums as well as orchids) have an Oriental as well as English aspect, in keeping with the décor of the rue La Pérouse. For the information on orchid cultivation which follows I am indebted to Reinikka's book, esp. pp. 1–33, 153–9 (Lindley), and 179–83 (Darwin).

after his patron. He named the particular species *Cattleya labiata*, after the large 'labellum' or lower 'lip' of the corolla.

Cattleya labiata, with its size and gorgeous beauty, was almost single-handedly responsible for starting the orchid craze of the nineteenth century, still going strong at the time of Odette's debut as a high-society courtesan in the late 1870s. Tropical orchids required the most sophisticated Victorian greenhouse technology to flourish; gardeners in wealthy English country houses, as well as English nurserymen, vied to find and propagate new species, drawing on an imperial network of exploration and exploitation (literally, in the case of orchid habitats, 'from China to Peru').[20] The Royal Horticultural Society sponsored the first Orchid Conference in South Kensington in 1885; its Orchid Committee was founded in 1889. The orchid trade across Europe was dominated by English growers, and this dominance is reflected in France. In his annual address to his subscribers, in January 1888, the editor of the journal *L'Orchidophile* took stock of the progress which orchid cultivation—and business—had made since the journal started: 'Eight years ago, the trade in orchids in France did not attain to 30,000 francs; today, it surpasses, by a wide margin, three hundred thousand francs!' *L'Orchidophile* is filled with articles translated from the *Gardeners' Chronicle* and other English magazines; its pages buzz with English words ('les *nurserymen*', 'les *market-growers*') and the names of English people and places. *L'Orchidophile* also shows the characteristic alliance of aristocracy and commerce: the journal was conducted by a commercial grower, Lebeuf, but its title-page also emphasizes its aristocratic patronage by the aptly named Comte du Buysson.[21]

I like to think, though there is no way of knowing, that Odette wears a bouquet of *Cattleya labiata* on the night when she and Swann first make love. They are in her carriage, and Proust describes in detail how their sexual intimacy begins:

Elle tenait à la main un bouquet de catleyas et Swann vit, sous sa fanchon de dentelle, qu'elle avait dans les cheveux des fleurs de cette même orchidée

---

[20] The discovery in the mid-century of cool-growing orchids in the highlands of Mexico put orchid-growing within the reach of the less well-off; in 1851 the *Gardeners' Chronicle* published a series of articles by Benjamin S. Williams called 'Orchids for the Millions'. But the cultivation of tropical species remained an expensive business.

[21] *L'Orchidophile. Journal des amateurs d'orchidées. Publié avec la collaboration de M. le Comte du Buysson par la maison V.-F. Lebeuf, d'Argenteuil. A. Godefroy-Lebeuf, gendre et successeur.* The journal ran from 1880 to 1892, but I have only been able to consult issues from 1886.

attachées à une aigrette en plumes de cygne. Elle était habillée, sous sa mantille, d'un flot de velours noir qui, par un rattrapé oblique, découvrait en un large triangle le bas d'une jupe de faille blanche et laissait voir un empiècement, également de faille blanche, à l'ouverture du corsage décolleté, où étaient enfoncées d'autres fleurs de catleyas. Elle était à peine remise de la frayeur que Swann lui avait causée quand un obstacle fit faire un écart au cheval. Ils furent vivement déplacés, elle avait jeté un cri et restait toute palpitante, sans respiration.

"Ce n'est rien, lui dit-il, n'ayez pas peur."

Et il la tenait par l'épaule, l'appuyant contre lui pour la maintenir; puis il lui dit:

"Surtout, ne me parlez pas, ne me répondez que par signes pour ne pas vous essouffler encore davantage. Cela ne vous gêne pas que je remette droites les fleurs de votre corsage qui ont été déplacées par le choc? J'ai peur que vous ne les perdiez, je voudrais les enfoncer un peu."

Elle, qui n'avait pas été habituée à voir les hommes faire tant de façons avec elle, dit en souriant:

"Non, pas du tout, ça ne me gêne pas."

Mais lui, intimidé par sa réponse, peut-être aussi pour avoir l'air d'avoir été sincère quand il avait pris ce prétexte, ou même commençant déjà à croire qu'il l'avait été, s'écria:

"Oh! non, surtout, ne parlez pas, vous allez encore vous essouffler, vous pouvez bien me répondre par gestes, je vous comprendrai bien. Sincèrement je ne vous gêne pas? Voyez, il y a un peu … je pense que c'est du pollen qui s'est répandu sur vous, vous permettez que je l'essuie avec ma main? Je ne vais pas trop fort, je ne suis pas trop brutal? Je vous chatouille peut-être un peu? mais c'est que je ne voudrais pas toucher le velours de la robe pour ne pas le friper. Mais, voyez-vous, il était vraiment nécessaire de les fixer, ils seraient tombés; et comme cela, en les enfonçant un peu moi-même … Sérieusement, je ne suis pas désagréable? Et en les respirant pour voir s'ils n'ont vraiment pas d'odeur, non plus? Je n'en ai jamais senti, je peux? dites la vérité."

[She was holding in her hand a bunch of cattleyas, and Swann could see, beneath the film of lace that covered her head, more of the same flowers fastened to a swansdown plume. She was dressed, beneath her cloak, in a flowing gown of black velvet, caught up on one side to reveal a large triangle of white silk skirt, and with a yoke, also of white silk, in the cleft of the low-necked bodice, in which were fastened a few more cattleyas. She had scarcely recovered from the shock which the sight of Swann had given her, when some obstacle made the horse start to one side. They were thrown forward in their seats; she uttered a cry, and fell back quivering and breathless.

"It's all right," he assured her, "don't be frightened." And he slipped his arm round her shoulder, supporting her body against his own. Then he went on: "Whatever you do, don't utter a word; just make a sign, yes or no, or you'll be out of breath again. You won't mind if I straighten the flowers on your bodice? The jolt has disarranged them. I'm afraid of their dropping out, so I'd like to fasten them a little more securely."

She was not used to being made so much fuss of by men, and she smiled as she answered: 'No, not at all; I don't mind in the least.'

But he, daunted a little by her answer, and also, perhaps, to bear out the pretence that he had been sincere in adopting the stratagem, or even because he was already beginning to believe that he had been, exclaimed, "No, no, you mustn't speak. You'll get out of breath again. You can easily answer in signs; I shall understand. Really and truly now, you don't mind my doing this? Look, there's a little—I think it must be pollen, spilt over your dress. Do you mind if I brush it off with my hand? That's not too hard? I'm not hurting you, am I? Perhaps I'm tickling you a bit? I don't want to touch the velvet in case I crease it. But you see, I really had to fasten the flowers; they would have fallen out if I hadn't. Like that, now; if I just tuck them a little farther down. ... Seriously, I'm not annoying you, am I? And if I just sniff them to see whether they've really got no scent? I don't believe I ever smelt any before. May I? Tell the truth, now."]

(I, 228–9; I, 279–80)

The scene unfolds in close-up and in what seems to be real time; the description of Odette's dress is minute, technical, one might say botanical. With the cattleyas she carries in her hand, and wears in her hair, and in her bosom (the point of entry for Swann's caresses), she is like an orchid herself, as exotic, as gorgeous, as expensive, and Swann her cultivator, her grower, her 'orchidophile'. And in his concern for the Odette-orchid, his dusting away of the pollen, he is like a collector carefully pollinating and fertilizing his precious specimen.

The fertilizing of orchids was the subject of intense study and controversy in the nineteenth century. Orchids had been associated with sexuality for a long time before that, because of the shape of the tubers; the Greek word ὄρχις (Latin *orchis*) means testicle, and English herbals record 'ballock's-grass', 'sweet ballocks', and 'dogstones' as names of orchids. The modern scientific study of orchids began in the late eighteenth century, and received its greatest contribution from Charles Darwin. Orchids play a prominent part in *Origin of Species* (1859) as examples of Darwin's contention that no higher plant could fertilize itself in perpetuity;

cross-fertilization was required, and the means were at hand in the form of insects. In 1862 Darwin published *On the Various Contrivances by which British and Foreign Orchids are Fertilized by Insects*, a work which had itself been fertilized by Darwin's study of the native orchids which grew near his home in Downe, Kent; his experiments had included the artificial pollination of flowers using a pencil or fine bristle; he had got as close to his flowers as Swann to Odette.[22]

L'Orchidophile of 1885 has a 'Note sur la fécondation des Orchidées' which may suggest the kind of botanical operation Proust had in mind. The author of the article, Alfred Bleu, one of the leading French cultivators, mentions the importance of insects for fertilization, but adds that there is another helpful phenomenon,

la mise à nu des masses de pollen par l'enlèvement de l'opercule qui les recouvre et qui peut être produit soit par un vent violent, soit par le battement de l'aile d'un oiseau dans son vol, etc. Dans ces conditions, les pollinies ou masses de pollen sont facilement mises en contact avec le stigmate et la fécondation est ainsi opérée.(Vol.6, p.82)

[the exposure of the masses of pollen by the removal of the operculum which covers them, and which can be produced either by a strong wind, or by the beating of a bird's wing in flight, etc. In these conditions, the pollen clusters or pollen masses are easily placed in contact with the stigma, and fertilization is thus accomplished.]

A gust of wind, the beating of a bird's wing—or the sudden swerve of a carriage, effecting the 'mise à nu' of the pollen on Odette's breast. 'Mais il est à remarquer,' M. Bleu goes on, 'qu'elle n'a lieu que sur un nombre de fleurs relativement très restreint' [But it should be noted that this takes place only in a small number of flowers]. Yet what is Odette to Swann, if not the most unusual of specimens?

For Swann and Odette, the association of orchids with their first lovemaking rapidly becomes a stereotyped or shorthand way of alluding to sexual intercourse. At first Swann simply repeats the gestures and phrases

---

[22] A French translation of Darwin's book on orchids appeared in 1870. Emily Eells, in *Proust's Cup of Tea*, 94–101, discusses Proust's interest in orchids (including cattleyas) and in Darwin, focusing on the episode of M. de Charlus's encounter with Jupien in the courtyard of the Hôtel de Guermantes at the beginning of *Sodome et Gomorrhe* (III, 4–9; IV, 3–8).

which he used in his first approach to her, with the comic indignity to which foreplay renders us liable:

Si elle avait des catleyas à son corsage, il disait: "C'est malheureux, ce soir, les catleyas n'ont pas besoin d'être arrangés, ils n'ont pas été déplacés comme l'autre soir . . ." Ou bien, si elle n'en avait pas: "Oh! pas de catleyas ce soir, pas moyen de me livrer à mes petits arrangements."

[If she had cattleyas pinned to her bodice, he would say: "It's most unfortunate; the cattleyas don't need tucking in this evening; they've not been disturbed as they were the other night . . ." Or else, if she had none: "Oh! no cattleyas this evening; then there's no chance of my indulging in my little rearrangements."]

(I, 230; I, 281)

In the course of time, the metaphorical cattleyas become a mere sign; 'faire cattleya', for Swann and Odette, is 'un simple vocable qu'ils employaient sans y penser quand ils voulaient signifier l'acte de la possession physique—où d'ailleurs l'on ne possède rien . . .'[a simple verb which they would employ without thinking when they wished to refer to the act of physical possession—in which, by the way, one possesses nothing . . .][23] Proust is tender of such linguistic survivals, because they indicate what belongs to each person's peculiar, individual apprehension of the world, including its pleasures; as tender as he is intolerant of the idea of physical 'possession'; only our ideas can truly belong to us, and then only if we guard against their falling into desuetude, their deflowering. For Swann, the best that can be said is that a nominal, a commemorative trace remains of his peculiar 'take' on (and taking of) Odette; but for Proust the matter does not end there.

Odette en fleurs

During his first holiday at Balbec, in *A l'ombre des jeunes filles en fleurs*, Marcel visits the studio of the painter Elstir. From the window he catches sight of the 'jeunes filles en fleurs' themselves, whom he has long yearned to meet, including the one who will become the object of his obsessive and tragic passion, Albertine. He realizes that Elstir knows the young girls and can introduce him to them; I discuss this connection in the next chapter, but what concerns us here is another unexpected connection, that between Elstir and Odette.

---

[23] In *Vintage* the last phrase reads 'in which, paradoxically, the possessor posseses nothing'.

Elstir agrees to accompany Marcel on a walk, giving him hope that they may catch up with Albertine and her friends. But first Elstir must finish the piece on which he is working. It is a study of flowers; in the final version of the novel they are not named, except negatively: 'C'était des fleurs, mais pas de celles dont j'eusse mieux aimé lui commander le portrait que celui d'une personne . . . aubépines, épines roses, bluets, fleurs de pommiers' [It was a study of some flowers, but not those of which I would rather have commissioned a portrait from him than one of a person . . . hawthorn white and pink, cornflowers, apple-blossom] (II, 203; II, 493). However, a cancelled passage makes clear what these flowers were, and makes explicit a connection with Odette which Proust chose in the end to leave tacit and sly:

fleurs de pommiers, mais des fleurs qui n'étaient pour moi que des fleurs de chez le fleuriste, des fleurs pour Mme Swann . . . des orchidées. Elstir tout en peignant s'éleva contre ce que je disais d'elles et commença à me raconter relativement à la merveille de leur fécondation de ces histoires que [ ] a contées, que d'autres suivants ont complétées et qu'enfin le livre de Metschnikof et les splendides essais de Maeterlinck ont rendues populaires. Il me parlait des ruses de celles qui forcent un insecte soit en lui donnant des morceaux charnus à manger après quoi elles le font trébucher dans un godet plein d'eau, d'où il ne peut s'échapper que par un couloir où il s'enduit les ailes de pollen . . . (II, 1441) [24]

[apple-blossom, but flowers which for me were nothing but flowers from the florist's shop, flowers for Mme Swann . . . orchids. Elstir while continuing to paint protested against what I said about them and told me, relative to the marvel of their fertilisation, stories such as [ ] has related, which others following him have completed, and which, finally, Metschnikoff's book and Maeterlinck's splendid essays have made common knowledge. He spoke to me of the ruses of those which force an insect either by giving it fleshy pieces to eat after which they make it stumble into a cup full of liquid, from which it can't escape except by a passage in which its wings become loaded with pollen . . .]

In the final version Elstir's elaborate account is reduced and abstracted: 'Elstir tout en peignant me parlait de botanique, mais je ne l'écoutais guère' [Elstir as he worked talked botany to me, but I scarcely listened] (II,

---

[24] The name which Proust left blank is almost certainly Darwin, who is mentioned later in the novel (see below). Two minor orthographical slips have been corrected. The passage was added to the proofs of the Gallimard edition of *À l'ombre des jeunes filles en fleurs* of 1918 (the penultimate set on which Proust worked), then crossed out. For a description of these proofs, see *Pléiade*, I, 1290–1.

203; II, 493). Marcel is indeed not paying attention; he is thinking not of these 'fleurs de chez le fleuriste' but of his 'jeunes filles en fleurs', who represent everything (he supposes) that Odette is not; he is blind to the connections between Elstir's art, and Odette's artifice, and the artfulness of the orchid; though he is about to stumble on a revelation about Odette's past, and Elstir's, which has an intimate connection with the flowers Elstir is painting, its full meaning will not be clear to him.[25]

As he wanders impatiently around the studio, waiting for Elstir to finish, Marcel turns over some sketches placed against the walls, and comes across a watercolour which dates from an earlier period of Elstir's life. It is the portrait of a young woman, not pretty but 'of a curious type', as it turns out, a portrait of Odette 'en demi-travesti', when she was a young actress (and *cocotte*) in 1872, playing the role of 'Miss Sacripant' in a 'revue des Variétés'.[26] Critical attention has concentrated on what Marcel calls the 'ambiguous character' of the model, and the fact that it reveals Elstir to be, in the elegant formula of the *Pléiade* editors, 'un peintre de l'indécision sexuelle' [a painter of sexual indecision] (II, 1442). I am more concerned, however, with the connection between this episode and one which takes place in a later volume of the novel, and which is introduced by Marcel's memory of the flowers to which he had been so inattentive in Elstir's studio.

In the fourth volume of *A la recherche*, *Le Côté de Guermantes II*, the princesse de Parme, a guest at a dinner party given by the duc et duchesse de Guermantes, expresses admiration for one of Mme de Guermantes's flowering plants. Marcel recognizes it as 'une plante de l'espèce de celles

---

[25] I have found my argument here anticipated in some respects by Pascale McGarry, 'Proust et Wilde—"Mr W. H." et "Miss Sacripant": étude de deux portraits imaginaires', *Études irlandaises* NS12/2 (Dec. 1987), 45–64; McGarry points out the connection between the flowers Elstir is painting and those that Marcel sees later at Mme de Guermantes' house, and the significance of the discussion which takes place there about their fertilization; she finely notices the quiet but potent relation of the phrases Marcel uses to describe his reluctant inspection of Elstir's work, 'je perdis un instant à les regarder . . . ces minutes perdues' to the great theme of 'temps perdu' in the novel; but she misses the connection between the cattleyas and Odette, and her focus is on English literature not language. For 'Mr. W.H.' see Ch. 3, pp. 149–50.

[26] *Sacripant* was a comic opera first produced in 1866, whose hero disguises himself as a woman. Neither Proust's date, nor his assigning the piece to the Théâtre des Variétés, are intended to be exact. On the popularity in *fin-de-siècle* Paris of nicknames beginning 'Miss' ('Miss Cocktail', 'Miss Flirt' etc.), see Tadié, 864 n. 318, citing an article by R. Veisseyre in the *Bulletin de l'Association Marcel Proust*, 19 (1969), 869.

qu'Elstir avait peintes devant moi' [a plant of the sort that I had watched Elstir painting] (II, 805; III, 596). Once again, Proust does not name the plant as an orchid, but the subsequent conversation establishes its identity, and to begin with its connection with Odette. In response to the princesse de Parme's compliment, Mme de Guermantes says: ' "Je suis enchantée qu'elle vous plaise; elles sont ravissantes, regardez leur petit tour de cou de velours mauve; seulement comme il peut arriver à des personnes très jolies et très bien habillées, elles ont un vilain nom et elles sentent mauvais. . . ." ' ["I'm so glad you like them; they are charming, do look at their little purple velvet collars; the only thing against them is—as may happen with people who are very pretty and very nicely dressed— they have a hideous name and a horrid smell. . . ."].

Mme de Guermantes, who remorselessly refuses to acknowledge Odette's social existence, has unwittingly welcomed this pretty, well-dressed woman into her home in metaphorical form (my extra-textual guess would be that the plant was a gift from Swann, who pines for Mme de Guermantes to relent and agree to 'know' Odette and their daughter Gilberte). The 'velours mauve' combines the 'flot de velours noir' of Odette's dress on the night of the 'cattleyas' with the 'larges pétales mauves' of the flower; even the word 'cou' in 'tour de cou' (the nuance is lost in the English 'collar') brings back the Botticellian inclination of Odette's neck in the act of sexual surrender.[27] The 'vilain nom' might be the 'vulgar' name of the species—Emily Eells (p. 110) points to the passage in Oscar Wilde's *The Picture of Dorian Gray* where Lord Henry Wotton laments that the orchid he cut for his buttonhole, 'a marvellous spotted thing, as effective as the seven deadly sins' turns out to be 'a fine specimen of *Robinsoniana*, or something dreadful of that kind'—but along with the bad smell there may also be a hint of Odette's shameful profession.[28] All this is unconscious on the part of Mme de Guermantes, but deliberate on Proust's, as the sequel of the conversation makes clear.

[27] The 'flot de velours noir' comes from the description of Odette's dress quoted above (I, 228; I, 279); 'Elle fléchissait le cou' [She bent her neck] (p. 229; p. 280); Swann hopes 'que c'était la possession de cette femme qui allait sortir d'entre leurs larges pétales mauves' [that it was the possession of this woman that would emerge for him from their large mauve petals] (p. 231; p. 282).

[28] The *Dorian Gray* passage is in chapter 17. It may also have influenced M. de Charlus's scornful comment to Morel in *Sodome et Gomorrhe*: 'Je suis assez sensible aux noms; et dès qu'une rose est un peu belle, on apprend qu'elle s'appelle la *Baronne de Rothschild* ou la *Maréchale Niel*, ce qui jette un froid' [I am rather susceptible to names; and whenever a rose

Mme de Guermantes explains to the princesse de Parme that her orchid is female, and that she will have to expose it to the open air where an insect may bring the pollen it needs from a male plant. All this talk reminds her of Swann, and of Odette whom she will not consent to receive:

—Je dirai à Votre Altesse que c'est Swann qui m'a toujours beaucoup parlé de botanique. Quelquefois, quand cela nous embêtait trop d'aller à un thé ou à une matinée, nous partions pour la campagne et il me montrait des mariages extraord-inaires de fleurs, ce qui est beaucoup plus amusant que les mariages de gens, et a lieu d'ailleurs sans lunch et sans sacristie. . . . Malheureusement dans l'intervalle il a fait lui-même un mariage encore beaucoup plus étonnant et qui rend tout dif-ficile. . . . Placée entre le renoncement aux promenades botaniques et l'obliga-tion de fréquenter une personne déshonorante, j'ai choisi la première de ces deux calamités.

["I must explain to Your Highness that it's Swann who has always talked to me a great deal about botany. Sometimes when we thought it would be too boring to go to an afternoon party we would set off for the country, and he would show me extraordinary marriages between flowers, which was far more amusing than going to human marriages—no wedding-breakfast and no crowd in the sac-risty. . . . Unfortunately, in the meantime he himself has made an even more astonishing marriage, which makes everything very difficult. . . . Faced with the alternatives of giving up my botanical expeditions and being obliged to call upon a degrading person, I chose the first of these two calamities. . . ."]

(II, 806; III, 597–8)

Less unwittingly this time, Mme de Guermantes associates Odette with a flower, though she cannot take the full measure of her analogy. The phrase 'sans lunch' gives the passage an added English twist; it makes a fashion-able secular pair with the religious ceremony of signing the register in the 'sacristie', and wittily suggests that the loose morals of flowers are more tolerable than marriage to 'une personne déshonorante'.[29] Mme de

is at all beautiful, one learns that it is called Baronne de Rothschild or Maréchale Niel, which casts a chill] (III, 395; IV, 469). It was a commonplace of the polemic against pros-titution that prostitutes stank; cattleyas, however, as Swann says in his overture to Odette, are scentless.

[29] The 'English ring' of the term 'lunch' is noticed by Eells (p. 96), who connects it with the allusion to Darwin later in the passage. The particular sense of *lunch* as a meal served at a reception dates from 1860 (Le Robert); Proust refers to the *lunch* at his brother's wedding in 1903 (*Corr.* III, 234).

Guermantes continues her anthropomorphic play on the 'choses inconvenantes' which take place even in her own garden between plants and insects, but the jokes are lost on the princesse de Parme, 'qui, n'étant pas familière avec les travaux de Darwin et de ses successeurs, comprenait mal la signification des plaisanteries de la duchesse' [who, not being famil- iar with the works of Darwin and his followers, was unable to grasp the point of the Duchess's pleasantries] (II, 807; III, 598). But in truth the real 'signification' escapes Mme de Guermantes, too. It lies in a tacit, oblique connection between the real and the painted flowers; between Odette and the orchids she loves, both painted by Elstir; between these paintings and Marcel's own latent understanding of art and life, whose unfolding takes him from his childhood through the history of the Swann marriage and his own experience of desire and loss, towards the discovery of his vocation.

Swann's way with words

For all his English affiliations, Swann, unlike Odette, never speaks English in the novel, never—with a single exception—utters an identifiably English word. Mme de Guermantes, that well of French undefiled, is capable, as we have just seen, of using the word 'lunch'—but not Swann. Marcel's grandmother, equally identified with the values of 'classic' French, uses an English word, albeit a quasi-naturalized one.[30] Even in his guise as Odette's vulgar, boastful husband Swann remains unaffected by her *anglomanie*; when Odette interpolates an English word into a trivial anecdote he is telling, he ignores it and continues with his story:

—C'est idiot. Vous savez que Mme Blatin aime à interpeller tout le monde d'un air qu'elle croit aimable et qui est surtout protecteur.—Ce que nos bons voisins de la Tamise appellent *patronizing*, interrompit Odette.—Elle est allée dernièrement au jardin d'Acclimatation . . . (I, 526)

[It's idiotic. You know that Mme Blatin likes to accost everyone in a way she thinks friendly and which is in fact condescending.—What our good neighbours by the Thames call *patronizing*, interrupted Odette.—She went to the Zoo recently . . .][31]

Odette and Gilberte speak English between themselves, to Marcel's confusion, but Swann is not present at these conversations; M. de Charlus

---

[30] The word is *budget*: see Ch. 3, p. 129.
[31] My translation; *Vintage* (II, 125), after Odette's interruption, has Swann say: 'Exactly. Well, she went the other day . . .' which is exactly wrong.

may utter an English word in order to disdain it, rejecting 'le vomitif appelé *cup* où on fait généralement traîner trois fraises pourries dans un mélange de vinaigre et d'eau de Seltz' [the emetic known as *cup*, which consists, as a rule, of three rotten strawberries swimming in a mixture of vinegar and soda-water] (III, 395; IV, 469);[32] but one of his catchwords is the absurd 'médiumnimique', which he deploys in the same passage to disparage his protégé Morel's insufficiently 'spiritualist' violin-playing: 'vous semblez ne pas apercevoir le côté médiumnimique de la chose' [you seem not to be aware of the mediumistic side] (III, 396; IV, 469).[33] Moreover, M. de Charlus cannot resist the charm of an English nickname, since he calls Charles Morel 'Charlie'.[34] But Swann is never 'Charlie'; Mme de Guermantes, when she wants to address him with affectionate familiarity, calls him 'mon petit Charles'.

Swann's linguistic chastity, or fastidiousness, is a paradoxical form of his Englishness. It is the complement of his reticence about his social position, his discretion, his ironic self-deprecation—qualities which were often opposed in the period to French 'franchise'.[35] In this sense the refusal to affect Englishness by using English words might be thought a truer indication than the monocle so admired by Odette of 'un vrai gentleman'.

Swann leaves it to others to denote him in this way, including the narrator. He is surrounded by English words, which form, so to speak, the

---

[32] Bonnaffé defines *cup* as an abbreviation of 'champagne-cup', and cites—who else?— Paul Bourget, in a more polite vein than M. de Charlus: 'Ils buvaient . . . un *cup* aromatisé d'herbes odorantes' [They drank . . . a *cup* scented with odorous herbs] (*Voyageuses*, 1897).

[33] The fact that M. de Charlus lengthens the word from the more usual 'médiumnique', which Bonnaffé first records in 1905, might suggest that Proust is making fun of his preciosity; but he has Marcel use the same form (II, 489; III, 216), apparently without irony. 'Médium' itself dates from 1856 and probably came from America, where the craze for spiritualism in the 1840s and 1850s originated.

[34] 'Charlie' first appears in *Sodome et Gomorrhe*, soon after *cup* (III, 399; IV, 473); Proust took the name from a young English manservant called Charlie Humphreys (Tadié, p. 626). Robert de Saint-Loup's mistress Rachel calls him 'Bobbey' in *Le Côté de Guermantes I* (II, 470; III, 175). I regret to say that Proust signed one of his youthful pieces in *Le Mensuel* 'Bob' ('Endroits publics', in *Écrits*, 59–62).

[35] For Ruskin's definition of 'franchise', see above, p. 83. One of Swann's literary precursors, Alfred Mosé in Paul Bourget's novel *Un cœur de femme* (1890), who like Swann comes from a converted Jewish family, is cherished by the aristocratic Mme de Candale 'pour sa discrétion, pour son ton véritablement exquis', and it is said of him that 'Il tenait son role de gentleman avec une irréprochable rigueur' (pp. 270–1).

contours of his social existence: he is 'le Swann que connurent à la même époque tant de clubmen'[the Swann whom so many *clubmen* knew at the same period] (I, 18),[36] a phrase which implies that Swann was a *clubman* himself but which doesn't say so outright. In the account of his love-life before Odette, we are told that when his mistress belonged to his own class, he would arrange for her to be invited 'dans les salons particulière-ment fermés où il avait ses habitudes, ses dîners hebdomadaires, son poker' [the most exclusive salons, to those houses where he himself went regularly for weekly dinners or for poker] (I, 192; I, 212).[37] An English word complements a French one in the description of these affairs: 'cha-cune de ces liaisons, ou chacun de ces flirts' [each of these liaisons, or each of these flirtations].[38] Swann's preferred carriage is a *victoria*, the open-topped two wheeler with which he is particularly associated; [39] Odette's

[36] My translation; *Vintage* (I, 19) has 'the Swann who was a familiar figure in all the clubs of those days'. When they meet towards the end of Swann's life, Marcel refers to him as 'le vieux clubman' [the old clubman] (II, 867; III, 670). Bonnaffé defines *clubman, club-woman* as 'celui, celle qui fait partie d'un club' [he or she who belongs to a club], but spec-ifies for the masculine form 'le sens d'homme élégant et mondain' [the sense of an elegant man of the world], citing (as expected) Paul Bourget: 'Elle avait trompé ce charmant homme avec un clubman très à la mode' [She had betrayed this charming man with a very fashionable clubman] (*Mensonges*, 1888). The term is applied to Saint-Loup, also in the context of sexual licence: 'la maîtresse d'un jeune clubman comme Saint-Loup' [the mis-tress of a young clubman like Saint-Loup] (II, 139; II, 417 where *Vintage* renders 'jeune clubman' as 'young blood').

[37] Bonnaffé has 'poker' from 1858, but a more recent citation from Paul Bourget is apposite here, since Swann is the son of a stockbroker: 'La Bourse ressemble au poker. Quand on est assez bête pour demander l'avis de son adversaire, il a bien raison de bluffer' [The Stock Exchange resembles poker. If you are stupid enough to ask your opponent for advice, he has every right to bluff] (*Idylle tragique*, 1896). Proust uses the noun *bluff* three times, twice in relation to the dangerous psychological game which Marcel plays with Albertine in the days preceding her flight (III, 856, 865; V, 404, 413–14).

[38] Bonnaffé dates 'flirt', in the sense of 'manège de coquetterie ou de galanterie', to 1879; he quotes from *Flirt*, a novel by Paul Hervieu (1890): 'Son sense très aiguisé de l'utile et du décent, en matière de flirt, ne lui interdisait pas de poursuivre les personnalités du demi-monde' [His finely honed sense of what was serviceable and decent in matters of flir-tation did not prohibit him from pursuing persons belonging to the *demi-monde*]. See also Ch. 1, p. 61.

[39] The 'victoria' is first recorded in French in 1867, but Bloch and Wartburg claim that the term was invented in France, pointing out that the earliest occurrences in English (from 1844) are in works relating to France. Seven out of the ten occurrences of the word in *A la recherche* are associated with Swann or Odette; another has M. Bloch *père* in an uncon-sciously burlesque imitation of Odette's elegance: 'M. Bloch louait à certains jours une vic-toria . . . et traversait le bois de Boulogne, mollement étendu de travers . . .' [M. Bloch used on special occasions to hire an open victoria . . . and would drive through the Bois de Boulogne, reclining indolently . . .] (II, 131; II, 407).

triumph over him is signalled, after her marriage, by her adoption of this fashionable vehicle, which Marcel sees in its full glory, and in which the 'petit groom' is himself an emblem of literary *anglomanie*:

emportée par le vol de deux chevaux ardents . . . portant établi sur son siège un énorme cocher fourré comme un cosaque, à côté d'un petit groom rappelant le "tigre" de "feu Beaudenord", je voyais . . . une incomparable victoria, à dessein un peu haute et laissant passer à travers son luxe "dernier cri" des allusions aux formes anciennes, au fond de laquelle reposait avec abandon Mme Swann . . .

[borne along by the flight of a pair of fiery horses . . . carrying on its box an enormous coachman furred like a cossack, and by his side a diminutive groom like "the late Beaudenord's tiger," I saw . . . a matchless victoria, built rather high, and hinting, through the extreme modernity of its appointments, at the forms of an earlier day, in which Mme Swann negligently reclined . . .]

(I, 411; I, 503)[40]

We have seen Odette describe Swann to the Verdurins as 'très *smart*'; Cottard, the naïvely snobbish and impressionable physician, discovers that Swann knows the President of the Republic, M. Grévy, and asks Mme Verdurin each time they sit down to dinner: ' "Verrons-nous ce soir M. Swann? Il a des relations personelles avec M. Grévy. C'est bien ce qu'on appelle un gentleman?" ' ["D'you think we shall see M. Swann here this evening? He's a personal friend of M. Grévy's. I suppose that means he's what you'd call a 'gentleman'?"] (I, 214; I, 260). Just as Swann never takes the letter from Twickenham out of his pocket, he refrains from adding insult to injury by informing Cottard that he and M. Grévy have a friend in common—the Prince of Wales (I, 213; I, 259).

The degree of protection which Swann is accorded in the linguistic sphere is confirmed by his never being called *snob*, a fate which no other main character in the novel escapes, except Marcel's grandmother. The word *snobisme*, too, passes him by. In an account (perhaps a little too admiring) of the unaffected polish of Swann's manners, the narrator generalizes

[40] The ' "tigre" de "feu Beaudenord" ' appears in two novels by Balzac, *La Maison Nucingen* and *Les Secrets de la princesse de Cadignan*; the latter features both in *A la recherche* where it is admired by M. de Charlus (III, 442–3, 445; IV, 525–6, 529–30), and in the pastiche of Balzac which Proust first published in 1908 and collected in *Pastiches et mélanges* in 1919; there the groom appears with his Irish name, Paddy. In Balzac he is a young man discharged by his first employer, an English nobleman, for his effeminacy, before being hired by the duc de Beaudenord. See the *Pléiade* note, I, 1279. The same combination of enormous coachman and diminutive groom appears in Bourget's *Lettres de Londres* (see Ch. 1, p. 61).

his portrait to include all those imbued with the values of 'la société élégante': 'Leur amabilité, séparée de tout snobisme' [Their good nature, freed from all taint of snobbishness'] (I, 199; I, 242). Again, when Forcheville is introduced at the Verdurins: 'Sans doute Forcheville était grossièrement snob, alors que Swann ne l'était pas' [Of course, Forcheville was a colossal snob, which Swann was not] (I, 246; I, 301). When Swann is thinking of marrying Odette, the only person whose possible disapproval causes him anxiety is Mme de Guermantes—'et non par snobisme' [and from no snobbish motive], Marcel emphasizes (I, 461; II, 48).

Swann's newspaper obituary—a masterly pastiche of the urbane commonplaces with which Parisian society papers such as *Le Gaulois* dispatched their readers—is the last occasion on which an English phrase swirls around Swann without touching him—without, in this case, the power to touch him: 'Sa physionomie spirituelle, comme sa notoriété marquante ne laissaient pas d'exciter la curiosité du public dans tout *great event* de la musique et de la peinture, et notamment aux "vernissages" dont il avait été l'habitué fidèle jusqu'à ces dernières années ...' [His witty and striking personality never failed to arouse the interest of the public at all the great events of the musical and artistic seasons, notably at private views, where he was a regular attendant until the last few years . . .] (III, 704; V, 222). The *great event* of Swann's death safeguards him from this last snobbish compliment. It's only a small remission; for Swann's own form of Englishness, though it does not contaminate his language, is one of the qualities which in Proust's unforgiving judgement cost him his soul.

'C'est bien ce qu'on appelle un gentleman?'

The question, we recall, was the vulgarian Cottard's. Swann is too much of a gentleman to use the word; the values of his world forbid it. These values also forbid other forms of speech, whether in English or French: boasting, bluster, dogmatic assertion. And behind these: pomposity, dullness, over-solemnity. Now the borderline between a linguistic vice and a moral principle begins to come into view. 'Over-solemnity', even 'dullness', may be the forms in which seriousness is stigmatized by those too shallow or frivolous to bear it, or bear with it. The flight from dogma may also involve a flight from passing any kind of judgement—intellectual, moral, political— or at any rate from doing so in public. In turn, the atrophy of judgement affects the heart. The relentless practice of tact may lead to a condition in which you are touched by nothing.

The refinement of a social manner which consists in the exquisite avoidance of banality, and in never expressing an opinion with unseemly feeling or force, is directly linked to the French concept of *le gentleman*. Its elements can be found in dozens of French observations on English manners from the mid-eighteenth century onwards, but it was given a particular twist in its adoption by the French aristocracy in the period after 1848. If Carlyle thought the English aristocracy had become effete through no longer fulfilling the task for which it was designed—namely, to rule—then the French aristocracy was in an even more hapless state. When, therefore, Swann is said to be the friend of both the comte de Paris and the Prince of Wales, this collocation means something more than a simple index of social rank. He is the friend of princes without power, of an ineffectual heir and an impotent pretender. All that such people truly possess is their manner; and manner unmaketh man.

The delicacy and discretion of Swann's manners are opposed to those of Odette in an implicit contrast between two forms of *anglomanie*. Because one is the object of satire it is easy to fall into the error of thinking that the other is to be approved. Swann's career in high society has left him with a desiccated heart, and with the inability to get past the surfaces of life; he will go to almost any lengths to avoid giving his real opinion on any serious matter, or expressing an unguarded emotion. He would rather give the precise dates of a painter's birth and death than pass judgement on his work. On the rare occasions when he betrays himself, Marcel remarks, 'il donnait alors à ses paroles un ton ironique comme s'il n'ad-hérait pas tout entier à ce qu'il disait' [but then he would cloak his words in a tone of irony, as though he did not altogether associate himself with what he was saying] (I, 207; I, 252). This substitution of the protocol of life for its core, the negation of warmth and personal commitment in favour of ironic detachment, is a recurring theme in the French charac-terization of the English gentleman's mentality, his well-bred reluctance to pass judgement or engage in heated debate and his liking for unemo-tional commonplaces. Swann is far more 'English' in this respect than Odette; she follows a fashion, but he has embraced something akin to a code.

It is true that this code safeguards Swann not just from vulgarity but from certain kinds of corruption; he will not renege on his adherence to the *faubourg Saint-Germain*, whatever the cost; a gentleman may hold his tongue while blasphemy is uttered in his presence, but must not utter it himself. For Mme Verdurin this reticence is itself a heresy; she wants Swann to betray his grand friends, to denigrate them in her presence so that she can feel better about not knowing them; but Swann won't do it. He goes to great lengths to avoid a 'scene', but on one occasion he is cornered and forced to acknowledge that he thinks the duchesse de La Trémoïlle 'intelligente'. Forcheville (anticipating Professor Joad and the Brains Trust by half a century) cuts in:

—Tout dépend de ce que vous appelez intelligence . . . Voyons, Swann, qu'entendez-vous par intelligence?
—Voilà! s'écria Odette, voilà les grandes choses dont je lui demande de me parler, mais il ne veut jamais.

["It all depends on what you call intelligence . . . Come now, Swann, tell us what you mean by intelligence."

"There," cried Odette, "that's the sort of big subject I'm always asking him to talk to me about, and he never will."]

(I, 256; I, 313)

It is an imbecilic question, posed by an imbecile and seconded by an ignoramus; but through its injustice we get an acute glimpse of Odette's very French indignation at Swann's refusal to discuss 'les grandes choses'. Years later (though it comes in an earlier part of the novel) Marcel will be troubled by this same reluctance of Swann to say what he really feels, which had seemed to him at first an elegant and Parisian attribute: 'Mais maintenant je trouvais quelque chose de choquant dans cette attitude de Swann en face des choses' [But now I found something shocking in this attitude of Swann when faced with things] (I, 97).[41] The alliterative sequence 'quelque chose de choquant' opposes the awkward rigour of the boy's judgement to the elegant and evasive 'Swann en face des choses'. Although Marcel will repeat many of Swann's mistakes in love, this will not be one of them.

L'israélite du Jockey

The one exception to Swann's avoidance of English words is the word *jockey*, or rather the phrase *le Jockey*, meaning the Jockey Club. It is true that even here the context in which Swann finally pronounces an English

---

[41] My translation; *Vintage* (I, 116) has 'But now I found myself slightly shocked'.

EDOUARD BONNAFFÉ

L'ANGLICISME ET L'ANGLO-AMÉRICANISME
DANS LA LANGUE FRANÇAISE

DICTIONNAIRE

ÉTYMOLOGIQUE
ET
HISTORIQUE

DES

ANGLICISMES

Préface de M. Ferdinand BRUNOT
DOYEN DE LA FACULTÉ DES LETTRES DE PARIS

PARIS
LIBRAIRIE DELAGRAVE
15, RUE SOUFFLOT, 15
1920

9a (*left*). Title-page from Bonnaffé's *Dictionnaire étymologique et historique des anglicismes*, 1920.

9b (*below*). Entry for 'Jockey-Club' from Édouard Bonnaffé's *Dictionnaire étymologique et historique des anglicismes*, 1920.

IRIDIUM — 78 — JOCKEY

S. m. - Élément dissocié par l'effet du courant électrique.

Ion: nom commun donné... aux deux corps dissociés par le courant électrique. (LAROUSSE, p. 779; 1873.) Les ions de Faraday se déplacent à travers la masse non décomposée. (JAMIN-BOUTY, Cours de Phys., t. IV, 1re part., p. 214; 1888.) Les éléments électrolytiques, les ions, sont les véhicules du courant. (DASTRE, R. des Deux-Mondes, CLVI, 700; 1899.)

ISM. — Faraday a créé, en même temps, les termes anion et cation pour désigner chacun des éléments - négatif et positif - dissociés par le courant électrique. Ces expressions sont peu usitées. Par contre, les physiciens ont été amenés à former un certain nombre de dérivés du mot « ion » et auj. d'emploi fréquent : L'état d'ionisation de l'électrolyte demeure constant. (L. POINCARÉ, Phys. Mod., p. 156, 1911.) Les particules d'un radium cessent d'insuler les gaz. (id., ibid., p. 272.) L'atome matériel... peut, sous certaines influences « ionisantes », être brisé en morceaux. (BRUNHES, Dégrad. de l'Énergie, p. 303; 1908.)

IRIDIUM [iridium, ainsi baptisé par Tennant, chimiste anglais, à cause de la variété des irisations qu'il donne, en dissolution].

S. m. — Corps simple, métal très dur et cassant.

L'iridium a été découvert et nommé par M. Tennant. (Ann. du Muséum d'Hist. Nat., VII, 404; 1806.) L'iridium est solide. (THÉNARD, Tr. de Chim., I, 427; 1827.) L'iridium fut découvert en 1803. (ACAD., 1878.)

J

JACK-KNIFE [jack-knife; de Jack, qui vient probt. du français Jacques, et sert, en angl., de préfixe à un grand nombre d'engins et d'appareils divers; et knife (couteau) = tent. knifed].

S. c. m. — Commutateur à chevilles, muni d'un ressort en lame de couteau, dont on fait usage dans les bureaux téléphoniques centraux pour mettre en communication les abonnés entre eux.

La disposition du Jack-knife switch est en partie française, car l'inventeur... est un Français du Canada appelé Rousseau.

(C. HASKINS, Lumière Electr., II, 136; 1880.) Les commutateurs... sont disposés en Jack-knifs. (DU MONCEL, id., V, 43; 1884.) Quand on veut donner la communication à deux abonnés, on réunit leurs Jackknives par une corde métallique. (NAUDET, Electricien, p. 568; 1882.)

Abrévt. : L'employé saisit la fiche... et la porte dans le jack de l'abonné demandé. (Éclair. Electr., x, 176; 1897.)

JERSEY [Jersey, île de la Manche; parce que la laine en question fut primitivement (vers la fin du XVIIe s.) fabriquée à Jersey].

S. m. — Laine anglaise. || Tissu ou vêtement fait de cette laine.

HIST. — Leurs moutons [de Jersey] ont de la laine fort blanche dont nous laissons notre Kersey ou Jersey. (BRUYN, Singularités Nat. d'Anglet., p. 311; 1667.)

Tricot en soie ou laine souple dont on fait emploi pour les corsages connus sous le nom de Jersey. (Mode Ill., p. 215, c. 2; 1881.) Petites têtes blondes aux cheveux frisés sur de grands cols anglais et les jerseys serrés de près. (MAURIN des Mauves, p. 96; 1901.)

JIGGER [jigger (cribleur); du v. to jig, dont l'étym. est très incertaine].

S. m. — 1° - Technol. : Cuve pour la teinture des tissus de coton.

On a généralement un batterie composée d'un nombre plus ou moins grand de jiggers pour chaque couleur. (LEFÈVRE, Teint. des Tissus de Coton, p. 32; 1911.)

2° - Electr. : Dans la télégraphie sans fil, transformateur spécial du poste récepteur.

Le jigger ou résonateur est constitué par un solénoïde en fil nu. (BOULANGER-FERRIÉ, Télégr. sans Fil, p. 238, 1907.) Le secondaire du jigger se compose de deux bobines distinctes. (H. POINCARÉ, Théorie de Maxwell, p. 93; 1907.)

JOCKEY [jockey, dim. de Jock, forme écos. de Jack ou John. L'acception actuelle (1°) remonte, en angl., à 1670].

S. m. — 1° - Cavalier professionnel qui monte dans les courses; postillon, laquais, palefrenier.

La Course ou les Jockeis. (LAUS DE

JOCKEY — 79 — JURY

BOISSY; 24 août 1776). On annonce la couleur des Jockeis ou palefreniers coureurs de chacun des concurrents. (MAIROBERT et ANGERVILLE, Mém. Secrets, x, 80; 1883 ... 1777.) Ils [les riches] veulent bien faire courir, parier, avoir des Jockeys. (LINGUET, Ann. Polit., I, 182; 1777.) On fait pleuvoir le jockei qui doit conduire, afin qu'il pèse moins. (MERCIER, Tabl. de Paris, ch. 421; 1783.) - ACAD., 1835. - Les équipages de la reine, conduits par des jockeys en veste rouge et or. (TH. GAUTIER, Caprices et Zigzags, p. 216; 1852.) Les jockeys, en nage de soie, tâchaient d'aligner leurs chevaux. (G. FLAUBERT, Educat. Sentiment., I, 357; 1869.)

HIST. — Il y a lieu de remarquer qu'en franç., jaquet, jacquet, a signifié d'abord « paysan, bouffon, domestique » au XVIe s., « petit laquais » au XVIIe, et finalement « postillon » au XVIIIe. Ces dernières acceptions ont forcément provoqué une confusion entre les deux mots jaquet et jockey, quand l'anglomanie a commencé à nous faire adopter les termes de courses en usage de l'autre côté du détroit : M. le Comte d'Artois... affecquent dans ta foule du peuple pour aller encourager un des jockeis aux jupets. (MERCY-ARGENTEAU, Lett. à Marie-Thérèse d'Autriche; 15 nov. 1776.) Depuis qu'un Jacquet, un Heyduque, un Coureur sont plus fêtés, chéris, que s'ils eu précéptaur. (CAILHAVA, Egoïsme, II, 7; 1777.) L'auteur ajoute en note : « Le mot anglois est Jockey et nous prononçons comme Jacquet. » Je signalerai comme fort bon le jockey à tige de fer que j'ai vu employer en Angleterre. (MONTIGNY, Man. des Piqueurs, p. 98; 1873.) Le jockey à charnière est le seul qui puisse être adopté. (Monit. de la Sellerie, p. 101, c. 1; 1893.)

3° - Ornement en forme de volant disposé au haut des manches d'un corsage et emprunté au costume des jockeys.

La première bouillon [de la manche] est à demi-cachée par le jockey garni d'une frange. (Caprice, p. 415, c. 2; 1836.) Double jockeys trouvés aux épaules. (Salon de la Mode, p. 91; fév. 1908.)

4° - Chapeau analogue à ceux que portaient les palefreniers ou postillons.

Chapeaux de femme pour le déshabillé : jocquay en oarson. (Cabinet des Modes, I, 8; 1785.) Voici le vrai moment du jockey gris, le chapeau chic par excellence. (R. de la Chapellerie, p. 353, c. 1; 1900.)

JOCKEY-CLUB.

S. c. m. — Cercle mondain d'amateurs du sport hippique, fondé à Paris, en 1833, sur le modèle du Jockey-Club anglais.

Les listes des courses sont dressées par une espèce de secrétaire reconnu par le jockey club [anglais]. (J. des Haras, p. 212; 1828.) Nous n'ignorons pas l'utilité du Jockey's Club. (GAYOT, Guide du Sportsman, p. 54; 1839.) Le Jockey-Club n'est pas, comme on semble le croire communément, une société de jeunes centaures. (TH. GAUTIER, Hist. de l'Art Dramat., V, 94; 1848.)

Abrévt. : Elle a compromis beaucoup d'hommes comme il faut... je t'ai enlevée à ces messieurs du Jockey. (A. DUMAS, Quest. d'Argent, II, 7; 1857.) Le monde, pur papa, commence à ceux qui sont du Jockey et finit à ceux qui n'en sont pas. (L. HALÉVY, Grand Mariage, p. 151; 1887.)

JOHN BULL [littéralement « Jean le Taureau ». Ce nom est emprunté à l'Hist. de John Bull, pamphlet de John Arbuthnot, médecin de la reine Anne, publié en 1712, et traduit en français par l'abbé Velly, en 1753].

S. m. — Sobriquet du peuple anglais.

Bull au fond était un honnête garçon, simple, uni, sans détours; mais colère, hargneux, brusque, inconstant. (Hist. de John Bull, p. 12; trad. 1753.) John Bull ne peut plus se vanter d'être le personnage exclusif du bon roast-beef. (SAINT-CONSTANT, Londres et les Angl., II, 322; 1804.) John Bull lançait des trognons de pommes à la divinité dont il encense aujourd'hui les images. (CHATEAUBRIAND, Ess. sur la Litt. Angl., XI, 586; 1836.) Probablement, aux yeux du gros John Bull... la peintre n'est pas un gentleman. (TAINE, Notes sur l'Anglet., p. 279; 1872.)

JURY [jury = v. franç. jurée, enquête juridique].

S. m. — 1° - La réunion des jurés d'un tribunal de justice.

word is somewhat ironic. On one of the last occasions on which Marcel sees him, shortly before his death, he asks Swann if he sees anything of Robert de Saint-Loup these days, and Swann, whose partisanship of Dreyfus in the great 'Affaire' has alienated him from many of his former aristocratic friends, replies:

—Non, jamais. Il m'a écrit l'autre jour pour que je demande au duc de Mouchy et à quelques autres de voter pour lui au Jockey, où il a du reste passé comme une lettre à la poste.
    —Malgré l'Affaire!
    —On n'a pas soulevé la question. Du reste je vous dirai que, depuis tout ça, je ne mets plus les pieds dans cet endroit.

["No, never. He wrote to me the other day asking me to persuade the Duc de Mouchy and various other people to vote for him at the Jockey, where for that matter he got through like a letter through the post."
    "In spite of the Affair!"
    "The question was never raised. However, I must tell you that since all this business began I never set foot in the place."]

(II, 871; III, 674–5)[42]

Only when he refuses to set foot in his old haunt does Swann actually say its name. Nevertheless *le Jockey* has in some sense been his life. It heads the list of his social distinctions, as Marcel records them on his first appearance, coming even before the mention of friendships with royalty; along with his *victoria*, it is transferred to Odette as an attribute of her status as Mme Swann. When Marcel sees her in her pomp, strolling in the Bois de Boulogne with Swann and the rest of her entourage, he catches the murmur of gossip which surrounds her:

"Vous savez qui c'est? Mme Swann! Cela ne vous dit rien? Odette de Crécy?
    —Odette de Crécy? . . . Je me rappelle que j'ai couché avec elle le jour de la démission de Mac-Mahon.

---

[42] Saint-Loup's family had worried that he would be blackballed at the Jockey Club because of his Dreyfusard sympathies and scandalous liaison with the actress Rachel; later on, in *Sodome et Gomorrhe*, we find M. de Charlus virtuously decrying his nephew's conduct, which had come close to getting him 'blackboulé au Jockey' (III, 91; IV, 107). *Blackbouler* had been established in French since the mid-19th cent. and has an entry in the 1877 edn. of Littré's standard dictionary (Bonnaffé).

—Je crois que vous ferez bien de ne pas le lui rappeler. Elle est maintenant Mme Swann, la femme d'un monsieur du Jockey, ami du prince de Galles.

["You know who that is? Mme Swann! That conveys nothing to you? Odette de Crécy, then?"

"Odette de Crécy! . . . I remember I slept with her on the day MacMahon resigned.

"I shouldn't remind her of it, if I were you. She's now Mme Swann, the wife of a gentleman in the Jockey Club, a friend of the Prince of Wales. . . ."]

(I, 413; I, 505)[43]

This is what Swann's celebrity has come down to. And it features in his obituary, of course: 'il sera unanimement regretté . . . au Jockey-Club dont il était l'un des membres les plus anciens et les plus écoutés' [he will be universally mourned . . . at the Jockey Club of which he was one of the oldest and most respected members] (III, 704; V, 222).

Swann's membership of the Jockey Club serves to shield Odette from contact with her past self, but it had already performed the same service for him. For though Swann dies one of the oldest members of the Jockey Club, he was not born one. Proust made no secret of the fact that a large part of the social personality of Swann, as well as his physical appearance, was based on the wealthy dilettante, art collector and *clubman* Charles Haas (1833–1902), who was elected to the Jockey Club in 1871, but only after four rejections and with a tide of sympathy for his service in the Franco-Prussian War.[44] References to Haas in Proust's letters single out his Jewishness as the surprising complement of his social prestige: 'Haas l'ami des princes, l'israélite du Jockey' [Haas the friend of princes, the Jew of the Jockey].[45] When Swann

[43] The presidency of the maréchal de MacMahon (the usual spelling) was engineered in 1873 by an alliance between Bonapartists and royalists; he resigned prematurely, a year before the expiry of his seven-year term, in 1879, after the victory of the republicans in the elections of 1877, and was succeeded by Swann's friend Jules Grévy (Zeldin, I, 563, 594). For another allusion to MacMahon's presidency, also linked to Odette's sexual history, see below, p. 114.

[44] Alfred Mosé, in Paul Bourget's *Un cœur de femme* (see above, p. 96 n. 35) 'avait réussi à forcer la porte du Jockey par une diplomatie de dix années' (p. 270).

[45] Letter to Harry Swann, 10/11 Dec. 1920, *Corr.* XIX, 660; I discuss this letter below, p. 109. In a letter to Mme de Brantes of 1 Sept. 1897, when he was working on *Jean Santeuil*, Proust asked for details of aristocratic disdain for use in his portrait of the duc de Reveillon: 'N'auraient-ils donné que la main gauche (ou d'autres marques de mépris que j'aimerais bien savoir) à M. Haas ou M. Schlumberger' [Would they have offered only the left hand (or other signs of disdain which I'd very much like to know) to M. Haas or M. Schlumberger?] (*Corr.* II, 215).

turns against the Jockey Club because of the Dreyfus Affair, he is reclaiming
an identity which he had had to sacrifice in order to gain admission in the
first place. He becomes as suspicious and intolerant of anti-Semitism as he
had been, in his heyday, indulgent or indifferent. In turn, his old friends and
supporters at the Jockey Club, notably the duc de Guermantes, are outraged
at his betrayal of his adopted, as opposed to his 'natural', caste: 'Patronné
jadis dans le monde par nous, par le duc de Chartres, on me dit qu'il est
ouvertement dreyfusard' [Although he was originally introduced into society by ourselves and the Duc de Chartres, they tell me now that he is openly
Dreyfusard] (III, 76; IV, 89). In the list which M. de Guermantes goes on
to give of the nine attributes that make Swann's Dreyfusism so hard for
him to believe—comically incongruous on his part, ordered and artful on
Proust's—membership of the Jockey Club comes in the exact centre:

Jamais je n'aurai cru cela de lui, de lui un fin gourmet, un esprit positif, un
collectionneur, un amateur de vieux livres, membre du Jockey, un homme
entouré de la considération générale, un connaisseur de bonnes adresses qui nous
envoyait le meilleur porto qu'on puisse boire, un dilettante, un père de famille.

[I should never have believed it of him, an epicure, a man of practical judgement,
a collector, a connoisseur of old books, member of the Jockey, a man who enjoys
the respect of all, a connoisseur of good addresses who used to send us the best
port you could wish to drink, a dilettante, a family man.]

(III, 76–7; IV, 89)

As well as being central to this list, 'membre du Jockey' is also grammatically
distinct, all the other features of Swann's identity being preceded by 'un';
membership of the Jockey Club is a kind of physical adherence (as the
etymology of 'membre' suggests in both French and English), which
makes Swann's dissent all the more shocking and painful.

Like Haas, Swann had to struggle to gain admittance to the Jockey
Club. There was a time, Marcel reflects, when Swann himself would have
been among those who ridiculed the kind of marriage he ended up making, 'Swann qui s'était donné du mal pour être reçu au Jockey et avait
compté dans ce temps-là faire un éclatant mariage qui eût achevé en con-
solidant sa situation de faire de lui un des hommes le plus en vue de Paris'
[Swann who had taken endless pains to get himself elected to the Jockey
Club and had reckoned at that time on making a brilliant marriage
which, by consolidating his position, would have made him one of the
most prominent figures in Paris] (I, 461; II, 47). Such a marriage would

have effaced, once and for all, the traces of Swann's Jewishness, a phenomenon which takes effect only after his death in the marriage of
Gilberte to Robert de Saint-Loup, by which time the name 'Swann' has
been disavowed by his only child. Indeed the name of Swann would be
finally lost were it not ironically rescued by the work of art in which its
effacement is recorded.

The rescue is ironic because of what membership of the Jockey Club
means to Swann. The qualities which surround it in M. de Guermantes's
list may reflect the dim glow of the Duke's intellect, but they also convey
the novelist's intellectual grasp of the frivolity of Swann's existence. The
commonplace phrases ('un homme entouré de la considération générale')
prefigure Swann's obituary; M. de Guermantes even adds the pompous
conventional tribute 'père de famille', a tellingly empty formula in
Swann's case. Paternity in him is not the sign of fecundity; his good taste
is not the sign of truthful perception; his connoisseurship is not the sign
of art. He belongs in, and to, *le Jockey.*

'D'origine anglaise'

In *Albertine disparue*, Marcel analyses the ironic reversal by which Mme
de Guermantes performs after Swann's death the one favour she refused
while he was alive, the only one which really mattered to him: to 'know'
his daughter Gilberte. But the price of this favour is the extinction of
Swann's name. After his death Odette marries Forcheville, so that
Gilberte becomes, for a time, Mlle de Forcheville; this in itself might not
have affected the survival of Swann's name in the Guermantes circle
(apart from the natural oblivion into which he would in any case have
fallen) but as soon as Mlle de Forcheville is admitted into that circle he
becomes unmentionable, a non-person. Gilberte herself actively colludes
in this collective forgetting. With the exception of Marcel himself, with
whom she feels able to speak of her 'véritable père', 'on n'osait plus devant
elle prononcer le nom de Swann' [no one now dared utter the name
Swann in her presence] (IV, 162; V, 667).

The Jewishness of 'l'israélite du Jockey' plays its part here too. When a
Jewish lady leaves her card at Mme de Guermantes's, the Duchess says to
Gilberte:

"Je ne saurais même pas vous expliquer qui c'est, vous ne la connaissez certainement pas, elle s'appelle Lady Rufus Israël." Gilberte rougit vivement: "Je ne la

connais pas", dit-elle (ce qui était d'autant plus faux que Lady Israël s'était, deux ans avant la mort de Swann, réconciliée avec lui et qu'elle appelait Gilberte par son prénom), mais je sais très bien, par d'autres, qui c'est, la personne que vous voulez dire."

["I really don't know how to explain to you who she is, you've certainly never heard of her, she's called Lady Rufus Israels."

Gilberte flushed crimson: "No, I don't know her," she said (which was all the more untrue in that Lady Israels and Swann had been reconciled two years before the latter's death and she addressed Gilberte by her first name), "but I know quite well, from hearing about her, who it is that you mean."]

(IV, 164–5; V, 669–70)[46]

Lady Israël, Swann's aunt and therefore Gilberte's great-aunt, had been just as ruthless as Mme de Guermantes in refusing to acknowledge Odette, but unlike her she had relented while Swann was still alive— probably, though Marcel isn't explicit, as a result of the Dreyfus Affair which had driven Swann himself back on his Jewishness and which had diminished Lady Israël's own social prestige.[47] The passage I have just cited represents a double act of betrayal, disingenuous on the part of Mme de Guermantes who pretends not to know Gilberte's relationship to Lady Israël, cowardly on the part of Gilberte who follows suit. In the manuscript draft, Proust wrote immediately after this sentence, then deleted: 'C'est que Gilberte était devenue très snob' [The fact is, Gilberte had become very snobbish] (IV, 1099).[48] He thought better of this over-insistence; on the other hand he reinforced the point about Swann's name in the passage which follows:

J'appris qu'une jeune fille ayant soit méchamment, soit maladroitement demandé quel était le nom de son père, non pas adoptif mais véritable, dans son trouble et

---

[46] Proust refers to the surname here as 'Israël'; elsewhere he has 'Israels' and 'Israëls'; all three forms were passed by him in proof. *Vintage* standardizes on 'Israels'. The Israëls are equivalent in the novel to the Rothschilds (who also appear by name), but their English title distinguishes them from the Rothschilds who had been naturalized in France for several generations and whose name is in any case of German origin.

[47] Proust describes Lady Israël's conduct in *A l'ombre des jeunes filles en fleurs I*, in a passage which both reveals her family relationship to Swann and throws light on his friendship with the Orléans branch of the French royal family (I, 508–9; II, 104–5), since we learn that the Israëls were the Orléans' bankers.

[48] This sentence in fact appears in both the *Vintage* text (as 'Gilberte was becoming very snobbish') and the recent translation by Peter Collier (Penguin, 2002, 549) though both are meant to be based on the new *Pléiade* edition.

pour dénaturer un peu ce qu'elle avait à dire, elle avait prononcé au lieu de Souann, Svann, changement qu'elle s'aperçut un peu après être péjoratif, puisque cela faisait de ce nom d'origine anglaise un nom allemand.

[Thus a girl having one day asked her out of tactlessness or malice what the name of her real, not her adoptive father was, in her confusion and in order to somewhat distort what she had to say, instead of pronouncing it "Souann" she said "Svann," a change, as she soon realised, for the worse, since it made this name of English origin a German patronymic.]

(IV, 165; V, 670)[49]

This is the second time in the novel that Swann's name is pronounced 'Svann'. M. de Norpois, at dinner with Marcel's parents, chooses his words carefully in referring to the fact that 'society' women won't visit Mme Swann: 'il y va cependant des femmes, mais … appartenant plutôt … , comment dirais-je, au monde républicain qu'à la société de Swann (il prononçait Svann)' [women do go to the house, but women who … belong rather—what shall I say—to the Republican world than to Swann's (he pronounced it "Svann's") circle] (I, 457; II, 42). It is not clear, however, whether this pronunciation is habitual with M. de Norpois, or that there is anything Teutonic about it; the conversion of 'w' to 'v' was (and is) a common feature of the French pronunciation of English words, as we have seen in Françoise's pronunciation of New York as 'Nev'York' (I, 437; II, 18).[50] Gilberte's use of 'Svann' does not conform to this practice, however; how could it, since she must have heard her name pronounced in the 'English' fashion ever since she could remember? Her realization that 'Svann' is even worse than 'Souann' probably refers to the period of the Great War, but even so her mispronunciation is ill-chosen, since Swann (like his model Charles Haas) served with distinction against the Germans in the Franco-Prussian War of 1870; we learn that he added a codicil to his will instructing that he be buried (in the church at Combray, as a Christian) with the military honours due to him as a 'chevalier de la Légion d'honneur' (III, 111; IV, 130). Even without this, however, Gilberte's distortion of her father's name would be, indeed, a

---

[49] *Vintage* has 'as though to euphemise the name a little', but 'dénaturer' requires a stronger term.

[50] See Ch. 1, p. 20. Remy de Gourmont cites 'tranvé' for 'tramway'; he approves of this process, since the native French alphabet has no 'w'; if 'bow-window', for example, were allowed to naturalize itself it would become 'beauvindeau' (p. 53). Mallarmé, in *Les Mots anglais*, cites Goldsmith's novel *The Vicar of Wakefield* as 'le Vicaire de Vakefield' (p. 10).

'denaturing'. This is the only explicit allusion to the English origin of Swann's name; it has been kept in reserve for this moment of cruel disfigurement.

The full name, Charles Swann, evidently sounds more English than French; this is what Proust intended all along, as he explained in his letter to a certain Harry Swann, who wrote to him in December 1920 to enquire whether Proust had borrowed his family name and could give him any information about the French Swanns. Proust (in fine ironic form) expressed his regret at being unable to oblige, and explained that, although some of the names in *Du côté de chez Swann* were indeed borrowed from those of real people, Swann's was not one of them; he knew no one of that name, and had a quite different motive for choosing it:

Le prototype de Swann était M. Charles Haas, Haas l'ami des princes, l'israélite du Jockey. Mais ce n'était qu'un point de départ. Mon personnage évolue bien entendu autrement. Malgré tout je voulus chercher un nom d'apparence qui pût être anglo-saxonne et donner à mon oreille la sensation de *blanc* de l'*a* précédé d'une consonne et suivi d'une autre (je vous dis tout cela confidentiellement bien qu'il n'y ait aucun secret, mais parce que après plusieurs années écoulées, je peux me tromper sur la chimie assez particulière qui se passe dans notre cerveau quand nous fabriquons un nom). Les deux *nn* étaient destinés à compenser les deux *a*, à éviter l'idée de cygne liée à Me de Guermantes . . . (*Corr.* XIX, 660–1)

[The prototype of Swann was M. Charles Haas, Haas the friend of princes, the Jew of the Jockey. But that was only a point of departure. My character, of course, evolves quite differently. Still, I wanted to seek out a name which could be Anglo-Saxon in appearance and give my ear the *blank* feeling of the *a* preceded by one consonant and followed by another (I tell you all this in confidence, not because there is any secret about it, but because after several years have gone by I may be deceiving myself as to the quite specific chemical process which takes place in our brain when we make up a name). The two *nn* were destined to compensate for the two *aa*, [and] to avoid the idea of the swan, which is linked to Mme de Guermantes . . .]

The name 'Haas' is German-Jewish in origin; the effect of changing it to 'Swann' is to create an emphatic English resonance which belongs to Proust's character, not his 'prototype'. The 'compensation' which the second 'n' in 'Swann' offers to the lost second 'a' of 'Haas' is purely notional, since not only has the orientation of the word changed, but so has its semantic field. Proust's statement that the spelling was meant to *prevent* people from thinking of swans must be disingenuous; he of all writers would have known that a semantic association could not be undone by a variant in orthography. French readers with any knowledge of English would inevitably make the connection; only readers who did not know any English might hesitate over both origin and pronunciation, but Proust's motive for making the point can hardly have been to enlighten them so late in the day.[51] He seems rather to have wanted to emphasize the English origin of Swann's name precisely at the moment when that name was about to become extinct.

Swann's name is the seal of an Englishness which marks his social personality and psychology, and which is in turn a sign of his fate. A person's fate is almost always, in the great myths, the story of their return to their origins; it is not a matter of discovery but rediscovery. This is the case with Swann, I would suggest, and it is also the case with Odette.

We never learn Odette's original name; when we first meet her as *la dame en rose* she has no name at all; later she is introduced as 'Odette de Crécy', a name which we assume at first to be simply her courtesan's *nom de guerre*. She is successively Mme Swann and Mme de Forcheville, and she has in the past been 'Miss Sacripant'. But her origins go back further than this; she too, like Swann, has an 'origine anglaise', though not of the same kind.

Let us go back first to 'Crécy'. During his second stay at Balbec, Marcel makes the acquaintance of the comte de Crécy, 'gentilhomme pauvre mais d'une extrême distinction' [an impoverished, but extremely distinguished nobleman] (III, 468; again 'gentilhomme', not 'gentleman').[52] M. de Crécy attaches himself to Marcel not just because of the excellent

---

[51] Whether by error or design, Proust also offers a misleading association between the swan and Mme de Guermantes; its association with Albertine is far more potent. The yacht which Marcel promises to buy for her before her flight, and with which he tries to lure her back, was to be called *Le Cygne* and to have verses from Mallarmé's poem of that name on its prow (IV, 38–9; V, 520–1). After Albertine's death, Marcel, tormented by thoughts of her sexual pleasure with other women, compares the curvature of her thigh to a swan's neck, which in turn evokes for him 'le col hardi d'un cygne, comme celui qui dans une étude frémissante cherche la bouche d'une Léda' [the bold neck of a swan, like the one that can be seen in a stirring sketch seeking the mouth of a Leda] (IV, 108; V, 603). My own belief is that the mysterious 'chemistry' to which Proust alludes created a link between the double *nn* in Swann and the missing *n* in Albertine's surname, Simonet; her family prides itself on spelling their name with only one *n* whereas the usual spelling is Simonnet (II, 201; II, 490–1). Marcel's two great sexual mentors are joined by this play on the *n* in their names, as they are by the 'sign' of the swan, a connection reinforced by the fact that 'signe' is a homonym of 'cygne'.   [52] My translation; *Vintage* (IV, 558) has 'gentleman'.

dinners which the young man is able to offer him, but because he has
finally found someone who understands his passionate knowledge of the
social hierarchy, who can detect, for example, the false pretensions of
Legrandin to nobility and who knows the real value of the Guermantes
connection, 'quelqu'un pour qui l'univers social existait' [somebody for
whom the social world existed] (III, 471; IV, 561). Marcel goes on:

Très modeste en ce qui concernait sa propre famille, ce ne fut pas par M. de Crécy
que j'appris qu'elle était très grande et un authentique rameau détaché en France
de la famille anglaise qui porte le titre de Crécy. Quand je sus qu'il était un vrai
Crécy, je lui racontai qu'une nièce de Mme de Guermantes avait épousé un
Américain du nom de Charles Crécy et lui dis que je pensais qu'il n'avait aucun
rapport avec lui. "Aucun, me dit il. Pas plus—bien, du reste, que ma famille n'ait
pas autant d'illustration—que beaucoup d'Américains qui s'appellent Montgommery,
Berry, Chandos ou Capel, n'ont de rapport avec les familles de Pembroke, de
Buckingham, d'Essex, ou avec le duc de Berry." Je pensai plusieurs fois à lui dire,
pour l'amuser, que je connaissais Mme Swann qui comme cocotte, était connue
autrefois sous le nom d'Odette de Crécy; mais . . . je ne me sentis pas assez lié avec
M. de Crécy pour conduire avec lui la plaisanterie jusque-là.

[He was extremely modest so far as his own family was concerned, and it was not
from M. de Crécy himself that I learned that it was a very noble family and an
authentic branch transplanted to France of the English family which bears the
title of Crecy. When I learned that he was a real Crécy, I told him that one of Mme
de Guermantes's nieces had married an American named Charles Crecy, and said
that I did not suppose there was any connexion between them. "None," he said.
"Any more than—not, of course, that my family is so distinguished—heaps of
Americans who are called Montgomery, Berry, Chandos or Capel have with the
families of Pembroke, Buckingham or Essex, or with the Duc de Berry." I thought
more than once of telling him, as a joke, that I knew Mme Swann, who as a courtesan had been known at one time by the name Odette de Crécy; but . . . I did
not feel that I was on sufficiently intimate terms with M. de Crécy to carry the
joke so far.]

(III, 471; IV, 561–2)

Marcel believes that Odette has even less entitlement to the Crécy name
than the American husband of Mme de Guermantes's niece, but he is
quite mistaken. The reason that M. de Crécy is in such reduced circumstances is that he was formerly married to Odette, who ran through his
fortune and deserted him. By marriage, at any rate, the *cocotte* is an
authentic Crécy, allied to one of the most ancient aristocratic families of

France, a family which is itself a branch of the English nobility. By the same token, the refined and fastidious *gentilhomme*, who speaks with such polite scorn of the accidental affinity of American names with their English aristocratic 'originals', has given his own illustrious name to a *cocotte* with no family name of her own at all.

The discovery that Odette really was 'de Crécy' is another of Proust's long-delayed revelations. It comes in *La Prisonnière*, during the long soirée at the Verdurins presided over by M. de Charlus for Morel's benefit, but which results in Morel's treacherous repudiation of him. While this mine is being laid, Brichot is given the task of distracting M. de Charlus in an adjoining room; Marcel accompanies them, though he is not a party to the plot (he finds himself, as so often in the novel, an 'accidental' voyeur). M. de Charlus regales them with scandalous assertions and insinuations about the homosexuality of persons both living and dead, and he also reminisces about Odette's career and her liaison with Swann. We discover in the course of this conversation the following facts: that M. de Charlus in his youth was bi-sexual or at least had occasional heterosexual encounters; that he saw Odette as 'Miss Sacripant', found her alluring in her 'demi-travesti', slept with her, and then introduced her to Swann to get her off his hands (and since we know from *Un amour de Swann* that Swann and Odette met at the theatre, it is possible that this occasion, too, was a performance of *Sacripant*); and that when he subsequently acted as Odette's escort he got into trouble because of the name she used (III, 803–4; V, 339–41). It is at this point that Marcel realizes the connection with the ruined *gentilhomme* he knew at Balbec. M. de Charlus is speaking:

C'était moi qui sortais Odette quand elle ne voulait pas voir Charles. Cela m'embêtait d'autant plus que j'ai un très proche parent qui porte le nom de Crécy, sans y avoir naturellement aucune espèce de droit, mais qu'enfin cela ne charmait pas. Car elle se faisait appeler Odette de Crécy et le pouvait parfaitement, étant seulement séparée d'un Crécy dont elle était la femme, très authentique celui-là, un monsieur très bien qu'elle avait ratissé jusqu'au dernier centime. Mais voyons, c'est pour me faire parler, je vous ai vu avec lui dans le tortillard, vous lui donniez des dîners à Balbec. Il doit en avoir besoin, le pauvre: il vivait d'une toute petite pension que lui faisait Swann, et je me doute bien que depuis la mort de mon ami, cette rente a dû cesser complètement d'être payée.

[It was I who used to take Odette out when she didn't want to see Charles. It was all the more awkward for me as I have a very close kinsman who bears the name

Crécy, without of course having any sort of right to it, but still he was none too well pleased. For she went by the name of Odette de Crécy, as she perfectly well could, being merely separated from a Crécy whose wife she still was—an extremely authentic one, he, a most estimable gentleman out of whom she had drained his last farthing. But why should I have to tell you about this Crécy? I've seen you with him on the twister,[53] you used to have him to dinner at Balbec. He must have needed it, poor fellow, for he lived on a tiny allowance that Swann made him, and I'm very much afraid that, since my friend's death, that income must have stopped altogether.]

(III, 804–5; V, 341)

It's perhaps a little odd of M. de Charlus to refer to the American who married Mme de Guermantes's niece as his 'proche parent', but the main point is the contrast between this respectable family member, who has no right to his name, with Odette, who perversely has a perfect right to hers. Odette's rapacity belongs to the early part of her career as a *cocotte*; she will not ruin Swann in the way that she ruined M. de Crécy (indeed she cannot be held responsible for Swann's fate; Proust doesn't let him off so lightly); on the other hand, in marrying Swann Odette is repeating herself, exchanging one name 'd'origine anglaise' for another. Only with her marriage to Forcheville will she become, so to speak, properly French.

Odette's *anglomanie*, which begins by presenting itself to the reader as a fashionable affectation, thus turns out to have deeper roots. One piece of the puzzle remains; it takes us back to a different kind of origin, the source of Odette's sexual nature.

Looked at objectively, and allowing for the element of caricature in Proust's method, there is something compulsive about Odette's recourse to English words and phrases, as though it answered an inner need rather than a mere wish to be *chic*. As Swann, in the grip of his jealousy, probes her past, he comes across 'certains bruits relatifs à la vie qu'Odette avait menée autrefois à Nice' [certain rumours with regard to the life that Odette had formerly led in Nice] (I, 307; I, 376), rumours which even suggest that she had had there, and in other resorts such as Baden, 'une sorte de notoriété galante' [a sort of amorous notoriety] (I, 307; I, 377). Nice is of particular interest to us; Odette constantly wears a gold medallion of Notre-Dame de Laghet to which she is superstitiously attached

---

53 The 'tortillard' or 'twister' is one of the many nicknames for the local railway which winds its way between Balbec and neighbouring towns and villages, and which plays a prominent part in Marcel's social life, especially during his second visit.

because the Virgin 'l'avait jadis, quand elle habitait Nice, guérie d'une maladie mortelle' [had once, when Odette was living at Nice, cured her of a mortal illness] (I, 218; I, 266).[54] Marcel's Uncle Adolphe used to spend the winter there; Odette engineers a quarrel between him and Swann just before he can tell Swann any details about her past life. But Swann does not need to be told of Nice's reputation as a pleasure resort; he can imagine, even if he cannot document, the early years of Odette's sexual career, 'ces années du début du Septennat pendant lesquelles on passait l'hiver sur la promenade des Anglais' [those early years of MacMahon's Presidency during which one spent the winter on the Promenade des Anglais] (I, 308; I, 377).[55] Nor would Swann need to be told that the 'Promenade des Anglais' had more than a symbolic meaning. Nice, and indeed the whole of the Riviera, had been for many years the winter playground of the English aristocracy, chief among them the Prince of Wales, the 'King of the Côte d'Azur'.[56] Queen Victoria's patronage of Nice (she went there five times in the 1890s) did little to affect the general perception that Nice welcomed the wealthy gamblers, sportsmen, and sexual tourists of *Outre-Manche*. Such tourism carried then, as it does now in other parts of the world, connotations of corruption and perversity; appalled by his discovery that Odette has had (and enjoyed) sexual encounters with other women, Swann attempts to excuse her depravity: 'Pauvre Odette! il ne lui en voulait pas. Elle n'était qu'à demi coupable. Ne disait-on pas que c'était par sa propre mère qu'elle avait été livrée, presque enfant, à Nice, à un riche Anglais?' [Poor Odette! He did not hold it against her. She was only half to blame. Had he not been told that it was her own mother who had sold her, when she was still hardly more than a child, at Nice, to a wealthy Englishman?] (I, 361; I, 442). Proust's syntax here has an extraordinary power of emphasis: Odette's initiation is compressed into a sequence of short phrases, separated by commas, which ring like hammer-blows: 'livrée, presque enfant, à Nice, à un riche Anglais'; I hear in the opening syllable of '*An*glais' a repetition of the

---

[54] Notre-Dame de Laghet is a pilgrimage site not far from Nice, with a monastery and church dating from the 17th cent. (*Pléiade* note, I, 1206).

[55] *Vintage* is probably correct in interpreting the 'Septennat' as the presidency of MacMahon which began in 1873 (see *Pléiade* note, I, 1228). Odette's sexual looseness is linked to the end of this period as it is to the beginning: see above, pp. 103–4.

[56] See Patrick Howarth, *When the Riviera was Ours* (London: Century, 1977), and Michael Nelson, *Queen Victoria and the Discovery of the Riviera* (London: I. B. Tauris, 2001).

double 'en . . . an' in 'enfant', a dreadful concord of sounds. Whoever he was, this anonymous *gentleman* or *milord* has left his linguistic mark on Odette. No wonder her tongue is infected with English words; each one returns her to that first denaturing transaction. Her way of life is 'd'origine anglaise' as much as Swann's, and their *mésalliance* the marriage of untrue minds.

3

Choses Normandes

The title of this chapter is that of an article which Proust contributed to *Le Mensuel*, a short-lived journal edited by a fellow student at the École Libre des Sciences Politiques.[1] The piece appeared in the final issue of the magazine, in September 1891; it was the first published work by Proust to be signed with his full name, 'Marcel Proust', as opposed to initials or a pseudonym. The epigraph to 'Choses Normandes' cites the *Guide Joanne* (a standard guide of the period) to the effect that the Normandy resort of Trouville has 6,808 inhabitants but can lodge more than 15,000 visitors in summer.[2] However, as Proust tells us at the start of the article, most of these visitors have left, 'puisqu'il est élégant de quitter les plages à la fin d'août pour aller à la campagne' [since it is fashionable to leave the seaside at the end of August to go to the country]. It is in sympathy with the sparse year-round inhabitants, therefore, that Proust evokes the beauty of landscape, seascape, and moonlight; one of his favourite phrases from Baudelaire, 'le soleil rayonnant sur la mer' [the sun shining radiantly upon the sea], makes its debut here, in a scene which anticipates Marcel's impressions of the coast at Balbec.[3] Among several anticipatory touches of the Normandy of *A la recherche*, the English note is not lacking:

Enfin il y a quelques habitations tout à fait désirables . . . Je ne parle point des maisons "orientales" ou "persanes" qui plairaient mieux à Téhéran, mais surtout des maisons normandes, en réalité moitié normandes moitié anglaises, où l'abondance des épis de faîtage multiplie les points de vue et complique la silhouette, où les fenêtres tout en largeur ont tant de douceur et d'intimité, où, des jardinières

[1] 'Choses normandes', in *Écrits*, 63–5; for *Le Mensuel* see Tadié, 111–21.
[2] Fifteen years later this number had quadrupled: see below.
[3] Charles Baudelaire, 'Chant d'Automne' II, 4, in *Les Fleurs du mal*; twice cited in *A la recherche* (II, 34, 67; II, 291, 331); see *Pléiade* note, II, 1354–5.

faites dans le mur, sous chaque fenêtre, des fleurs pleuvent inépuisablement sur les escaliers extérieurs et sur les halls vitrés. (*Écrits*, 64–5)[4]

[Lastly there are a few eminently desirable houses … I am not speaking of "Oriental" or "Persian" houses which would be more pleasing in Tehran, but rather of Norman houses, in reality half-Norman half-English, where the abundance of roof-top turrets multiplies the viewpoints and complicates the silhouette, where there is such a gentle and intimate look to the wide windows, where, from window-boxes built into the wall, beneath each window, flowers rain down inexhaustibly on the outer staircases and the glazed hallways.]

In the pastiche of the Goncourts' journal which sparkles in the opening pages of *Le Temps retrouvé*, Proust made an oblique act of contrition for his own juvenile snobbery and preciosity; Mme Verdurin, as the 'Goncourts' report her, goes into ecstasies over 'cette Normandie qu'ils ont habitée, une Normandie qui serait un immense parc anglais, à la fragrance de ses hautes futaies à la Lawrence … une Normandie qui serait absolument insoupçonnée des Parisiens en vacances…' [the Normandy in which they once lived, a Normandy, so she says, like an immense English park, with the fragrance of tall woodlands that Lawrence might have painted … a Normandy absolutely unsuspected by the Parisian holiday-makers…] (IV, 291; VI, 27). The image of Normandy as 'un immense parc anglais' is stigmatized here as the product of a particularly odious form of snobbery, in which the Verdurins specialize, the snobbery of inside knowledge and privileged access denied to the common herd.[5] But an English Normandy does exist in *A la recherche*, though not as it is here projected by Mme Verdurin's self-regard and naïvely relayed by the 'Goncourts'. We need to look for it elsewhere, and to begin with in the very places where the despised Parisians, including Marcel, go 'en vacances', the seaside towns of the *Côte Fleurie*: Trouville, Deauville, Cabourg—and Balbec.

---

[4] The epithet 'persan' was transferred to the church at Balbec, as Swann describes it to Marcel (I, 378; I, 463). 'Hall' was one of the least obtrusive English imports into French: it was used first in the sense of a medieval or baronial hall, then to designate a hallway; both usages date from the 18th cent., but the second only became common in the 19th.

[5] Once again, Proust includes his own earlier tastes in his criticism of others': in *Les Plaisirs et les jours*, the poem on Gluck in 'Portraits de musiciens' begins: 'Temple à l'amour, à l'amitié, temple au courage | Qu'une marquise a fait élever dans son parc | Anglais' [Temple to love, to friendship, temple to courage, which a marquise has had built in her English-style park] (*JS* 82).

Balbec as found

Marcel first hears of Balbec from Legrandin, the neighbour at Combray whose sister has married a Norman nobleman. I have discussed Legrandin's snobbery in Chapter 1; what concerns us here is the double image of Balbec for which he is partly responsible. In his unwitting rhapsody on Balbec (unwitting because he doesn't realize that Marcel's parents are planning to send him there on holiday and may therefore ask him for a letter of introduction to his ennobled sister) Legrandin evokes an image of primitive wildness which is, as such images tend to be, intensely literary:

Balbec! la plus antique ossature géologique de notre sol, vraiment Ar-mor, la Mer, la fin de la terre, la région maudite qu'Anatole France—un enchanteur que devrait lire notre petit ami—a si bien peinte, sous ses brouillards éternels, comme le véritable pays des Cimmériens, dans l'*Odyssée*. De Balbec surtout, où déjà des hôtels se construisent, superposés au sol antique et charmant qu'ils n'altèrent pas, quel délice d'excursionner à deux pas dans ces régions primitives et si belles.

[Balbec! the most ancient bone in the geological skeleton that underlies our soil, the true Ar-mor, the sea, the land's end, the accursed region which Anatole France—an enchanter whose works our young friend ought to read—has so well depicted, beneath its eternal fogs, as though it were indeed the land of the Cimmerians in the *Odyssey*. Balbec; yes, they are building hotels there now, superimposing them upon its ancient and charming soil which they are powerless to alter; how delightful it is to be able to make excursions into such primitive and beautiful regions only a step or two away!]

(I, 129; I, 156)

Legrandin is quite wrong, as we shall see, to suggest that the presence of hotels does anything to alter the 'primitiveness' of the landscape, but in any case Marcel pays the hotels no mind. He is swept away by Legrandin's confected lyricism; at home in Paris he dreams of Balbec as the epitome of wild nature, again reshuffling Legrandin's sonorous formulas which are themselves pastiches of Anatole France and Chateaubriand:

"On y sent encore sous ses pas, disait-il, bien plus qu'au Finistère lui-même (et quand bien même des hôtels s'y superposeraient maintenant sans pouvoir y modifier la plus antique ossature de la terre), on y sent la véritable fin de la terre française, européene, de la Terre antique. Et c'est le dernier campement des pêcheurs, pareils à tous les pêcheurs qui ont vécu depuis le commencement du monde, en face du royaume éternel des brouillards de la mer et des ombres."

["You still feel there beneath your feet," he had told me, "far more than at Finistère itself (and even though hotels are now being superimposed upon it, without power, however, to modify that oldest ossature of the earth) you feel there that you are actually at the land's end of France, of Europe, of the Old World. And it is the ultimate encampment of the fishermen, the heirs of all the fishermen who have lived since the world's beginning, facing the everlasting kingdom of the sea-fogs and shadows of the night."]

(I, 377; I, 462–3)[6]

There is a significant variation in this expanded version of Legrandin's words, the substitution of 'la terre française, européene' for the vaguer 'notre sol' or the more general 'terre'. The boundaries of modern nations have nothing to do with 'la Terre antique'; 'la terre française', in particular, never existed in isolation from 'la terre anglaise'; the 'royaume éternel des brouillards de la mer' was an unromantic inconvenience in the way of war, trade, or migration. We might go further and point out that Normandy, of all places in France, ought to be the least susceptible to this kind of mythifying flummery, since its concrete historical circumstances have included owning, and being owned by, 'la terre anglaise'.

'La terre française' in this sense is like 'la langue française', an entity whose autonomy or purity is hard to establish outside the confines of myth. In the final chapter of this book I discuss the way in which *A la recherche* engages with contemporary debates about the French language, particularly Marcel's discovery that etymology breaks down the very concept of purity, whether racial, national, or aesthetic. One example from the academician Brichot's numerous, learned, prolix etymological explanations may be taken out of sequence for our purpose here, because it concerns the name of Balbec.

"Balbec est probablement une corruption de Dalbec, me dit-il. Il faudrait pouvoir consulter les chartes des rois d'Angleterre, suzerains de la Normandie, car Balbec dépendait de la baronnie de Douvres, à cause de quoi on disait souvent Balbec d'Outre-Mer, Balbec-en-Terre. Mais la baronnie de Douvres elle-même relevait de l'évêché de Bayeux . . ."

["Balbec is probably a corruption of Dalbec," he told me. "One would have to consult the charters of the Kings of England, suzerains of Normandy, for Balbec was a dependency of the barony of Dover, for which reason it was often styled

---

[6] For the parallels with Anatole France's novel *Pierre Nozière*, and with Chateaubriand's *Mémoires d'Outre-tombe*, see the *Pléiade* note (I, 1263–4).

Balbec d'Outre-Mer, Balbec-en-Terre. But the barony of Dover itself came under the bishopric of Bayeux . . ."]

(III, 327; IV, 388)

Proust made use of several scholarly treatises on etymology and place-name formation for this part of *A la recherche*, but the *Pléiade* editors note that he made up this particular derivation himself (III, 1529). The key word *corruption* tells us about the action of time on language and also the nature of that action, eroding and reshaping, preserving meaning through deformity and disguise. Having postulated 'Dalbec' as the original form, Proust was then able to draw on his sources for Brichot's further explanations: both *dal* and *bec* are words of German origin, meaning 'valley' and 'stream' respectively;[7] Brichot (for once) doesn't elaborate, but the reader will see that these are roots of common English words ('dale' and 'beck') which survive in French only in the form of place-names. Is 'Balbec', then, an English word? The matter is more complicated than that. Both historically and linguistically, Balbec 'belongs' both to England and France; it is both 'en-Terre' and 'Outre-Mer'; the feudal ties which make its ownership so difficult to unravel exemplify the double-ness, the complexity which is intrinsic to the human condition. Brichot is over-optimistic if he thinks that being able to consult a royal charter would clear this matter up.

Swann, kindly and tactful, intimates that Balbec is a place not of nature and myth but of history and art; he sidesteps Marcel's naïve question as to whether Balbec is the best spot for witnessing the most violent storms and proffers instead an urbane tribute to its celebrated church, 'le plus curieux échantillon du gothique normand, et si singulière, on dirait de l'art persan' [the most curious example to be found of our Norman Gothic, and so singular, one thinks of Persian art] (I, 378; I, 463).[8] Marcel is delighted to discover that the landscape he had thought of as timeless and immemorial actually features in the known sequence of historical periods, but it's not enough to overthrow the imaginative construct which the name of Balbec evokes for him; indeed, the two forms of the romantic sublime, Nature and the Gothic, end by joining forces. By a powerful mental elision

[7] I report Brichot's terms here: *bec* 'la forme normande du Germain *Bach*'; *dal* 'une forme de *Thal*'; the *OED* gives a Scandinavian origin for 'beck'; 'dale' is from OE 'dael', related to Old High German 'tal' and Gothic 'dal'.

[8] The last phrase is my translation; *Vintage* has 'so singular that one is tempted to describe it as Persian in its inspiration'.

Marcel situates the church at Balbec at the very edge of the ocean, as though it 'grew' on the cliff top, so that he can indulge two fantasies at once, mingling 'le désir de l'architecture gothique avec celui d'une tempête sur la mer' [the desire for Gothic architecture as well as for a storm upon the sea] (I, 378; I, 464). The power of such a fantasy can only be broken by personal experience, not another's opinion—especially when that opinion is delivered by a master of the received idea and the conventional phrase such as M. de Norpois. When Marcel meets the old Ambassador at dinner, he learns that Balbec has made great strides in recent years—'On commence à y construire des villas fort coquettes' [They are beginning to build some very attractive little villas there] (I, 456; II, 41)—and that the church is nothing special, chiefly notable for the tomb of Tourville, a seventeenth-century admiral (which is actually in Paris). Marcel ignores these disenchanting hints that Balbec belongs to the modern social world, and he is right to do so, because even disenchantment, to have any lasting value, must be experienced first-hand.

Accordingly, it is only when Marcel travels to Balbec that he feels the full force of the collision between his fantasy and the reality. The first thing he discovers is that there are two Balbecs—Balbec-le-Vieux, also known as Balbec-en-Terre, and Balbec-Plage—and that the church which he had situated at the ocean's edge is inland, in the middle of a town square, miles from the sea; he had always assimilated its bell-tower to a sheer cliff face, beaten by the waves, whereas in reality 'il se dressait sur une place où était l'embranchement de deux lignes de tramways, en face d'un café qui portait, écrit en letters d'or, le mot "Billard" . . .' [(it) stood on a square which was the junction of two tramway routes, opposite a café which bore, in letters of gold, the legend "Billiards" . . .] (II, 19; II, 273). This concentrated image of vulgar modernity, which Marcel will learn from the painter Elstir *not* to despise, is marked on the one hand by mobility and interchange (the junction of the two tramway routes is one of the many prefigurings of the 'two ways' which unite at the end of the novel) and on the other by the solid, static facts of French provincial life. But Marcel cannot yet read the golden letters in which this vision is offered to him.

From Balbec-le-Vieux Marcel gets back on the train and travels on to Balbec-Plage, since it is (of course) the modern hotel, not the medieval church, which is next to the sea, if not perched gothically on a cliff-top. With his aesthetic disappointment exacerbated by physical and mental fatigue, and by the terror of having to adjust to a new dwelling, Marcel must now confront the hotel which Legrandin had dismissed as being merely 'superimposed' on the ancient soil of France.

Le Grand-Hôtel de Balbec-Cabourg

Balbec is based largely (though by no means exclusively) on Cabourg, and its Grand Hotel corresponds (with fewer variations) to the Cabourg hotel which now features in *les pèlerinages proustiens en France*.[9] Life (or commerce) has hastened to conform to art, as Christian Pechenard records in *Proust à Cabourg*: the famous 'digue', the seafront promenade on which Marcel first glimpses the 'jeunes filles en fleurs', has become 'la promenade Marcel-Proust', though with commendable resistance, and a greater degree of Proustian authenticity, it is still referred to as 'la digue'.[10] The Grand Hotel itself has rooms named after 'Guermantes' and 'Cambremer', and of course a 'chambre Marcel Proust', a unique feature of the hotel, as its website (www.cabourg-web.com/grandhotel) declares: 'le décor de cette magnifique chambre a été reconstitué scrupuleusement suivant la description qu' en faisait l'auteur. La Pléiade y est disponible, le temps semble s'y être arrêté' [the décor of this magnificent room has been scrupulously reconstituted following the description of it made by the author. The Pléiade edition is available in it, and time seems to have stopped there]. Needless to say the unique room is also uniquely expensive. Whatever Proust would have felt about all this—that last phrase especially—the one emotion he would probably not have experienced is surprise.

Pechenard points out that whereas Proust stayed in two hotels at Cabourg, Marcel stays in only one at Balbec. The hotel where the 10-year-old Proust stayed with his maternal grandmother, Mme Nathé Weil, in 1881, had been built in 1861 with the intention of making Cabourg a rival of Deauville; but twenty years later Cabourg was still, in Pechenard's pitying phrase, 'une plage de famille, formule dont on ne comprend pas ce qu'elle peut avoir de consternant' [a family resort, a phrase whose full awfulness is hard to grasp] (p. 20). Proust returned to Cabourg for several

[9] I borrow the phrase from Proust's article 'Pèlerinages ruskiniens en France' which appeared in *Le Figaro*, 13 Feb. 1900 (*CSB* 441).

[10] The 'digue' had formerly been 'la promenade de l'Impératrice' but after the fall of the Second Empire in 1870 was renamed 'la promenade des Anglais'; that would have been its official name when Proust stayed there.

10. The Grand Hotel at Cabourg, the model for the Grand Hotel at Balbec.

childhood holidays, but after 1886 we know of only two brief visits, in 1890 and 1891, during neither of which he stayed at the hotel. In 1892 another attempt was made to redevelop Cabourg. Pechenard: 'Le passé est une ruine. Proust le reconstruira. Charles Bertrand aussi. À partir de 1892, Charles Bertrand achète. Il achète tout. Il deviendra maire de Cabourg' [The past is a ruin. Proust will rebuild it. So will Charles Bertrand. Charles Bertrand starts buying in 1892. He buys everything. He will become Mayor of Cabourg] (p. 22). Pechenard records the progress of 'improvements' at Cabourg through the bulletins of *L'Écho de Cabourg*, from electric light to pedalos. More significant was the spread of those attractive little villas mentioned by M. de Norpois. Eventually M. Bertrand got round to the Grand Hotel; it was demolished and rebuilt in 1907.

Bertrand knew about modern publicity; he made sure the new hotel got noticed. *Le Figaro* ran a daily column of seaside news and gossip, but this wasn't enough; Bertrand (I guess) arranged for a long article, exclusively devoted to the opening of the Grand Hotel, and modestly titled 'Une brillante inauguration', which appeared on 10 July 1907.[11] We know that Proust, who wrote occasionally for *Le Figaro*, read it every day, and we can be reasonably sure that he read this article. He responded with (for him) extraordinary promptness and decision—it took him a mere three and half weeks to leave for Cabourg. But if he was making a pilgrimage to the Cabourg of his childhood, he would have found as violent a clash between image and reality as Marcel at Balbec.

To quote from André Nède's article is to seem to pastiche it, so completely does it belong to its time and type; its splendid, empty flourishes remind you of M. de Norpois. Cabourg is 'ce décor charmant que connaissent tous les Parisiens, et qui a fait, depuis longtemps, surnommer cette coquette petite ville, la Reine des Plages' [this charming setting which all Parisians know, and which for many years has given this pretty little town the title of Queen of the Seaside]. The Grand Hotel offers 'à sa brillante clientèle de baigneurs et touristes toutes les perfections et toutes les merveilles que le progrès moderne a pu réaliser' [to its brilliant clientele of bathers and tourists all the perfections and all the marvels which

[11] The article is signed André Nède. It seems a fair bet that it was placed and paid for by Bertrand, judging by the general conditions in which such press coverage was obtained in France: see Zeldin, II, 513. It is pleasing to note that advertisements which did not pretend to be anything else were known as 'English advertisements'; they were (of course) the cheapest. The main part of the article is reprinted in Pechenard, 27–30.

modern progress has brought about]. The brochure phrases roll on: 'un ameublement du goût le plus riche et le plus recherché' [furnishings in the richest and most sought-after taste], 'les magnifiques jardins du Casino' [the magnificent gardens of the Casino], 'toutes les commodités que l'hydrothérapie, chaude ou froide, rend aujourd'hui si agréablement pratiques' [all the conveniences which modern hydrotherapy, both hot and cold, makes both pleasant and practical].[12] Naturally an English phrase, 'un déjeuner ultra-select', pops up to describe the snob-appeal of the inaugural lunch.[13] But there are also passages of greater resonance for Proust and for readers of *A la recherche*: the paradoxical image of the hotel as 'un véritable palais des Mille et une Nuits' [a veritable Arabian Nights palace], for example, or the way in which the sea is described as a theatrical backdrop seen from the entrance hall. The theatrical motif would in any case be evident in Nède's treatment from the presence of words such as 'programme', 'décorations', and 'façades', but this image directly compares the setting of the hotel to a painted spectacle:

on aperçoit la mer comme tableau de fond—je pourrais dire comme toile de fond, si l'on songe que ce merveilleux panorama qu'offre l'horizon de Cabourg . . . a été maintes fois porté au théâtre . . . Preuve évidente—car les auteurs dramatiques s'y connaissent—que c'est le plus joli décor que l'on puisse imaginer . . .

[you perceive the sea as a background—I might almost say a painted backdrop, if you think that the marvellous panorama offered by the horizon at Cabourg . . . has frequently been used in the theatre . . . Proof positive—for playwrights know their business—that it's the prettiest scene you could imagine . . .][14]

---

[12] The hotel prospectus which Marcel miserably peruses on the day of his arrival has the same tone and some of the same details: his eye falls on phrases such as 'un séjour de délices', 'la chère exquise', and 'le coup d'œil féerique des jardins du Casino' (II, 25).

[13] When the dowager marquise de Cambremer attends a Balbec party, the proud family plants an item in *Le Gaulois* about 'la matinée ultra-select' (III, 163; IV, 192). The sculptor, Ski, tries to dissuade the Verdurins from admitting M. de Charlus to their 'salon si "select"' (III, 296; IV, 349). Bonnaffé's first citation for 'select' in the sense of 'choisi, élégant' dates from 1869; his next, from *Les Morts qui parlent*, a novel by vicomte Eugène-Melchior de Vogüé published in 1899, sneers at a social-climbing banker: 'Aussi voyait-on chez lui ce défilé de cinématographe que les journaux à sa dévotion proclamaient "une réunion très *select*" [Thus his house was filled with a cinematographic stream of people, which the newspapers who supported him proclaimed as 'an ultra-select gathering']. The same phrase ('une sorte de défilé cinématographique des choses' [a sort of procession of things upon the screen of a cinematograph] occurs in *Le Temps retrouvé*, where it denotes naïve literary realism (IV, 461; VI, 237).

[14] Pechenard, 28. 'Panorama' is a Greco-English word, coined by a Scotsman, Robert Barker, in 1789; in his 1787 patent he called it *La Nature à coup d'Œil* (*OED*).

Proust responded to this image, not just in the stage-entrance of Robert de Saint-Loup against the backdrop of the sea, which I quote later in this chapter, but in a longer passage in *Sodome et Gomorrhe*, during Marcel's second visit to Balbec:

Je comprenais très bien le charme que ce grand palace pouvait offrir à certaines personnes. Il était dressé comme un théâtre, et une nombreuse figuration l'animait jusque dans les cintres. Bien que le client ne fût qu'une sorte de spectateur, il était mêlé perpétuellement au spectacle, non même comme dans ces théâtres où les acteurs jouent une scène dans la salle, mais comme si la vie du spectateur se déroulait au milieu des somptuosités de la scène. Le joueur de tennis pouvait rentrer en veston de flanelle blanche, le concierge s'était mis en habit bleu galonné d'argent pour lui donner ses lettres. Si ce joueur de tennis ne voulait pas monter à pied, il n'était pas moins mêlé aux acteurs en ayant à côté de lui pour faire monter l'ascenseur le lift aussi richement costumé.

[I could well appreciate the charm that this great hotel might have for certain persons. It was arranged like a theatre, and was filled to the flies with a numerous and animated cast. For all that the visitor was only a sort of spectator, he was perpetually involved in the performance, not simply as in one of those theatres where the actors play a scene in the auditorium, but as though the life of the spectator was going on amid the sumptuosities of the stage. The tennis-player might come in wearing a white flannel blazer, but the porter would have put on a blue frock-coat with silver braid in order to hand him his letters. If this tennis-player did not choose to walk upstairs, he was equally involved with the actors in having by his side, to propel the lift, its attendant no less richly attired.]

(III, 170; IV, 200)

I will come shortly to the figure of 'le lift', and in the next section of this chapter to 'le joueur de tennis'; what I want to emphasize here is how the element of spectacle in the Grand Hotel actually works. It does not dissolve the boundary between real life and show, but gives the impression that real life is taking place within a show; the key word is *mêlé*, 'mêlé perpétuellement au spectacle . . . mêlé aux acteurs', as though the Grand Hotel performs itself, and the guests are caught up in this performance. This is not what Nède had in mind when he praised the hotel's contemporary feel—'Il est impossible de se figurer une plus complète compréhension de la vie moderne' [It is impossible to imagine a more complete grasp of modern life]—but to Proust the essence of modern life, at least in its social aspect, lies in such mixed effects, in which individuals find themselves spectators of a performance and part of its 'figuration'.

The Grand Hotel may be especially 'modern' because the nature of its performance is not straightforward. There is something factitious about the 'play' which it puts on, and Proust's imagination was always kindled by the fake and the nearly-real. It is a quality conveyed by the use of the English word 'palace' (pronounced in French with the accent on the second syllable: pa'láss). Jules Cesari, the manager of the Grand Hotel at Cabourg, came, as Nède emphasizes, from the Élysée-Palace in Paris; purists loathed 'palace' because it had re-entered French from English after dropping out in favour of 'palais'; it was reserved for luxury hotels and cinemas, and represented a toxic mixture of the cosmopolitan and the modern. As a result, the interaction of 'performers' and 'spectators' in the Grand Hotel play is subject to dislocations which are the result, so to speak, of miscasting. In *A l'ombre des jeunes filles en fleurs*, when the genuinely aristocratic M. de Cambremer first visits the Grand Hotel at Balbec, he is badly treated by the staff who are 'frais débarqué de la Côte d'Azur' [freshly imported from the Riviera]: 'Non seulement il n'était pas habillé en flanelle blanche, mais par vieille manière française et ignorance de la vie des Palaces, entrant dans un hall où il y avait des femmes, il avait ôté son chapeau dès la porte . . .' [Not only was he not wearing white flannels, but, with old-fashioned French courtesy and in his ignorance of the ways of grand hotels, on coming into the hall in which there were ladies sitting, he had taken off his hat at the door . . .] (II, 43; II, 301).

Nède's *Figaro* article is not addressed to M. de Cambremer, of course, but to readers who might themselves be fresh—if that is the right word—from the Côte d'Azur.[15] He does not mean to suggest that there might be something inauthentic about the whole performance, but Proust emphatically does. Nède describes the hall as being 'd'aspect grandiose et d'une sobre décoration Louis XVI' [imposing in appearance and soberly decorated in Louis XVI style]; when Marcel, by contrast, arrives in 'le hall du Grand-Hôtel de Balbec', he observes that the staircase is of imitation marble. The manager wears '[le] smoking du mondain' [a smart dinner-jacket],

---

[15] Le Robert, who dates the appearance of 'palace' as designating a luxury hotel to 1903, adds that it is is linked to the popularity of the Côte d'Azur among wealthy English travellers. From 1891 Queen Victoria chose to stay in hotels rather than private villas, though like Mme de Villeparisis she insulated herself within her own household, bringing her own china and linen with her (Howarth, 62). Proust compounds the indignity of 'palace' by using the word to designate the high-class brothel which opens near Balbec, and which is made the occasion of an elaborate joke about a traveller who mistakes it for a luxury hotel (III, 462; IV, 550).

and in his voice can be heard a variety of accents 'dus à des origines lointaines et à une enfance cosmopolite' [acquired from an alien ancestry and a cosmopolitan upbringing]. Like the other members of staff at the hotel, he is incapable of discerning the true social status of his guests, taking 'les grands seigneurs pour des râleux et les rats d'hôtels pour des grands seigneurs' [the grandees for haggling skinflints and the flashy crooks for grandees]; he relies on a code of dress and behaviour which consists in ostentatious mimicry of aristocratic bearing, 'comme de ne pas se découvrir en entrant dans le hall, de porter des knickerbockers, un paletot à taille, et de sortir un cigare ceint de pourpre et d'or d'un étui en maroquin écrasé' [such as not taking one's hat off when one came into the hall, wearing knickerbockers or an overcoat with a waist, and taking a cigar with a band of purple and gold out of a crushed morocco case] (II, 23–4; II, 277–8).[16]

The rebuilding of the Grand Hotel formed part of Bertrand's ambition to make Cabourg the peer of Trouville and Deauville. The number of summer visitors around the time of Proust's 1907 visit was between 6,000 and 8,000, compared to 20,000 at Deauville and 60,000 at Trouville; in 1908, the stake at the Casino amounted to 400,000 francs, far less than at Trouville.[17] A lot of energy went into this (ultimately unsuccessful) effort, and it was in full swing when Proust arrived. The hotel, and the town, to which he returned were therefore not those of his childhood, but it was this hotel and town, and not the former ones, which he reconstructed in *A la recherche*. The relationship between Marcel and his grandmother relates to the 1880s, but the stage on which it is acted out is that of 1907.[18] The Grand Hotel is the luxurious 'palace' of the early twentieth century, and the social scene both in the hotel itself and Balbec generally is dominated not by family values but by those of cosmopolitan fashion, centring on the Casino, the golf course, the racecourse, and the regatta. All of these—but especially the last three—are imbued with Englishness

---

[16] Bonnaffé traces *knickerbockers* to Cruikshank's illustrations of the old-fashioned Dutch knee-breeches in Washington Irving's *History of New York* (1809); Irving's comic pseudonym was 'Diedrich Knickerbocker'. By Proust's time they were not only fashionable, but identified with sporting and outdoor pursuits, for whose popularity at Balbec see below. I would guess that the crushed-leather cigar case is of English manufacture.

[17] Tadié, 491 and 882 n. 52.

[18] Marcel, in the novel, is older than Proust was by perhaps four or five years; it is a young adolescent, already sexually awakened, who goes to Balbec for the first time in *A l'ombre des jeunes filles en fleurs*, not a child.

(in spirit and vocabulary). Within the hotel the central means of communication—mechanical and personal—turns on a single English term, misapplied and mispronounced—*le lift*.

Marcel's room is high up in the Grand Hotel. It is one of the cheaper rooms; Marcel has already suffered the humiliation of his grandmother telling the manager that the prices are 'beaucoup trop élevés pour mon petit budget' [far too high for my little budget]—the only time an identifiably English word escapes her, 'sur une intonation artificielle' [in an artificial tone of voice] (II, 24; II, 278).[19] Marcel himself resorts to English vocabulary to signify his alienation: sitting on a bench while his grandmother chaffers, he watches with a miserable sense of inferiority the other, posher guests, 'tous ces gens pour qui c'était regagner leur *home* que de gravir les degrés en faux marbre' [all these people for whom climbing those imitation marble stairs meant going home]. But Marcel does not climb the fake staircase:

le directeur vint lui-même pousser un bouton: et un personnage encore inconnu de moi, qu'on appelait "lift" (et qui au point le plus haut de l'hôtel, là où serait le lanternon d'une église normande, était installé comme un photographe derrière son vitrage ou comme un organiste dans sa chambre), se mit à descendre vers moi . . .

[the manager himself came forward and pressed a button, whereupon a personage whose acquaintance I had not yet made, known as "lift" (who at the highest point in the building, where the lantern would be in a Norman church, was installed like a photographer behind his curtain or an organist in his loft) began to descend towards me . . .]

(II, 25; II, 280)

We have already seen how the Grand Hotel at Balbec occupies the site which Marcel's fantasy had assigned to the church; Proust makes this substitution explicit here, and offers Marcel a peculiarly modern figure as guide. Bonnaffé's first citation for *lift* as a piece of machinery is dated 1904; its metonymic application to the employee who operated the lift was even more recent, the first citation being dated 1910.[20] As the lift passes each floor, Marcel glimpses the corridors of the hotel fanning out,

[19] For *budget*, see Ch. 1, n. 5.
[20] Proust only uses *lift* in this metonymic sense; when he refers to the machine itself he uses 'ascenseur' (e.g. II, 42; II, 300, where the correct translation of 'ascenseur' as 'lift' effaces this small distinction).

and chambermaids carrying bolsters; the only lighting comes from the windows of 'l'unique water-closet de chaque étage' [the solitary water-closet on each landing] (II, 26; II, 280). Sexual desire, shame, and secrecy fuse with social inadequacy, and Marcel babbles uncontrollably to the lift-boy, who keeps an enigmatic silence. When he reaches his room Marcel is intimidated by its furnishings and its size, which give it 'un caractère quasi historique qui eût pu la rendre appropriée à l'assassinat du duc de Guise, et plus tard à une visite de touristes conduits par un guide de l'agence Cook' [a quasi-historical character which might have made it a suitable place for the assassination of the Duc de Guise, and afterwards for parties of tourists personally conducted by one of Thomas Cook's guides] (II, 27; II, 282).

Marcel will gradually get used to his room—it will become, if not his *home*, then at least his *chez-soi*—and he will get used to *le lift*, too, who is also *le liftier* and *le liftman*, a character who contributes with surprising persistence not just to the atmosphere of the Grand Hotel but to the plot of the novel. His function deviates, you might say, from the vertical to the horizontal, as he brings messages and goes on errands for Marcel, almost always in a context which is suggestive of sexual desire or intrigue. The adolescent Marcel lives in a perpetual state of longing amongst a host of fleeting female shapes, among them a milkmaid who comes to the hotel from a nearby farm. One day he receives a letter, and the plebeian writing on the envelope convinces him it must be from this peasant girl; alas, it is only from the great writer Bergotte, who hadn't wanted to disturb him and had left 'un mot charmant pour lequel le liftman avait fait une enveloppe que j'avais crue écrite par la laitière' [a few charming lines for which the lift-boy had addressed an envelope which I had supposed to have been written by the milk-girl] (II, 74; II, 339). Bergotte and the *lift* are also joined in the sly comedy of Marcel's first encounters with M. de Charlus, in the course of which the baron lends Marcel a volume of Bergotte, then asks for it back; it is the 'liftier' who executes this commission (II, 126; II, 400–1).

It is not just the 'lift's' handwriting which is ill-educated; as befits a character tagged with an English name, his French is execrable, full of pretentious euphemisms which disguise the indignity he feels at being a servant (II, 157–8; II, 438–9); Marcel is able to record these euphemisms because, in a reversal of their relation on the night of his arrival, it is now he who keeps silent while the 'lift' chatters incessantly. This feature of his character, together with his message-bearing function, dominates his appearances during Marcel's second visit to Balbec, in *Sodome et Gomorrhe*. Here we learn among other things that the 'lift' cannot pronounce the French word for lift, *ascenseur*, correctly (III, 187; IV, 220).[21] But his more important role now is to carry messages from Marcel to Albertine, even to fetch her and bring her to the hotel; in a virtuoso sequence Proust alternates Marcel's minute observation of the 'lift's' linguistic deformations with the progress of his own liaison with Albertine, a passage which leads directly to his account of the first occasion on which he became conscious of the possibility that Albertine might desire other women, might be the lover of Andrée (III, 186–90; IV, 219–25).

In *À l'ombre des jeunes filles en fleurs*, the 'lift' as the bearer of messages comes to the attention of Bloch, who announces that he will pay Robert de Saint-Loup a visit at the hotel, and adds: ' "Comme je ne peux pas supporter d'attendre parmi le faux chic de ces grands caravansérails, et que les tziganes me feraient trouver mal, dites au "laïft" de les faire taire et de vous prévenir de suite." ' ["As I cannot endure to be kept waiting among all the false splendour of these great caravanserais, and the Hungarian band would make me ill, you must tell the "lighft-boy" to make them shut up, and to let you know at once"] (II, 97; II, 367). Bloch's unspeakable vulgarity is constantly emerging in his speech, and Proust enjoys hoisting him with his own petard—in this instance the affectation of knowing how to pronounce English. Remy de Gourmont (p. 60 n. 8) makes fun of French people who can't, claiming to have asked several people to pronounce 'plum-pudding', with the following results: *plum, pleum, plome, ploume*; *poudigne, poudinègue, poudine, poudingue*.[22] But here the joke has a particular sting, as Marcel goes on to explain:

Pour ce qui est de "laïft", cela avait d'autant moins lieu de me surprendre que quelques jours auparavant, Bloch m'ayant demandé pourquoi j'étais venu à Balbec . . . comme je lui avais dit que ce voyage répondait à un de mes plus anciens désirs, moins profond pourtant que celui d'aller à Venise, il avait répondu: "Oui, naturellement, pour boire des sorbets avec les belles madames, tout en faisant semblant de lire les *Stones of Venaïce* de Lord John Ruskin, sombre raseur et un des

---

[21] Nor could Proust spell it, incidentally: see his letter to his father of September 1898, *Corr.* II, 256–7.

[22] When Hippolyte Taine, author of the standard *Histoire de la littérature anglaise* (1863), asked for potatoes in England, he got buttered toast (Zeldin, II, 104). On our side of the Channel the joke has been going since Chaucer's Prioress with her 'French of Stratford-atte-Bowe'.

plus barbifiants bonshommes qui soient." Bloch croyait donc évidemment qu'en Angleterre non seulement tous les individus du sexe mâle sont lords, mais encore que la lettre *i* s'y prononce toujours *aï*.

[As regards the word "lighft," I had all the less reason to be surprised at Bloch's pronunciation in that, a few days before, when he had asked me why I had come to Balbec . . . and I had explained to him that this visit was a fulfilment of one of my earliest longings, though one not so deep as my longing to see Venice, he had replied: "Yes, of course, to sip iced drinks with the pretty ladies, while pretending to read the *Stones of Venighce* by Lord John Ruskin, a dreary bore, in fact one of the most tedious old prosers you could find." Thus Bloch evidently thought that in England not only were all the inhabitants of the male sex called "Lord," but the letter "i" was invariably pronounced "igh."]

(II, 99; II, 369)[23]

Marcel refrains from pointing out that Bloch's misjudgement of the value of *The Stones of Venice* is more serious than his mispronunciation of its title; it is as though he has taken on the identity of Swann, who would similarly confine himself to such 'objective' details and avoid as far as possible passing any judgement which came from his heart. In Marcel's impassive phrasing, 'laïft' and 'Venaïce' appear on a level; it is important not to commit such solecisms, not to expose oneself to ridicule, whether pronouncing the name of a hotel employee or a work of genius.

The context of the passage makes this anxiety easier to understand but harder to forgive. In between Bloch's initial mispronunciation of *laïft*, and Marcel's comment which adds the Ruskin example, comes a passage

---

[23] In a letter to Antoine Bibesco of 3 Apr. 1903, which is packed with Ruskinian quotations and references to English friends, Proust (or, as I have heard many times in England, 'Prowst') attributes the mispronunciation 'Venaïce' to one of the two Henraux brothers, probably Lucien, the future curator of the Louvre, whom he seems to have known socially (*Corr.* III, 284–6). Another joke about *lords* occurs in Proust's pastiche of Émile Faguet in *Pastiches et mélanges*: 'Un grand savant anglais, moitié physicien, moitié grand seigneur, un lord anglais, comme dit l'autre (mais non, madame, tous les lords sont Anglais, donc un lord anglais est un pléonasme; ne recommencez pas, personne ne vous a entendue) . . .' [A great English scientist, half natural philosopher, half nobleman, an English lord as they say (no, no, Madam, all lords are English, therefore an English lord is a pleonasm; don't do it again, no one heard you . . .] (*CSB* 30). Francis Wey (p. 63) had fulminated for real on this point as far back as 1845: 'Nous disons un *mylord*, c'est comme qui dirait *un mon seigneur*; car les Anglais disent *a lord*, un lord. Il n'est rien de pis, si ce n'est de dire comme les journaux: *un mylord anglais*, sans doute afin de le distinguer d'un *mylord turc*' [We say *un mylord*, as who should say *un mon seigneur*; for the English say *a lord*, *un lord*. There is nothing worse, unless it is to say like the newspapers: *un mylord anglais*, no doubt to distinguish him from *un mylord turc*].

which links Bloch's vulgarity with his Jewishness, indeed with his belonging to a 'colonie juive' at Balbec. This Jewish colony doesn't mix with the
other social groups at the resort; its members flash their money around
and wear loud clothes; the men are irredeemably Jewish-looking 'malgré
l'éclat des smokings et des souliers vernis' [despite the brilliance of their
dinner-jackets and patent-leather shoes] (II, 98; II, 368). Bloch's language is thus of a piece with his unwelcome appearance at the hotel, and
his intrusion into the high-minded friendship between Marcel and Saint-
Loup is marked by his jumped-up put-down of Ruskin. Marcel's intoler-
ance contrasts with Saint-Loup's generous embarrassment on Bloch's
behalf; Saint-Loup blushes at Bloch's error because he knows, or thinks he
knows, that Bloch would blush if it were pointed out to him; he himself
attributes the error to a kind of lofty indifference on Bloch's part towards
trivial social graces, yet he is simultaneously aware that Bloch himself
would be far from indifferent to being laughed at:

Car il pensait bien que Bloch attachait plus d'importance que lui à cette faute. Ce
que Bloch prouva quelque temps après, un jour qu'il m'entendit prononcer "lift",
en interrompant: "Ah! on dit lift." Et d'un ton sec et hautain: "Cela n'a d'ailleurs
aucune espèce d'importance."

[For he assumed that Bloch attached more importance than he to this mistake—
an assumption which Bloch confirmed some days later, when he heard me pronounce the word "lift," by breaking in with: "Oh, one says 'lift,' does one?" And
then, in a dry and lofty tone: "Not that it's of the slightest importance."]

(II, 99; II, 369)

Marcel knows perfectly well that this last phrase means the opposite of
what it pretends; but isn't Bloch right despite himself? Saint-Loup understands that Bloch would be chagrined at being caught out in a social
solecism even though it didn't really matter; Marcel, a few days later,
teaches his comrade a lesson.[24]

---

[24] I don't have space to go fully into the subject of the 'lift's' later appearances in the
novel, both in *Sodome et Gomorrhe* and *Le Temps retrouvé*; these belong in any case more to
the topic of 'Anglosexuality', to use Emily Eells's word. In the course of his prolonged, elaborate reconstructions of Albertine's past, and in the light of his knowledge of Saint-Loup's
homosexuality, Marcel learns that the 'lift' was involved in bisexual intrigue at Balbec both
with Saint-Loup and with other guests at the hotel. Marcel reflects that if this is true, then
Saint-Loup had another reason for blushing when Bloch mentioned the 'laïft' (IV, 260–1;
V, 786). But his 'knowledge' itself is questionable, and every affirmation made by or about
people in these later portions of the novel is radically uncertain.

Le sport

It is high season in Balbec. No one is braving the storms raging on the edge of the known world, or peering moodily into the realms of eternal fog; they are sunning themselves on the boardwalk, where a band plays every morning outside the hotel. And Balbec is sports-mad. Marcel, like his author, takes a book onto the beach; at most he goes for an occasional bathe; everyone else is playing tennis, golf, or polo, riding horses or bicycles, sailing on yachts, going to the races. When she first gets to know him, Albertine condescends to Marcel: 'Vous ne faites rien ici? On ne vous voit jamais au golf, aux bals du Casino; vous ne montez pas à cheval non plus. Comme vous devez vous raser! Vous ne trouvez pas qu'on se bêtifie à rester tout le temps sur la plage?' [Don't you do anything here? We never see you playing golf, or dancing at the Casino. You don't ride either. You must be bored stiff. You don't find it too deadly, idling about on the beach all day?] (II, 231; II, 527–8).[25] Marcel has already noticed that the *jeunes filles en fleurs*, whom he desires and envies, are keen on sport. His first sight of them is marked by (with apologies to the Scots) the most English of French sporting imports:

Une de ces inconnues poussait devant elle, de la main, sa bicyclette; deux autres tenaient des "clubs" de golf; et leur accoutrement tranchait sur celui des autres jeunes filles de Balbec, parmi lesquelles quelques-unes, il est vrai, se livraient aux sports, mais sans adopter pour cela une tenue spéciale.

[One of these unknown girls was pushing a bicycle in front of her; two others carried golf-clubs; and their attire generally was in striking contrast to that of the other girls at Balbec, some of whom, it is true, went in for sports, but without adopting a special outfit.]

(II, 146; II, 426)

The *Pléiade* editors have a note on the debate which raged in France at the turn of the century about what dress was proper for female cyclists, but they say nothing about what 'tenue spéciale' might have been envisaged for female golfers. Fortunately Proust himself supplies a clue, in the form of a snide remark by none other than the anglophile Odette. When Marcel praises the artistry of her dresses, she of all people responds with scorn of an English fad which, for once, she cannot embrace, since it

---

[25] It is in this conversation that Marcel observes the 'affectation juvénile de flegme britannique' in Albertine's voice (II, 232; II, 528).

conflicts with an even higher priority: ' "Je ne joue pas au golf comme plusieurs de mes amies, disait-elle. Je n'aurais aucune excuse à être, comme elles, vêtue de sweaters." ' ["I don't play golf," she would answer, "like so many of my friends. So I should have no excuse for going about in *sweaters* as they do"] (I, 610; II, 228).[26]

Marcel may not recall Odette's backhanded concession that golf is an acceptable pastime in her milieu; at any rate he does not yet know where to place the girls of the 'petite bande' on the social scale. One of his hypotheses is that they are 'les très jeunes maîtresses de coureurs cyclistes' [the very juvenile mistresses of racing cyclists] (II, 151; II, 431).[27] When he eventually meets Albertine and hears her use a locution which indicates that she comes from a bourgeois background, he has to revise his first impression of her as 'la bacchante à bicyclette, la muse orgiaque du golf' [the bacchante with the bicycle, the orgiastic muse of the golf-course] (II, 228; II, 524). But even at their first appearance he judges that the members of the group have been brought together by their love of physical activity, and that their energy and confidence may belong to a wider social phenomenon, '[les] habitudes nouvelles de sport, répandues même dans certains milieux populaires' [new sporting habits, now prevalent even among certain elements of the working class] (II, 149; II, 428)—a cult of sporting prowess with which Balbec is imbued and which has its origin in a particular aspect of *anglomanie*. I use the word 'cult' advisedly; when Marcel dreams of making an assignation with one of the *jeunes filles en fleurs*, he imagines it taking place 'avant la messe ou après le golf' [before church or after golf] (II, 242; II, 541).

The modern concept of 'le sport' in France came from England. 'Par le mot de *sports*, dont l'équivalent n'existe pas en notre langue . . . on désigne la chasse, les courses, le combat de boxeurs' [The word *sport*, whose equivalent does not exist in our language . . . denotes hunting, horse-racing, boxing-fights], stated the *Journal des haras* in 1828; 'haras' means 'stud-farm' and the predominant application of the term *sport* in

---

[26] Bonnaffé has 'sweater' from 1910, specifically as an outfit for sports; Le Robert dates this sense to 1902 and says that by 1910 the sense extended to what we would now call a cardigan. Albertine later expresses the same view from the opposite perspective: she ridicules the aristocratic 'demoiselles d'Ambresac' for their lack of sporting dress-sense: ' "Et puis elles s'habillent d'une manière ridicule. Elles vont jouer au golf en robes de soie!" ' ["And then they dress in the most absurd way. Fancy going to play golf in silk frocks!"] (II, 239; II, 537).

[27] He later adds, for good measure, 'de champions de boxe' (II, 200; II, 490).

France was initially to horse-racing. *Le Sport*, founded in 1854, was
essentially a racing paper aimed at aristocratic patrons of *le turf*—some of
whom would be members of *le Jockey-Club*.[28] The new vocabulary
attracted hostile attention: young men spoke 'un argot incompréhensible
[an incomprehensible slang], *sport, turf, handicap*', wrote Théophile
Gautier in 1848; the poet Jean-Pons-Guillaume Viennet, in *Épître à
Boileau sur les mots nouveaux*, argued that the Anglo-French alliance in the
Crimean War didn't mean that France had to surrender its linguistic
autonomy: 'Faut-il, pour cimenter un merveilleux accord, | Changer
l'arène en *turf* et le plaisir en *sport*' [Must we, to cement an admirable
accord, change *l'arène* to *turf*, and *le plaisir* to *sport*?].[29] This last, more
general definition of *sport* as *plaisir* may be a poeticism, but it suggests that
the term was widening its application; a note to the French translation of
Thackeray's *Pendennis*, published in 1875, defines it as 'Les courses de
chevaux, la chasse, le pêche, le tir, en un mot tous les plaisirs du gentleman' [Horse races, hunting, fishing, shooting, in a word all the amusements of a gentleman].[30] Gradually, the concept of sport as practised by
les gentlemen in England, and the ideals associated with it, made their way
into French culture, giving 'English' sports an aristocratic tinge; at the
same time, counter-impulses were at work, both in defence of native
forms of exercise and in opposition to sporting prowess as such, as an
enemy of intellectual and artistic values. Albert Dauzat, writing in 1912,
claimed not to approve of the split between intellectuals and *les sportifs*,
but he could not resist a dig at the English; speaking of 'la renaissance
sportive' in France, which he dates to the period 1890–5, he says that its
theoreticians 'réhabilitent le culte de l'énergie et nous donnent pour
modèles nos voisins d'outre-Manche, peu férus d'humanités antiques,
mais en revanche admirablement dressés à la vie pratique et à la conquête
du monde' [rehabilitate the cult of physical energy and give us as models
our neighbours across the Channel, not very keen on classical learning,
but on the other hand admirably set up for the practical business of
life and the conquest of the world] (p. 8). Unfair to Victorian classical

---

[28] Zeldin, II, 560. As a *Guide du sportsman* put it in 1839, 'Le genre de *sport* qui donne,
en quelque sorte, la vie à tous le autres . . . c'est le *turf*.' This latter term arrived at the same
time as *sport* itself, in 1828, also in the *Journal des Haras*; Balzac has it in *Béatrix*, 1845
(Bonnaffé).

[29] Both citations from Bonnaffé; for more on Viennet's poem, see Ch. 1, pp. 12–13.
[30] Cited in Mackenzie, 132.

scholarship, certainly, but a routine jibe; and Dauzat goes on to differentiate French from English sports according to national temperament: 'tandis que le snobisme soutenait seul chez nous les sports anglais de jeu et de lutte, l'esprit d'initiative de notre race choisissait ou créait ses sports, propres à développer nos qualités individualistes . . . alpinisme, cyclisme, automobilisme, aviation' [while snobbery alone sustained in our country the English sports of gambling and fighting, the spirit of initiative of our race chose or invented its own sports, fit to develop our individualist qualities . . . mountaineering, cycling, motoring, aviation] (pp. 10–11).

Proust is not above making literary fun of Philistine young gentlemen who haven't a brain in their virile heads. In *Sodome et Gomorrhe*, at the princesse de Guermantes's soirée, Marcel witnesses M. de Charlus, smitten by Mme de Surgis's two handsome sons, doing his best to discern in them a smidgin of intellectual culture. One of them, Victurnien, does indeed know his name to be that of a character in Balzac, though that is all of Balzac he knows; M. de Charlus lauds him for his literary gifts, and turns to his brother Arnulphe:

"Et vous lisez vous aussi? Qu'est-ce que vous faites?" demanda-t-il au comte Arnulphe qui ne connaissait même pas le nom de Balzac. Mais sa myopie, comme il voyait tout très petit, lui donnait l'air de voir de très loin, de sorte que, rare poésie en un sculptural dieu grec, dans ses prunelles s'inscrivaient comme de distantes et mystérieuses étoiles.

"Si nous allions faire quelques pas dans le jardin, Monsieur", dis-je à Swann, tandis que le comte Arnulphe, avec une voix zézayante qui semblait indiquer que son développement au moins mental n'était pas complet, répondait à M. de Charlus avec une précision complaisante et naïve: "Oh! moi, c'est plutôt le golf, le tennis, le ballon, la course à pied, surtout le polo." Telle Minerve, s'étant subdivisée, avait cessé, dans certaine cité, d'être la déesse de la Sagesse et avait incarné une part d'elle-même en une divinité purement sportive, hippique, "Athénè Hippia". Et il allait aussi à Saint-Moritz faire du ski, car Pallas Tritogeneia fréquente les hauts sommets et rattrape les cavaliers.

["And are you a reader too? What do you do?" he asked Comte Arnulphe, who had never even heard the name of Balzac. But his short-sightedness, since it caused him to see everything very small, gave him the appearance of seeing great distances, so that—rare poetry in a statuesque Greek god—remote, mysterious stars seemed to be engraved upon his pupils.

"Suppose we took a turn in the garden," I said to Swann, while Comte Arnulphe, in a lisping voice which seemed to indicate that mentally at least his development was incomplete, replied to M. de Charlus with an artlessly obliging precision: "Oh, you know, mainly golf, tennis, football, running, and especially polo." Thus had Minerva, having subdivided herself, ceased in certain cities to be the goddess of wisdom, and had become partly incarnated in a purely sporting, horse-loving deity, Athene Hippia. And he went to St Moritz also to ski, for Pallas Tritogeneia frequents the high peaks and outruns swift horsemen.]

(III, 102; IV, 120)

The comic contrast between Arnulphe's physical beauty and his brainless addiction to English sports (not a single individualistic French activity among them) is only part of the effect of this passage. It tells us about Marcel's, and Proust's, impulse to aestheticize stupidity, and to make it the subject of intellectual contemplation: Arnulphe's myopic gaze (a liability on the polo field, you would think) is filled with a poetry he knows nothing about; a characteristic Proustian simile links his 'nobility' (of social station) with classical divinity, a divinity divorced from its intellectual pretensions but, despite the satire, still divine. Just as Albertine is truly, in at least one of her 'incarnations', 'la muse orgiaque du golf', so Arnulphe here incarnates a 'divinité purement sportive', at which we are free to laugh but which we should recognize as a part of that reality outside himself to which Marcel is so strongly drawn. And we should acknowledge that the goddess who appears divided here may reunite her elements in a different figure. When Marcel first sees Robert de Saint-Loup, he describes him in terms of his physical beauty and energy, and also in terms of an aesthetic 'framing' which resembles, except for its tone, the treatment of Arnulphe de Surgis:

Il venait de la plage, et la mer qui remplissait jusqu'à mi-hauteur le vitrage du hall lui faisait un fond sur lequel il se détachait en pied, comme dans certains portraits où des peintres prétendent, sans tricher en rien sur l'observation la plus exacte de la vie actuelle, mais en choisissant pour leur modèle un cadre approprié, pelouse de polo, de golf, champ de courses, pont de yacht, donner un équivalent moderne de ces toiles où les primitifs faisaient apparaître la figure humaine au premier plan d'un paysage.

[He was coming from the beach, and the sea which filled the lower half of the glass front of the hall made a background against which he stood out full-length, as in certain portraits whose painters attempt, without in any way falsifying the most accurate observation of contemporary life, but by choosing for their sitter an appropriate setting—a polo ground, golf links, a race-course, the bridge of a yacht—to furnish a modern equivalent of those canvases on which the old masters used to present the human figure in the foreground of a landscape.]

(II, 89; II, 357)

Although the background to Saint-Loup here is the sea,[31] the analogy which Marcel draws with modern painters who place their figures against the background of sporting landscapes suggests that such landscapes, too, would be a 'cadre approprié' for Saint-Loup. Yet this golden young nobleman is (at least in this phase of his life) the very reverse of Arnulphe de Surgis; in him, as Marcel soon discovers, the two aspects of Minerva are not separated but united: 'Ce jeune homme qui avait l'air d'un aristocrate et d'un sportsman dédaigneux n'avait d'estime et de curiosité que pour les choses de l'esprit' [This young man who had the air of a disdainful aristocrat and sportsman had in fact no respect or curiosity except for the things of the mind] (II, 92; II, 360).[32]

The ease with which both Arnulphe and Marcel mingle English and French terms—'le golf, le tennis, le ballon, la course à pied, surtout le polo' from Arnulphe; 'pelouse de polo, de golf, champ de courses, pont de yacht' from Marcel—suggests a linguistic fluidity which is characteristic of the vocabulary of sport in the period. But the history of French sport in the nineteenth century is also one of the supplanting of native species by foreign imports, often accompanied by linguistic 'forgetting'. Rugby was introduced in 1872 by English residents in Normandy, who formed the Havre Athletic Club; it displaced *la soule*, or *mellé*, the 'game' between neighbouring parishes which, as one writer put it, 'allows one to kill an enemy without losing one's right to Easter communion'.[33] The word used by the server to his opponent in the *jeu de paume*, which goes back to the fourteenth century, 'tenez' ('take this', 'here it comes') is accepted by the *OED*, with some caution, as the origin of the English word 'tennis'; this suggestion was first made by nineteenth-century etymologists and is found in Bonnaffé; the usual exasperation was expressed that the French were reimporting their own word in an English guise, especially since the English *tennis* conforms to the stress pattern of *tenez*, with the accent on the first syllable, whereas the French pronunciation of *tennis* lengthens the second syllable and places the stress there: *tenníce* (as in Odette's home

---

[31] For this image of the sea as a backdrop, see the *Figaro* article on the Grand Hotel cited above, n. 11.

[32] Le Robert dates 'sportsman' to 1823, with the same link to racing as 'sport' (see above); the more general sense of 'amateur de sports' dates from 1872, 'évoquant la période 1870–1930'; it was eventually replaced by *sportif* 'qui n'a pas la même connotation sociale distinguée, liée à l'anglomanie'.

[33] Zeldin, II, 685–6. Subsequent information also comes from this section of Zeldin's work.

town).[34] 'Des vocabulaires entiers sont gâtés par l'anglais' [Entire vocabularies are spoiled by English], Remy de Gourmont claimed:

Tous les jeux, tous les *sports* sont devenus d'une inélégance verbale qui doit les faire entièrement mépriser de quiconque aime la langue française. *Coaching, yachting*, quel parler! Des journalistes français ont fondé il y a quelques années un cercle qu'ils baptisèrent *Artistic-cycle-club*: ont-ils honte de leur langue ou redoutent-ils de ne pas la connaître assez pour lui demander de nommer un fait nouveau? (pp. 53–54)

[All games, all *sports* have become linguistically inelegant to the point where they must be held in complete contempt by anyone who loves the French language. *Coaching, yachting*, what parlance! A few years ago some French journalists founded a club which they named *Artistic-cycle-club*: are they ashamed of their own language or are they afraid of not knowing it well enough to ask it to supply a name for something new?]

The extremity of Gourmont's own language, here as elsewhere in his book, betrays him into pomposity ('quiconque aime la langue française', as though there were only one way of loving it) and reveals a blind spot; Proust, by contrast, recognized what a fertile literary resource the *parler* of sport offered him. The social world which Marcel enters at Balbec is in any case defined by an 'inélégance verbale' which takes many forms, from the hotel manager's macaronic malapropisms to the self-satisfied conversations of the 'regulars', not to mention the reappearance of Marcel's school-friend Bloch, with his defective pronunciation of English names and words. The distinctiveness of the vocabulary of sport signifies to Marcel the inaccessibility (to him) of a particular mentality, which by that very token becomes an object of intense desire; like all the other 'worlds' from which Marcel (as subject) is excluded, but over which Proust (as writer) presides, it is guarded by linguistic demons which must be propitiated, tamed, and subsumed into the novel's own vast, encompassing *parler*.

Proust himself never played an 'English' sport, though many of his friends did. Jeanne Pouquet, who became the wife of Gaston Arman de

---

[34] Bonnaffé dates *tennis* (as an abbreviation of *lawn-tennis*) to 1836 when it was described as a little-known ball-game; even thirty years later, the supplement to the *Dictionnaire de l'Académie* was still fairly vague: 'sorte de jeu de balle, dans lequel on se sert de raquettes' [a sort of ball-game, in which one makes use of rackets]. Paul Bourget reminds us, again, of the social aspect: 'Ils [les gens de cercle] savent s'habiller, jouer au tennis, parler sport' [They (society people) know how to dress, play tennis, talk about sport] (*Mensonges*, 1888); his Proustian *cocotte* Gladys Harvey (see Ch. 1, p. 23) is a renowned *joueuse de tennis*.

Caillavet and was one of the models of Gilberte, told her daughter: 'If one was to substitute "The tennis club on the Boulevard Bineau" for the "Champs-Elysées" in the account of Marcel's love for Gilberte, I can trace almost word for word the evocations of his love for me . . .'.[35] Proust used to frequent this club, but not to play tennis; he would bring sandwiches and cakes, and loiter with his particular brand of charged flirtatiousness; there is a fine photograph of him at the club, kneeling in troubadour pose at the feet of Jeanne Pouquet (who stands on a chair to give her divinity greater mock-dignity) and strumming on a racket as though it were a lute. The duc de Guiche took him to a polo match at Cabourg in 1907, and the following year secured his election to a club called the Polo de Bagatelle; in the last year of his life an English newspaper asked him for a photograph 'à cheval en train de jouer au polo' [on horseback and playing polo]. None was to hand.[36] He also accompanied friends around the golf course at Cabourg, but without understanding the rules, as we shall see; and one of the oddest reflections in the novel is that 'Le golf donne l'habitude des plaisirs solitaires' [Golf gives one a taste for solitary pleasures] (II, 282; II, 589).[37] In *A la recherche* the young Marcel is not physically inactive, but the games he plays are old-fashioned children's games, the kind whose French names Remy de Gourmont would have savoured: *le jeu de barres* ('Prisoner's Base') with Gilberte and her friends in the Champs-Élysées, *La Tour prends garde* ('King of the Castle') and *le furet* ('Hunt-the-Slipper') with the *jeunes filles en fleur* on their outings at Balbec. But he never plays tennis or golf with Albertine; the 'muse orgiaque du golf' remains, as a Muse should, untouched by her worshipper.

The golf course featured prominently in publicity for Cabourg and the Grand Hotel. An item in the journal *Comœdia* in 1913 lays it on thick:

On nous écrit de Cabourg: Le Golf de Cabourg qui comptait parmi les plus beaux de la Côte peut prétendre maintenant être un des plus beaux Golfs de France. M. H.

---

[35] Tadié, 101.

[36] Letter to Bernard Faÿ, 12 Aug. 1922, *Corr.* XXI, 412–13. See also Tadié, 449 and note.

[37] For a sighting of Proust on the golf course, wrapped in his violet velvet cloak, see Painter, II, 172–3. *Diabolo* is an example of Gourmont's Revenge, or the reimportation of a word from French into English: despite its Italian name, the modern version of the game was invented by a Frenchman and replaced the old English 'devil upon two sticks'; the first *OED* citations come by a pleasing coincidence from 1907, the year of Proust's return to Cabourg. It is perhaps easier to see the relation of the diabolo than of golf to the other occupations which Marcel mentions as requiring 'une inviolable solitude: la lecture, la rêverie, les larmes et la volupté' [an inviolable solitude: reading or day-dreaming, tears or sensual pleasure] (I, 12; I, 12).

11. Proust serenades Jeanne Pouquet at the tennis club on boulevard Bineau.

Ruhl qui préside aux destinées de Cabourg n'a reculé devant aucun sacrifice pour le réorganiser totalement. A grands frais, il fit venir cet hiver une équipe d'ouvriers anglais qui a travaillé d'arrache-pied sous la haute direction de M. Colt, l'architecte paysagiste anglais bien connu. Le Grand Hôtel, le Casino et le Golf sont autant d'attraits uniques qui font comprendre la vogue croissante de Cabourg.

[News reaches us from Cabourg: the golf course of Cabourg which ranked among the finest on the Côte [Fleurie] can now claim to be one of the finest golf courses in France. M. H. Ruhl who presides over the destinies of Cabourg has spared no expense to reorganize it completely. At great expense, he brought over during the winter a team of English workmen which worked flat-out under the high command of M. Colt, the well-known English landscape architect. The Grand Hotel, the Casino, and the Golf Club form an ensemble of unique attractions which help to explain the growing vogue of Cabourg.][38]

Golf had arrived relatively recently in France, in the 1870s; the fact that the Cabourg course had been redesigned by an Englishman gave it the double prestige of authenticity and fashion. Proust knew that this fashionableness was localized both in social and topographical terms. It might be *chic* at the seaside, where its English provenance was a strong part of its appeal;[39] but in Paris, as we have seen from Odette's disparaging comment on *sweaters*, it would be trumped by a stronger suit. Nevertheless Marcel does at least clarify the issue of respectability when he sees one of the girls being marched home by her governess. Not only the sport, but the markers of social status are 'done' in English here:

au coin d'une des petites rues qui débouchent, perpendiculairement, sur la plage, nous croisâmes une jeune fille qui, tête basse comme un animal qu'on fait rentrer malgré lui dans l'étable, et tenant des clubs de golf, marchait devant une personne autoritaire, vraisemblablement son "anglaise", ou celle d'une de ses amies, laquelle ressemblait au portrait de *Jeffries* par Hogarth, le teint rouge comme si sa boisson favorite avait été plutôt le gin que le thé . . .

[at the corner of one of the little streets which ran down at right angles to the beach, we passed a girl who, hanging her head like an animal that is being driven reluctant to its stall, and carrying golf-clubs, was walking in front of an authoritarian-looking person, in all probability her or one of her friends' "Miss," who resembled the portrait of Jeffreys by Hogarth, with a face as red as if her favourite beverage were gin rather than tea . . .]

(II, 185; II, 472)[40]

The girls are old enough to be sexually enticing, young enough still to be provided with the English governess (here, 'anglaise'; elsewhere referred

---

[38] *Comœdia*, 8 June 1913, from a column called 'Échos'; cited in *Corr.* XII, 244 n. 5. Henri Ruhl had succeeded Jules Cesari as manager of the Grand Hotel.
[39] In this, as in other aspects of the Grand Hotel's operations, the influence of the Riviera is strong: see Howarth, 62–4.
[40] The reference is to Hogarth's portrait of the lawyer John Jeffreys and his family; this is another small example of the transpositions of gender which run through *A la recherche*, many of which have, as here, an English flavour. *Vintage* has 'suggested a portrait of Jeffreys'.

to as 'Miss')[41] who was *à la mode* (or even *de rigueur*). Marcel thinks that this particular young girl, who is wearing 'un polo noir', may be Mlle Simonet (i.e. Albertine); at any rate he decides to fix his desire, which floats among the whole of the 'petite bande', on 'celle aux clubs de golf . . . les yeux brillants sous son "polo"' [the one with the golf-clubs . . . her eyes sparkling beneath her polo-cap] (II, 186; II, 472–3).[42]

The use of *polo* here to mean a kind of hat is French, not English; the *OED* cites the *Daily Chronicle* in 1905: 'The small round hat that the French milliners call the "polo" and we in this country term the porkpie'—for the French are more elegant even in their vulgarity.[43] *Golf* is similarly adapted in French to the game, the course, and the Golf Club or club-house: ' "Celui-ci joue très bien au golf" ' ["This one plays golf quite well"] (II, 234; II, 531); ' "Elle est sur sa chaise longue, mais par ubiquité ne cesse pas de fréquenter simultanément de vagues golfs et de quelconques tennis" ' ["She is outstretched on her couch, but in her ubiquity has not ceased to frequent simultaneously vague golf-courses and dubious tennis-courts"] (II, 235; II, 533); 'un goûter donné au golf', [a tea-party at the golf-club] (II, 248; II, 547).[44] This linguistic economy allows

[41] Albertine says of Gisèle: 'elle repart tantôt pour Paris . . . elle et Miss, parce qu'elle a à repasser ses examens' [She's going back to Paris later today . . . she and 'Miss,' because she's got to take her exams again]; Marcel immediately conceives the fantasy of meeting Gisèle on the train and making a pass at her 'tandis que Miss sommeillerait' [while 'Miss' dozed] (II, 243; II, 542–3; *Vintage* has 'while the governess dozed').

[42] Proust's use of quotation marks around English words is inconsistent. The clubs carried by the young girls when Marcel first sees them are ' "clubs" de golf', later simply 'clubs de golf'; again at first sight, one of them wears 'un "polo" noir', which in the later passage from which I have just quoted is successively 'un polo noir' and 'son "polo" '. This inconsistency forms part of a larger uncertainty which Proust, and his printers, would have shared as to what exactly constituted a naturalized foreign word.

[43] Bonnaffé: 'Petite coiffure ronde portée par les jouers de polo ou d'autres sports', with a citation from 1897, 'Coiffés de "polos" à la dernière mode'.

[44] Le Robert dates the first appearance of *golf* meaning the game to 1872, and as 'golf-course' to 1901, but does not give the third sense of 'club-house'. Much later in the novel, in *La Prisonnière*, Marcel will register that *golf*, too, has become an item of clothing; when he is attracted to a young dairymaid and summons her to his apartment on the pretext of sending her on an errand, he glimpses 'la manche rouge de sa jaquette' [the red sleeve of her jersey] and asks her what she calls it: 'Elle me répondit: "C'est mon golf." Car par une déchéance habituelle à toutes les modes, les vêtements et les mots qui, il y a quelques années, semblaient appartenir au monde relativement élégant des amies d'Albertine, étaient maintenant le lot des ouvrières' [She replied: "It's my *golf*. For, by a slight downward tendency common to all fashions, the garments and words which a few years earlier seemed to belong to the relatively smart world of Albertine's friends, were now the currency of working-girls] (III, 650; IV, 156–7; *Vintage* has 'It's my sweater'). This sense of *golf* is dated by Le Robert to 1909.

Marcel to take part in the sport without actually playing it: 'maintenant je m'intéressais extrêmement au golf et au tennis' [I now showed a keen interest in golf and tennis], he says in the first phase of his infatuation with the *jeunes filles en fleurs* (II, 189; II, 477), but he doesn't mean he takes up these sports, only that their location (and language) become part of his imaginative life. In turn, this prepares the ground for Elstir's revelation that the vulgar elements of modernity are as capable of artistic transfiguration as the most perfect works of art—that the painting of a sporting occasion may not be less valuable in aesthetic terms than that of a cathedral. Already Bloch's deliciously overdone phrase, 'de vagues golfs et de quelconques tennis', is a step in this direction. Marcel is severe on him: 'Comme beaucoup d'intellectuels il ne pouvait pas dire simplement les choses simples. Il trouvait pour chacune d'elles un qualificatif précieux, puis généralisait'. [Like many intellectuals, he was incapable of saying a simple thing in a simple way. He would find some precious qualifier for every statement, and would then generalise] (II, 235; I, 941).[45] But isn't this what the greater artist does, in his greater way? For Albertine to become, for Marcel, 'la muse orgiaque du golf' required a transformation just as fanciful, but more powerful; the artist of *A la recherche* escapes from the preciosity in which Bloch is mired only because he is stronger and fleeter of foot.

Elstir's lesson and example take pride of place in the development of Marcel's artistic sensibility at Balbec, but another character, as sports-mad as the dim-witted Arnulphe, proves capable of a surprising development of his own. This is Octave, popularly known as 'Dans les choux' ('I'm a wash-out'), a friend of Albertine and the other *jeunes filles*, and a nephew of M. Verdurin. Octave rarely appears without a jingling of English words:

Un jeune homme aux traits réguliers, qui tenait à la main des raquettes, s'approcha de nous. C'était le joueur de baccara dont les folies indignaient tant la femme du premier président. D'un air froid, impassible, en lequel il se figurait évidemment que consistait la distinction suprême, il dit bonjour à Albertine. "Vous venez du golf, Octave? lui demanda-t-elle. Ça a-t-il bien marché? Étiez-vous en forme? — Oh! ça me dégoûte, je suis dans les choux, répondit-il. —Est-ce qu'Andrée y était? —Oui, elle a fait soixante-dix-sept. —Oh! mais c'est un record. —J'avais fait quatre-vingt-deux hier."

[45] *Vintage* has 'and would sweep from the particular to the general'.

[A young man with regular features, carrying a bag of golf-clubs, sauntered up to us. It was the baccarat-player whose fast ways so enraged the senior judge's wife. In a frigid, impassive tone, which he evidently regarded as an indication of the highest distinction, he bade Albertine good day. "Been playing golf, Octave?" she asked. "How did it go? Were you in form?" "Oh, it's too sickening; I'm a wash-out," he replied. "Was Andrée playing?" "Yes, she went round in seventy-seven." "Why, that's a record!" "I went round in eighty-two yesterday."]

(II, 233; II, 529)[46]

Bloch's *vagues golfs* indeed! Perhaps Proust deduced that the aim of golf was to score as highly as possible from the standard of play he witnessed. At any rate Octave continues to be associated with this sport and with a whole way of thinking and behaving whose consummate frivolity fascinates Marcel:

Je fus frappé à quel point chez ce jeune homme . . . la connaissance de tout ce qui était vêtements, manière de les porter, cigares, boissons anglaises, chevaux . . . s' était développée isolément sans être accompagnée de la moindre culture intellectuelle. Il n'avait aucune hésitation sur l'opportunité du smoking ou du pyjama, mais ne se doutait pas du cas où on peut ou non employer tel mot, même des règles les plus simples du français.

[I was struck by the extreme degree to which, in this young man . . . the knowledge of everything that pertained to clothes and how to wear them, cigars, English drinks, horses . . . had been developed in complete isolation, unaccompanied by the least trace of any intellectual culture. He had no hesitation as to the right time and place for dinner-jacket or pyjamas, but had no notion of the circumstances in which one might or might not employ this or that word, or even of the simplest rules of grammar.]

(II, 233; II, 530)[47]

---

[46] The opening sentences refer to Octave's first appearance in the novel, where, not yet named, he figures as a consumptive *fin-de-siècle* decadent who goes each day to the Casino 'dans un veston nouveau, une orchidée à la boutonnière' [in a new jacket, with an orchid in his buttonhole], losing enormous sums at baccarat, 'pâle, impassible, un sourire d'indifférence aux lèvres' [pale, impassive, a smile of indifference on his lips] (II, 38; II, 295; *Vintage* has 'in a new suit of clothes' and 'a smile of complete indifference'). Both the orchid and the affectation of indifference are 'English' signs; the latter in particular derives from the *dandy* of the earlier 19th cent. The phrase 'en forme', as used here, was a borrowing from English, first to describe the good condition of a horse (1858), then of a sportsman (1884). Le Robert dates *record* as used here to 1893.

[47] 'Pyjama(s)', from an Urdu and Persian word, entered English around 1800 with wildly varying spellings (peijammahs, pie-jamahs, pyjamahs, etc.); 'pajamas', the American form, influenced the first appearances of the word in French, dated by Le Robert

It is entirely germane to Proust's design that Octave's faulty French should accompany his expertise in words borrowed from another language; not surprisingly he wins first prize at the Casino in all the dance competitions, 'de boston, de tango, etc.';[48] on the other hand he dislikes being greeted by his cousin M. Verdurin in authentically vulgar French:

· il parla avec dédain des fameux mercredis, et ajouta que M. Verdurin ignorait l'usage du smoking ce qui rendait assez gênant de le rencontrer dans certains "music-halls" où on aurait autant aimé ne pas s'entendre crier: "Bonjour, galopin" par un monsieur en veston et en cravate noire de notaire de village. (II, 238)

[he spoke disdainfully of the famous Wednesdays, adding that M. Verdurin had no idea of when to wear a dinner-jacket, which made it a bit embarrassing to come across him in certain music-halls, where one would just as soon not be greeted with a 'Hello, young whipper-snapper!' by a gentleman in a lounge suit and a black tie like a village notary's.] [49]

Given this concentration of English affectations, which Marcel initially takes as a firm indication of Octave's intellectual nullity, his subsequent history in the novel takes a surprising turn. When we next hear of him directly, in *La Prisonnière*, Marcel is still referring to him as 'ce jeune homme si savant en choses de courses, de jeux, de golf, si inculte dans tout le reste' [the young man so learned in matters of racing, gambling and golf, so uneducated in everything else] (III, 568; V, 60). Later on he becomes the lover of the actress Rachel, formerly Saint-Loup's mistress,

to 1882; *le pyjama* became the dominant form in the 1890s. The original sense is that of loose drawers or trousers, usually of silk or cotton, then (with the addition of a jacket) applied to night wear; but Octave may mean a daytime or evening garment worn by women (which would fit with *le smoking*), or even a form of beachwear. A striking example of linguistic cross-over is found in one of the *OED* citations for 'pyjamas', from E. S. Bridges' *Round the World in Six Months* (1879): 'I relinquished my English *chemise de nuit* and took to pyjamas'; Bridges is in Japan at the time.

48 The *boston* was a slow waltz; Bloch and Wartburg date it to 1882. Gilberte's fierce determination to go to a dance class rather than stay home with Marcel is the occasion of their final quarrel, and is sarcastically attributed to 'une inclination sentimentale pour le boston' [a sentimental attachment to the boston] (I, 573; II, 182).

49 My trans., borrowing the excellent 'whipper-snapper' from James Grieve (*In the Shadow of Young Girls in Flower*, Penguin 2002, 461); *Vintage* (II, 535–6) incorrectly renders 'ignorait l'usage du smoking' as 'had never even heard of dress-clothes'. In the 12th cent. a 'galopin' was a messenger on horseback; in the 14th cent., an errand-boy; in the 17th cent., a street urchin; in the 19th cent., a familiar endearment ('young rascal'). 'Galopin' has a secondary degree of authentic 'Frenchness' in *A la recherche*: it is the name of the *pâtissier* in Combray (I, 56; I, 66, and *Pléiade* note, I, 1128).

then leaves her for Albertine's closest friend (and, probably, lover), Andrée; later still Marcel will learn (as far as he learns anything for certain) that Octave had hoped at one time to marry Albertine, and that her flight from Marcel's house had been made with him in mind. All these complications bring Octave into the maze of the novel's sexual intimacies, and, as though to match this development, we are told of his creative flowering: 'Ce jeune homme fit représenter de petits sketches, dans des décors et avec des costumes de lui, et qui ont amené dans l'art contemporain une révolution au moins égale à celle accomplie par les Ballets russes' [This young man produced certain sketches for the theatre, with settings and costumes designed by himself, which effected in contemporary art a revolution at least equal to that brought about by the Russian ballet] (IV, 184; V, 693). By a witty reversal, Octave's English affectations are superseded by another English word, *sketches*;[50] it seems so unlikely to many of those who knew him at Balbec, where he passed all his time 'au baccara, aux courses, au golf ou au polo', that they think these *sketches* must have been ghost-written, either by Andrée or a professional hack; 'Mais tout cela était faux; et ce jeune homme était bien l'auteur de ces œuvres admirables' [But all this was untrue, and this young man was indeed the author of those admirable works] (IV, 185; V, 694). Marcel himself recognizes that Octave's authentic talent may not be psychologically incompatible with his former (apparent) shallowness, and that genius may already have been present in the young man whose interests at Balbec had seemed confined to such matters as 'la correction des attelages et . . . la préparation des cocktails' [turning out a smart carriage and pair and mixing cocktails]. He ought perhaps to have realized this earlier; for he had before him the example of a greater artist than Octave, that of Elstir.

The painter of modern life

I am not concerned here with Elstir's revelation to Marcel of a new way of seeing, the young man's discovery, in Elstir's Balbec studio, of the painterly 'metaphors' by which the stale world of habitual perception is abolished and recreated afresh. Elstir is not simply a model and precursor for the aesthetic of *A la recherche*; indeed, if he were simply that he could

---

[50] Le Robert dates *sketch* in the theatrical sense to 1879; it elbowed out the old French 'saynète'. Bloch and Wartburg's date is considerably later, 1903.

not even be that. He figures so largely in Marcel's life, and in the development of his art, because he offers him more than one revelation, or, to put it another way, because the revelation he offers turns out to be multi-faceted, to be capable itself of metaphorical transformation. Elstir teaches Marcel not only how to look, but what to look at; he shows him a modern world stripped of social prejudice and *a priori* aesthetic judgements; he enlarges Marcel's imaginative scope to include the shapes of the material world in every one of their aspects, indifferent to aesthetic categorization as 'beautiful' or 'ugly'. Nor is it solely a question of shape or surface, but of spirit, of that which, in any 'picture' of life, whether in paint or words, gives us its inner meaning.

We have already seen how, on his first visit to Elstir's studio, Marcel discovered the painter's connection not only to the *jeunes filles en fleurs*, but to Odette, whom he evidently knew at the time of her affair with Swann.[51] The connection with Odette was made both indirectly, through the orchids which Elstir was painting, and directly, through the watercolour of 'Miss Sacripant'; Marcel makes the further leap, as he reflects on the provenance of this portrait, that Elstir must be the same as the crassly vulgar painter, 'M. Biche', who frequented the Verdurins' salon, he of 'le petit *speech*' so admired by Forcheville. Elstir's corruption extends further than his language, though; Marcel 'forgets' (though Proust does not) the painter's pleasure at the thought that Swann's liaison with Odette will happen under his eye: ' "Rien ne m'amuse comme de faire des mariages, confia-t-il, dans l'oreille, au docteur Cottard, j'en ai déjà réussi beaucoup, même entre femmes!" ' ["Nothing amuses me more than match-making," he confided to Cottard. "I've brought off quite a few, even between women!"] (I, 199; I, 242). The verb 'réussi' creates a link to the difficult 'marriages' of plants to which horticulturalists devoted their labours;[52] it links Elstir to Odette's sexual ambiguity in the past, and to Albertine's lesbianism in the present and the future.

Elstir's name is contained within that of Whistler—for Proust, as for many of his contemporaries, an English, not American painter, whom Proust refers to as 'le maître de Chelsea' (II, 163; II, 445)—and there is a speculative, but suggestive Englishness about the remaining letters,

---

[51] See Ch. 2, pp. 90–2.
[52] In the 'Note sur la fécondation des Orchidées' from the journal *L'Orchidophile* which I cited in the previous chapter (p. 89) we find phrases such as 'cet élément de réussite pour la fécondation' and 'l'opérateur tient à assurer la réussite de son expérience'.

'w h'.[53] I am thinking of 'Mr. W.H.', the 'onlie begetter' of Shakespeare's sonnets, and of Oscar Wilde's 'Portrait of Mr. W.H.' (1889); though Pascale McGarry, in her article on ' "Mr W.H." et "Miss Sacripant" ', is rightly cautious as to whether Proust knew the story directly, the connections between him and Wilde were extensive enough for Proust to have been aware of it from friends such as Douglas Ainslie, or the painter Jacques-Émile Blanche who knew both Wilde and Whistler, and who was himself one of the models for Elstir. Proust would have known of the Sonnets, independently of Wilde, if not from his own reading of Shakespeare then from a poem by Montesquiou with an English title, 'Sugared', in *Les Chauve-Souris* (1893); Montesquiou does not use the initials 'W.H.' but takes for granted that the dedicatee of the *'sonnets sucrés* d'origine bizarre' [*sugared sonnets* with their bizarre origin] was the Earl of Southampton, Henry Wriothesly, and names him in its first and last lines. There was also a 'Mr. W.H.' closer to Proust's heart, Willie Heath, whose fleeting friendship and early death Proust commemorated in the dedication to *Les Plaisirs et les jours*, in which Willie is himself compared to a melancholic English nobleman in a portrait by Van Dyck.[54]

Elstir at Balbec is marked by other English associations than his name. Marcel has read a study of him in 'une revue d'art anglaise qui traînait sur la table du salon du Grand-Hôtel' [an English art-journal which lay on the reading-room table of the Grand Hôtel] (II, 191; II, 479), and the *patron* of the restaurant at Rivebelle where Marcel and Saint-Loup spot Elstir has become gradually aware of his growing fame through 'les questions de plus d'une Anglaise de passage, avide de renseignements sur la vie que menait Elstir' [the questions asked by more than one English lady-visitor, athirst for information as to the life led by Elstir] (II, 183; II, 469). To these relatively dignified details we can add one from the garden of

[53] I am not quite sure whether my point is strengthened or weakened by the fact that Proust habitually misspelled 'Wisthler'.

[54] 'C'est au Bois que je vous retrouvais souvent le matin, m'ayant aperçu et m'attendant sous les arbres, debout, mais reposé, semblable à un de ces seigneurs qu'a peints Van Dyck, et dont vous aviez l'élégance pensive' [It is in the Bois that I would often find you in the morning, having caught sight of me and waiting for me beneath the trees, upright, but restful, like those noblemen whom Van Dyck has painted, and whose pensive elgance was yours] (*JS* 5–6). These portraits are again evoked in the poem on Van Dyck in 'Portraits de peintres' (pp. 81–2), specifically the portrait of James Stuart, the future Duke of Richmond, known as 'L'Homme au pourpoint', which Proust saw in the Louvre in 1891; a phrase from the dedication, 'debout, mais reposé', was borrowed from the poem. For Bourget's allusion to Van Dyck, see Ch. 1, n. 23.

Elstir's spanking new villa, which Marcel notices as he arrives: 'une petite tonnelle sous laquelle des rocking-chairs étaient allongés devant une table de fer' [a little arbour beneath which rocking-chairs were drawn up round an iron table] (II, 190; II, 478).[55]

The paintings which Marcel admires most on this first visit, those that initiate him into Elstir's aesthetic philosophy as opposed to his social and sexual past, are marine landscapes, and though they are intensely English in terms of technique, influenced as much by Turner as by Monet, they are less significant, for my purpose, than the ones which Marcel describes later in the novel, and about whose subjects Elstir himself discourses.[56] I would go further and point to a significant absence of English words from Marcel's description of these marine paintings. Remy de Gourmont had lamented the proliferation of English nautical terms in literature: 'La langue de la marine s'est fort gâtée en ces derniers temps, j'entends la langue écrite par certains romanciers' [Nautical language has become very spoiled in recent times, I mean the written language employed by certain novelists] (p. 56); but he would have nothing to reproach Proust with here. We have as words for ships *bateaux, vaisseaux, navires, barques*, but no *yachts*, though Elstir does not at all despise *le yachting*, as we shall see; words such as *mâts, bassin de calfatage, coques, grève, jetée, matelots, voiles* [masts, dry dock, hulls, shore, jetty, sailors, sails] deploy an impeccable French lexicon; I am tempted to take one last speculative step and point to the triple occurrence of the word *golfe*, its final 'e' indicating its proper French meaning of 'gulf' and segregating it from its sporting English homonym.[57]

Proust keeps his English vocabulary in reserve until he has established the connection between Elstir and Albertine. When Marcel glances out of the window of the studio he sees Albertine on her bicycle, wearing her *polo*; in the aftermath of his discovery that Elstir knows her and her friends he finds, as we have seen, the portrait of Odette as 'Miss Sacripant'; Elstir's

---

[55] Le Robert, usually so reliable, is wrong to state that *rocking-chair*, dated to 1851 in French, only features in an American context; it is true that rocking-chairs were an American colonial invention (Benjamin Franklin's excited great interest in Paris in 1766), but this example shows that the term had wider currency. Proust also uses the abbreviated form *le rocking* (II, 39; II, 296).

[56] For the English aesthetic of Elstir's paintings, see Eells, 113–42, and bibliography, 211–12.

[57] The description of Elstir's marine paintings is in II, 191–6 (II, 479–85); 'golfe' appears on pp. 192, 195, 196. The English word 'gulf' is French in origin.

English credentials are now established in his social life both past and present. In a conversation with Marcel some time after this first visit, he uses at least one English word, and arguably two. Marcel describes catching Andrée out in a social lie; she had told him she couldn't go out with him because her mother was ill, but Elstir (not deliberately) exposes the fib: ' "elle avait accepté un pique-nique à dix lieues d'ici où elle devait aller en break et elle ne pouvait plus se décommander" ' ["she had promised to go for a picnic somewhere miles from here. They were to drive over in a break, and it was too late for her to get out of it"] (II, 240; II, 539).[58] The next step is a long account of the change in Marcel's sensibility brought about by the experience of getting to know both the *jeune filles en fleurs* and Elstir. Marcel explains that he now looked forward to outings in fine weather with Albertine and her friends—complete with picnics featuring 'des sandwiches au chester' (II, 250; II, 551)[59]—having given up his former dream of Balbec as a primitive land shrouded in eternal mist:

Mais maintenant, tout ce que j'avais dédaigné, écarté de ma vue, non seulement les effets de soleil, mais même les régates, les courses de chevaux, je l'eusse recherché avec passion pour la même raison qu'autrefois je n'aurais voulu que des mers tempétueuses, et qui était qu'elles se rattachaient, les unes comme autrefois les autres à une idée esthétique. C'est qu'avec mes amies nous étions quelquefois allés voir Elstir, et les jours où les jeunes filles étaient là, ce qu'il avait montré de préférence,

[58]   The *OED* has a note on 'picnic': 'The chronology of the word in French and English, with the fact that our earliest instances refer to the Continent, and are sometimes in the French form *pique-nique*, show that the word came from French (although some French scholars, in ignorance of these facts, have, in view of the obscurity of its derivation, conjectured that the French word was from English)'. But Le Robert distinguishes between original and transferred senses: *faire un repas à pique-nique* originally meant a meal where everyone brought a dish, and dates from the early 18th cent.; English borrowed this term and gave it the modern meaning of an open-air party or excursion, and French then reborrowed it. Mackenzie dates *break* to 1830; Bonnaffé cites Flaubert's *Education Sentimentale* (1869): 'Mme de Remoussot, mise à la mode par son procès, trônait sur le siège d'un break en compagnie d'Américains' [Mme de Remoussot, who had become fashionable in the wake of her trial, was queening it on the seat of a break in the company of some Americans]. In *Sodome et Gomorrhe*, the Verdurins replace their *break* with an automobile at the request of Morel's friend, the nefarious chauffeur (III, 417; IV, 495).

[59]   'Sandwich(e)' is found in French from 1802; it was feminine in form up to the 1870s (Le Robert). Purists vainly pointed out the linguistic (and gastronomic) superiority of the *tartine*. 'Chester' like 'footing' (walking for exercise) and 'plus-value' (increment), is an English word with a meaning peculiar to French: it means Cheshire cheese. 'Les sandwiches au chester' featured in older texts of *Sodome et Gomorrhe*, at a reception given for King Edward VII where Marcel distinguishes himself by his tact (III, 62; IV, 73), but have, alas, been taken off the menu by the new *Pléiade* edition (see textual note, III, 1362).

c'était quelques croquis d'après de jolies yachtswomen ou bien une esquisse prise sur un hippodrome voisin de Balbec. J'avais d'abord timidement avoué à Elstir que je n'avais pas voulu aller aux réunions qui y avaient été données. "Vous avez eu tort, me dit-il, c'est si joli et si curieux aussi. D'abord cet être particulier, le jockey, sur lequel tant de regards sont fixés, et qui devant le paddock est là morne, grisâtre dans sa casaque éclatante . . . " Puis il s'extasia plus encore sur les réunions de yachting que sur les courses de chevaux et je compris que des régates, que des meetings sportifs où des femmes bien habillées baignent dans la glauque lumière d'un hippodrome marin, pouvaient être, pour un artiste moderne, un motif aussi intéressant que les fêtes qu'ils aimaient tant à décrire pour un Véronèse ou un Carpaccio.

[But everything that I had hitherto despised and thrust from my sight, not only the effects of sunlight upon sea and shore, but even regattas and race-meetings, I now sought out with ardour, for the same reason which formerly had made me wish only for stormy seas: namely, that they were now associated in my mind, as the others had once been, with an aesthetic idea. For I had gone several times with my new friends to visit Elstir, and, on the days when the girls were there, what he had selected to show us were drawings of pretty women in yachting dress, or else a sketch made on a race-course near Balbec. I had at first shyly admitted to Elstir that I had not felt inclined to go to the meetings that had been held there. "You were wrong," he told me, "it's such a pretty sight, and so strange too. For one thing, that peculiar creature the jockey, on whom so many eyes are fastened, and who sits there in the paddock so gloomy and grey-faced in his bright jacket . . ." After which he waxed more enthusiastic still over the yacht-races, and I realised that regattas, and race-meetings where well-dressed women might be seen bathed in the greenish light of a marine race-course, might be for a modern artist as interesting a subject as the festivities they so loved to depict were for a Veronese or a Carpaccio.]
(II, 251–2; II, 551–2)

If English words were banished from the description of paintings so influenced by English artists, here they return in full force for the description of paintings influenced by French ones—Degas and Manet, of course, but also the now less known Paul Helleu, whose studio at Deauville Proust visited, and who painted scenes very similar to those which Elstir evokes in this passage.[60] This is the first occurrence in the

---

[60] The link between Elstir and Helleu is made in *Sodome et Gomorrhe*, at a dinner at the Verdurins' house in Normandy, La Raspelière; Saniette says of Elstir: '— Il restitue la grâce du XVIIIᵉ, mais moderne . . . Mais j'aime mieux Helleu. —Il n'y a aucun rapport avec Helleu, dit Mme Verdurin' ["He has revived the grace of the eighteenth century, but in a modern form . . . but I prefer Helleu." "There's not the slightest connexion with Helleu," said Mme Verdurin] (III, 329; IV, 390).

12. Degas, *Before the Race*, c.1893, pastel.

novel of the word *jockey* in its literal sense, as opposed to the name of the club; it is reinforced by *paddock*, and also by *meeting*, which was last encountered as a typical affectation of Odette's: 'une réunion mondaine chez des amis des Swann (ce que celle-ci appelait "un petit meeting")' [some social gathering given by a friend of Mme Swann's (what the latter called "a little *meeting*")] (I, 516; II, 114).[61] The sporting occasions which are so repugnant to Marcel are rescued for art, and it is as though the bad

[61] Elstir's liking for the jockey's attire and demeanour is referred to once more, at II, 256 (II, 558); the only other occurrence of the literal sense, though still located at Balbec, is less aesthetic; it comes in *Sodome et Gomorrhe*, and refers to M. de Charlus's sexual tastes (III, 377; IV, 447). Mackenzie dates *paddock* to 1709, but it was still being stigmatized as an English word in Proust's day. For Proust's dislike of the social use of *meeting*, see Ch. 1, p. 42. The slight grammatical incoherence in the French text, which leaves the referent of 'celle-ci' in the parenthesis unclear, results from an oversight; 'des amis de Swann' was originally 'une amie de Mme Swann' (*Pléiade* note, I, 1376).

taste of English vocabulary becomes more palatable, can even be savoured. Elstir's passion for *le yachting* is especially marked; in one speech he uses the words *yacht* and *yachting* almost to excess, in one of the most concentrated clusters of English words in the whole of *A la recherche*:

Le plus grand charme d'un yacht, de l'ameublement d'un yacht, des toilettes de yachting, est leur simplicité de choses de la mer, et j'aime tant la mer! Je vous avoue que je préfère les modes d'aujourd'hui aux modes du temps de Véronèse et même de Carpaccio. Ce qu'il y a de joli dans nos yachts—et dans les yachts moyens surtout, je n'aime pas les énormes, trop navires . . . c'est la chose unie, simple, claire, grise . . . Les toilettes des femmes sur un yacht, c'est la même chose; ce qui est gracieux, ce sont ces toilettes légères . . .

[The great charm of a yacht, of the furnishings of a yacht, of yachting clothes, is their simplicity, as things of the sea, and I do so love the sea. I must confess that I prefer the fashions of to-day to those of Veronese's and even of Carpaccio's time. What is so attractive about our yachts—and the medium-sized yachts especially, I don't like the huge ones, they're too much like ships . . . is the uniform surface, simple, gleaming, grey . . . And it's the same with women's clothes on board a yacht; what's really charming are those light garments . . .]

(II, 253; II, 554)

The English word so insistently deployed here is preferred to the French ('trop navire'). Marcel had hitherto tried literally not to see what Elstir shows him in this scene, 'd'expulser du champ de ma vision . . . les yachts aux voiles trop blanches comme un costume de plage' [to expel from my field of vision . . . the yachts with their too dazzling sails]; but that was before seeing Elstir's ravishing seascape with its 'jeune femme, en robe de barège ou de linon, dans un yacht arborant le drapeau américain' [young woman in a dress of white serge or linen, on the deck of a yacht flying the American flag' (II, 255; II, 557).[62] As for Albertine, her pleasure in Elstir's painting connects to her acuity in matters of fashion, and to her greed: ' "Comme j'aimerais être riche pour avoir un yacht! dit-elle au peintre. Je vous demanderais des conseils pour l'aménager. Quels beaux voyages je ferais! Et comme ce serait joli d'aller aux régates de

---

[62] In his carriage drives along the coast with his grandmother and Mme de Villeparisis—again, before his meeting with Elstir—Marcel had found his would-be aesthetic views of the sea spoiled by 'tant d'enclaves vulgaires et que mon rêve n'admettait pas, de baigneurs, de cabines, de yachts de plaisance' [so many vulgar adjuncts that had no place in my dream—bathers, cabins, pleasure-yachts] (II, 67; II, 331). There is another cluster of yachts in Marcel's letter to Albertine, IV, 38–9 (V, 520).

Cowes! . . ." ' ["How I should love to be rich and to have a yacht!" she said to the painter. "I should come to you for advice on how to do it up. What lovely trips I'd make! And what fun it would be to go to Cowes for the regatta! . . ."] (II, 254; II, 555). Much later in the novel, when Marcel, in his desperation to keep Albertine 'imprisoned', talks of buying her a yacht, he consults Elstir, recalling that his taste in the furnishing of yachts was exacting: 'Il n'y admettait que des meubles anglais' [he would allow only English furniture] (III, 870; V, 420).[63]

Marcel never asks, and we never in fact discover, how Elstir comes to know Albertine and the other *jeunes filles en fleurs*. They are evidently not his models (though Marcel will 'see' Albertine in one of Elstir's paintings); their friendly visits to Elstir's studio are not 'placed' within the social world either of Balbec or elsewhere. Unlike his former friendships with Odette and with Swann, which are rationally accounted for by their meeting at the Verdurins', this link is enigmatic and, in some respects, unlikely. We have been told of Elstir's solitude, of his withdrawal from 'ordinary' social intercourse or family life: 'il vivait dans un isolement, avec une sauvagerie que les gens du monde appelaient de la pose et de la mauvaise éducation, les pouvoirs publics un mauvais esprit, ses voisins de la folie, sa famille de l'egoïsme et de l'orgueil' [he lived in an unsociable isolation which fashionable people called pose and ill-breeding, the authorities a recalcitrant spirit, his neighbours madness, his family self-ishness and pride] (II, 184; II, 471). Yet the occasion on which Marcel finally meets Albertine is a party which he persuades Elstir to host;[64] this event, with its buffet loaded with strawberry tarts and coffee éclairs, its music, and its vague assemblage of other guests amongst whom Marcel singles out only the old gentleman to whom he offers the rose in his buttonhole, seems poised somewhere between a pastiche and a dream; it gives the impression of having been manufactured for the occasion, like a theatrical set, and is in any event never repeated.

It is possible to construct a hypothetical route by which Elstir could have met Albertine—she is the niece of Mme Bontemps, a friend of Mme Cottard, whom Elstir knew when he frequented the Verdurins' salon; he

[63] He promises to buy her a car, too; needless to say it is a Rolls-Royce.
[64] The word Marcel uses takes us back, once more, to the 'marriages' of plants: 'Quand . . . j'eus *réussi* à ce qu'Elstir donnât une petite matinée où je recontrerais Albertine' [When . . . I had succeeded in persuading Elstir to give a small party at which I should meet Albertine] (II, 224; II, 519).

also knew Odette there, of course, and when she becomes Mme Swann Odette cultivates Mme Bontemps; we hear of 'la fameuse Albertine' at school from Gilberte, she who will surely be so *fast* (I, 503; II, 98).[65] The trouble is that none of these possible connections are activated in the novel. Unlike the writer Bergotte, Elstir does not form part of Mme Swann's salon, and indeed there is no indication that he and Odette meet at all after her marriage to Swann, or that he maintains any links with the Cottards.

In a novel where connections between the characters are traced with minute exactness, and where such connections often matter a good deal in terms of narrative or psychological development, this gap in the circuit is unusual, and may be purposive. That is, the connection between Elstir and Albertine is left unexplained because its 'motivation' is something they have in common, not something which belongs to an external system of social or familial relations. It is an elective affinity whose elements are sexual ambiguity and the fluidity of the self. The superimposition of different perspectives, both in space and time, creates a psychological kinship between Elstir and Albertine such that the story of Marcel's love for Albertine seems the working out in time of the spatial metaphors in one of Elstir's paintings; in Elstir's artistic career, in turn, the layering of his different 'manners'—mythological, *japonisant*, Impressionist, Post-Impressionist—resembles the different, mysterious, apparently incompatible 'selves' of Albertine as Marcel successively discovers them: 'la muse orgiaque du golf', the well-brought up young lady, the sexually willing companion, the prisoner, the fugitive, the ghost.

The 'English' note in the affinity between Elstir and Albertine is only one among many, but though I don't want to exaggerate its significance I do want to 'isolate' it, as a particular element whose presence can be detected in this aspect of the novel as in others. Certain familiar characteristics of Englishness as Proust understands it are vividly apparent in the way Elstir and Albertine appear at Balbec: vulgarity, for example, and affectation; but they appear in guises susceptible of extraordinary transmutation. Just as Elstir reveals to Marcel the aesthetic pleasure to be gained in the imaginative apprehension of jockeys on a racecourse, or of young women in fashionable outfits on yachts, so Albertine reveals to him the savour, the taste of 'Balbec-Plage', the world of golf, tennis, *sandwiches*

---

[65] For this use of 'fast', see the Introduction, pp. 6–7.

au chester, and cocktails at the Casino. These things shed their vulgarity in the transmutation of desire; but the price which Marcel pays for this knowledge is high. The painter who enjoyed matchmaking 'even between women' will reveal to Marcel the contours of an alien sexual pleasure from which he is excluded; bound in the past to 'Miss Sacripant' and linked at Balbec to 'la muse orgiaque du golf', women whose fleeting, suggestive, shape-changing persona is like an emblem of his art, he will bequeath his imaginative legacy to his young disciple—with a necessary though unwanted coefficient of suffering.

4

Les Mots retrouvés

Un englische; un English
To begin with, a twice-told tale.

Un jour que, de Josselin où j'étais chez les Rohan, nous étions allés à un pèlerinage, il était venu des paysans d'un peu toutes les parties de la Bretagne. Un grand diable de villageois du Léon regardait avec ébahissement les culottes beiges du beau-frère de Robert. "Qu'est-ce que tu as à me regarder? je parie que tu ne sais pas qui je suis", lui dit Léon. Et comme le paysan disait que non: "Hé bien, je suis ton prince. —Ah!" répondit le paysan en se découvrant et en s'excusant, "je vous avais pris pour un englische."

["Once when I was staying at Josselin, with the Rohans, we all went over to a place of pilgrimage to which peasants had come from pretty well every part of Brittany. A great hulking villager from Léon stood gaping at Robert's brother-in-law in his beige breeches. 'What are you staring at me like that for?' said Léon, 'I bet you don't know who I am.' The peasant admitted as much. 'Well,' Léon said, 'I'm your Prince.' 'Oh!' said the peasant, taking off his cap and apologising. 'I thought you were an *Englische*.'"]

(III, 545–6; V, 32)

Proust was so fond of this story that, forgetting he had placed it in *La Prisonnière*, he gave it again in *Albertine disparue*:

Je vous disais que Basin était alors tout rasé; un jour à un pèlerinage ... mon beau-frère Charlus, qui aime assez causer avec les paysans, disait à l'un, à l'autre: "D'où est-tu, toi?" ... Alors, je dis à Basin: "Voyez, Basin, parlez-leur un peu aussi." Mon mari qui n'est pas toujours très inventif ... —Merci Oriane, dit le duc sans s'interrompre de la lecture de mon article où il était plongé— ... avisa un paysan et lui répéta textuellement la question de son frère: "Et toi, d'où es-tu? —Je suis des Laumes. —Tu es des Laumes? Eh bien, je suis ton prince." Alors le paysan regarda la figure toute glabre de Basin et lui répondit: "Pas vrai. Vous, vous êtes un English."

["I was telling you that in those days Basin was clean-shaven. One day, at a
pilgrimage . . . my brother-in-law Charlus, who always enjoys talking to peasants,
was saying to one after another: 'Where do you come from?' . . . So then I said to
Basin: 'Come, Basin, say something to them too.' My husband, who is not always
very inventive ..." ("Thank you, Oriane," said the Duke, without interrupting
his reading of my article in which he was immersed) "... went up to one of the
peasants and repeated his brother's question in so many words: 'Where do you
come from?' 'I'm from Les Laumes.' 'You're from Les Laumes? Why, I'm your
Prince.' Then the peasant looked at Basin's hairless face and replied: 'That ain't
true. *You*'re an English.' "]

(IV, 164; V, 669)[1]

In each version the speaker is Mme de Guermantes, and the occasion is a
pilgrimage to a provincial shrine, though the subject of the anecdote, and
its location, are different: the first takes place in Brittany, the second in the
Saône-et-Loire region; the 'hero' of the first is the prince de Léon, of the
second Mme de Guermantes's husband. Both versions have a French aristocrat announcing his authentic rank to a French peasant, only for the
peasant to deny the claim—apologetically in the first version, forcefully
in the second. In the first version it is the aristocrat's 'culottes beiges', in
the second his 'figure toute glabre', which suggest to the peasant that he is
not French at all, but English.[2] It is a richly packed story, which speaks of
the aristocrat's post-Revolutionary yearning for recognition of his
authenticity, and of the comic anxiety to which it gives rise. Moreover it
tells us that, however fashionable the English *gentleman* or *milord* may be,
the French aristocrat wants to be known as prince of his own land and
people, in a context—that of Catholic devotion—which traditionally
binds the upper and lower classes together. 'Un English' is any old
English; it is not a compliment but a demotion.

The first anecdote has for its frame Marcel's account of his visits to
Mme de Guermantes, whom he has long ago ceased to love, and who has
dwindled in his life to a charming, friendly neighbour. Marcel appreciates
her now for the flavour of her speech, which he relishes as though it were

---

[1] Proust did not live to see either *La Prisonnière* or *Albertine disparue* through the press.
His brother Robert spotted the duplication and deleted the second occurrence of the anecdote, but then changed his mind. The 'article' which the Duke is reading has been published in *Le Figaro*: see below, p. 171.

[2] The English at this period were held to have abandoned their beards, except the
(francophile) Prince of Wales (*Pléiade* note, IV, 1099).

'un livre écrit en langage d'autrefois' [a book written in the language of long ago]:

J'avais assez de liberté d'esprit pour goûter dans ce qu'elle disait cette grâce française si pure qu'on ne trouve plus, ni dans le parler, ni dans les écrits du temps présent. J'écoutais sa conversation comme une chanson populaire délicieusement française, je comprenais que je l'eusse entendue se moquer de Maeterlinck . . . comme je comprenais que Mérimée se moquât de Baudelaire, Stendhal de Balzac, Paul-Louis Courier de Victor Hugo, Meilhac de Mallarmé. Je comprenais bien que le moqueur avait une pensée bien restreinte auprès de celui dont il se moquait, mais aussi un vocabulaire plus pur. Celui de Mme de Guermantes . . . l'était à un point qui enchantait. Ce n'est pas dans les froids pastiches des écrivains d'aujourd'hui . . . qu'on retrouve le vieux langage et la vraie prononciation des mots, mais en causant avec une Mme de Guermantes ou une Françoise. J'avais appris de la deuxième, dès l'âge de cinq ans, qu'on ne dit pas le Tarn, mais le Tar, pas le Béarn, mais le Béar. Ce qui fit qu'à vingt ans, quand j'allai dans le monde, je n'eus pas à y apprendre qu'il ne fallait pas dire, comme faisait Mme Bontemps: Madame de Béar*n*.

Je mentirais en disant que ce côté terrien et quasi paysan qui restait en elle, la duchesse n'en avait pas conscience et ne mettait pas une certaine affectation à le montrer. Mais de sa part, c'était moins fausse simplicité de grande dame qui joue la campagnarde et orgueil de duchesse qui fait la nique aux dames riches méprisantes des paysans qu'elles ne connaissent pas, que goût quasi artistique d'une femme qui sait le charme de ce qu'elle possède et ne va pas le gâter d'un badigeon moderne. C'est de la même façon que tout le monde a connu à Dives un restaurateur normand, propriétaire de *Guillaume-le-Conquérant*, qui s'était bien gardé—chose très rare— de donner à son hôtellerie le luxe moderne d'un hôtel et qui, lui-même millionnaire, gardait le parler, la blouse d'un paysan normand et vous laissait venir le voir faire lui-même dans la cuisine, comme à la campagne, un dîner qui n'en était pas moins infiniment meilleur et encore plus cher que dans les plus grands palaces. . . .

S'il n'y avait aucune affectation, aucune volonté de fabriquer un langage à soi, alors cette façon de prononcer était un vrai musée d'histoire de France par la conversation. "Mon grand-oncle Fitt-jam" n'avait rien qui étonnait, car on sait que les Fitz-James proclament volontiers qu'ils sont de grands seigneurs français et ne veulent pas qu'on prononce leur nom à l'anglaise. . . .

Une fois que je demandais à Mme de Guermantes qui était un jeune homme exquis qu'elle m'avait présenté comme son neveu et dont j'avais mal entendu le nom, ce nom, je ne le distinguai pas davantage quand, du fond de sa gorge, la duchesse émit très fort, mais sans articuler: "C'est l' . . . i Éon, frère à Robert. Il prétend qu'il a la forme du crâne des anciens Gallois." Alors je compris qu'elle avait dit: c'est le petit Léon (le prince de Léon, beau-frère, en effet, de Robert de Saint-Loup). "En tout cas, je ne sais pas s'il en a le crâne, ajouta-t-elle, mais sa façon de s'habiller, qui a du reste beaucoup de chic, n'est guère de là-bas. Un jour que, de Josselin . . .

[I was sufficiently detached to enjoy in what she said that pure charm of the French language which we no longer find either in the speech or in the writing of the present day. I listened to her conversation as to a folk song deliciously and purely French; I understood why I should have heard her deriding Maeterlinck . . . as I understood why Mérimée had derided Baudelaire, Stendhal Balzac, Paul-Louis Courier Victor Hugo, Meilhac Mallarmé. I was well aware that the critic had a far more restricted outlook than his victim, but also a purer vocabulary. That of Mme de Guermantes . . . was enchantingly pure. It is not in the bloodless pastiches of the writers of today . . . that we recapture the old speech and the true pronunciation of words, but in conversing with a Mme de Guermantes or a Françoise. I had learned from the latter, when I was five years old, that one did not say "the Tarn" but "the Tar"; not "Béarn" but "Béar." The effect of which was that at twenty, when I began to go into society, I had no need to be taught there that one ought not to say, like Mme Bontemps, "Madame de Béarn."

It would not be true to say that the Duchess was unaware of this earthy and quasi-peasant quality that survived in her, or was entirely innocent of affectation in displaying it. But, on her part, it was not so much the false simplicity of a great lady aping the countrywoman, or the pride of a duchess bent on snubbing the rich ladies who express contempt for the peasants whom they do not know, as the quasi-artistic preference of a woman who knows the charm of what she possesses and is not going to spoil it with a coat of modern varnish. In the same way, everybody used to know a Norman innkeeper, landlord of the "William the Conqueror" at Dives, who had carefully refrained—a rare thing indeed—from giving his hostelry the modern comforts of a hotel, and, albeit a millionaire, retained the speech and the smock of a Norman peasant and allowed you to enter his kitchen and watch him prepare with his own hands, as in a farmhouse, a dinner which was nevertheless infinitely better, and even more expensive, than in the most luxurious hotel. . . .

If there was no affectation, no deliberate effort to fabricate a special language, then this style of pronunciation was a regular museum of French history displayed in conversation. "My great-uncle Fitt-jam" was not at all surprising, for we know that the Fitz-James family are proud to boast that they are French nobles and do not like to hear their name pronounced in the English fashion. . . .

On one occasion when I asked Mme de Guermantes who a young blood was whom she had introduced to me as her nephew but whose name I had failed to catch, I was none the wiser when from the back of her throat the Duchess uttered in a very loud but quite inarticulate voice: "*C'est l'*. . . *i Eon, frère à Robert.* He claims to have the same shape of skull as the ancient Welsh." Then I realised that she had said: "*C'est le petit Léon,*" and that this was the Prince de

Léon, who was indeed Robert de Saint-Loup's brother-in-law. "I know nothing about his skull," she went on, "but the way he dresses, and I must say he does dress very well, is not at all in the style of those parts. Once when I was staying at Josselin . . .]

(III, 543–5; V, 29–32)

And so the first version of the anecdote follows. The context for the second version is very different. It forms part of the episode in which, after Swann's death, Mme de Guermantes finally agrees to receive his daughter Gilberte. Marcel becomes aware of this development when he pays a visit to Mme de Guermantes and finds Gilberte there; and in the course of the conversation Gilberte makes a reference to M. de Guermantes's fine beard:

—Oui, il porte la barbe maintenant que tout le monde est rasé, dit la duchesse, il ne fait jamais rien comme personne. Quand nous nous sommes mariés, il se rasait non seulement la barbe mais la moustache. Les paysans qui ne le connaissaient pas ne croyaient pas qu'il était français. Il s'appelait à ce moment le prince des Laumes.—Est-ce qu'il y a encore un prince des Laumes?" demanda Gilberte qui était intéressée par tout ce qui touchait des gens qui n'avaient pas voulu lui dire bonjour pendant si longtemps. "Mais non, répondit avec un regard mélancolique et caressant la duchesse.—Un si joli titre! Un des plus beaux titres français!" dit Gilberte, un certain ordre de banalités venant inévitablement, comme l'heure sonne, dans la bouche de certaines personnes intelligentes. "Eh bien oui, je regrette aussi. Basin voudrait que le fils de sa sœur le relevât, mais ce n'est pas la même chose; au fond ça pourrait être parce que ce n'est pas forcément le fils aîné, cela peut passer de l'aîné au cadet. Je vous disais que Basin était alors tout rasé . . .

["Yes, he wears a beard now that everybody else is clean-shaven," said the Duchess. "He never does anything that other people do. When we were first married, he shaved not only his beard but his moustache as well. The peasants who didn't know him by sight thought he couldn't be French. At that time he was called the Prince des Laumes."

"Is there still a Prince des Laumes?" asked Gilberte, who was interested in everything that concerned the people who had refused to acknowledge her existence during all those years.

"Why, no," the Duchess replied with a melancholy, caressing gaze.

"Such a charming title! One of the finest titles in France!" said Gilberte, a certain sort of banality springing inevitably, as a clock strikes the hour, to the lips of certain quite intelligent persons.

"Ah, yes, I'm sorry too. Basin would like his sister's son to adopt it, but it isn't the same thing; though it would be possible, since it doesn't have to be the eldest son, it can be passed to a younger brother. I was telling you that in those days Basin was clean-shaven . . .]

(IV, 163–4; V, 668–9)

The second version of the anecdote now follows. When it is finished Marcel adds a comment, which in turn leads into an episode which we have already encountered:

On voyait ainsi dans ces petits récits de la duchesse ces grands titres éminents, comme celui de prince des Laumes, surgir, à leur place vraie, dans leur état ancien et leur couleur locale, comme dans certains livres d'heures on reconnaît, au milieu de la foule de l'époque, la flèche de Bourges. On apporta des cartes qu'un valet de pied venait de déposer. "Je ne sais pas ce qui lui prend, je ne la connais pas. C'est à vous que je dois ça, Basin. Ça ne vous a pourtant pas si bien réussi ce genre de relations, mon pauvre ami", et se tournant vers Gilberte: "Je ne saurais même pas vous expliquer qui c'est, vous ne la connaissez certainement pas, elle s'appelle Lady Rufus Israël." Gilberte rougit vivement . . .

[In these little anecdotes of the Duchess's, such great and eminent titles as that of Prince des Laumes seemed to stand out in one's mind's eye in their true setting, in their original state and their local colour, as in certain Books of Hours one recognises amid the medieval crowd the soaring steeple of Bourges. Some visiting-cards were brought to her which a footman had just left at the door. "I can't think what's got into her, I don't know her. It's to you that I'm indebted for this, Basin. Although that sort of acquaintance hasn't done you much good, my poor dear," and, turning to Gilberte: "I really don't know how to explain to you who she is, you've certainly never heard of her, she's called Lady Rufus Israels." Gilberte flushed crimson . . .]

(IV, 164; V, 669–70)[3]

I have discussed this last incident in Chapter 2; it concerns Gilberte's shameful repudiation of her own great-aunt, Lady Israël, an action which signifies her willingness to cut herself off from her father's name, race, and memory. It is a bleaker frame for Mme de Guermantes' 'petit récit', as *Albertine disparue* is a bleaker volume than *La Prisonnière*, but the two versions of the story communicate eloquently with each other and tell us something which goes beyond the painful social comedy of *A la recherche*, piercing though that is; preoccupied with words and names, they suggest something profound, constitutive, about the language from which the novel is made.

---

[3] *Vintage* standardizes on 'Israels' for this name; see Ch. 2, n. 45.

Let us return to the context of the first anecdote, Marcel's relish for Mme de Guermantes's old-fashioned speech. Already, in *Le Côté de Guermantes II*, he had spoken of this pleasure, noting that Mme de Guermantes 'n'usait guère que du pur vocabulaire dont eût pu se servir un vieil auteur français' [rarely strayed beyond the pure vocabulary that might have been used by an old French writer] (II, 785; III, 572). Here again, the term *pur* recurs: 'cette grâce française si pure qu'on ne trouve plus, ni dans le parler, ni dans les écrits du temps présent . . . un vocabulaire plus pur'. Mme de Guermantes's vocabulary is pure 'à un point qui enchantait'. Marcel recognizes that this purity is, in some respects, artificial, but it is excusably so because it is not a snobbish affectation but '[un] goût quasi artistique'; and he compares it to the deliberate (and extremely profitable) old-fangledness of a restaurateur in Normandy who knew better than to spoil a good thing by modernizing his business.

Dives is the neighbouring town to Cabourg, and there really was a restaurant named 'Guillaume-le-Conquérant'; Dives was the port from which William the Conqueror sailed in 1066. Whether these real names would have survived had Proust seen this volume through the press cannot be known. That of the restaurant, at least, is felicitous, because it alludes to a victory over the English—and, in the French form of William's name, a victory over English, too.[4] The victory is completed by the fact that this cannily authentic French restaurant is better *and more expensive* than 'les plus grands palaces'—for 'palace', remember, was an English import, one which Proust applies to luxury establishments such as the Grand Hotel at Balbec.[5] Yet this historical allusion also reminds us that, after all, the main *linguistic* result of the Norman conquest of England was not the preservation of 'purity' but its opposite.

The point about the restaurant fits into a pattern of allusion to issues of national identity between France and England; the pronunciation of

---

[4] Mallarmé's historical survey, in *Les Mots anglais*, begins with this point: 'Tout le monde sait bien que l'ancien Français entre pour une portion pas médiocre dans l'Anglais actuel . . . et que cela résulte de la Conquête de l'Angleterre par les Normands, sous la conduite de Guillaume-le-Conquérant en 1066. Combats, défaites et victoires entre les mots ainsi qu'entre les hommes' [Everyone knows that Old French is largely present in modern English . . . and that this results from the Conquest of England by the Normans, under the command of William the Conqueror in 1066. Combats, defeats and victories between words as well as between men] (pp. 11–12). See below for more on Mallarmé's work. One of Proust's favourite books in adolescence was Augustin Thierry's *Histoire de la conquête de l'Angleterre par les Normands*.   [5] For 'palace' see Ch. 3, n. 15.

'Fitt-Jam' for the naturalized 'Fitz-James' is one such issue, and the mistaking of the prince de Léon for 'un englische' is another. The story about the prince de Léon, however, opens up another front. Mme de Guermantes makes fun of a young man dressed in the latest fashion who lays claim not simply to feudal homage, but to an even more ancient and primitive status. 'Il prétend qu'il a la forme du crâne des anciens Gallois,' Mme de Guermantes says. She is mocking the fashion for racial and ethnic 'science' which was such a feature of late nineteenth-century intellectual culture, and which in France took the form of analysing the different characteristics of the three 'races' which supposedly made up France, the Franks, the Gauls, and the Celts. Paul Broca, who founded the Anthropological Society in 1869, was the main proponent of craniology in this field; he published works such as *Instructions craniologiques et craniométriques* (1869), and his method could be applied with surreal refinement: one enthusiast claimed to be able to make 5,000 measurements on a single skull.[6] The prince de Léon is claiming racial solidarity with the Celtic inhabitants of Brittany; his *chic* outfit, however, is not of a piece with Breton peasant wear. The irony of his being mistaken for an Englishman is politically, socially, and linguistically barbed.

It is in Mme de Guermantes's conversation that Marcel finds the true 'old' French, as opposed to 'les froids pastiches des écrivains d'aujourd'hui'. For good measure he adds the conversation of Françoise, the family servant who, along with Mme de Guermantes, represents a form of archetypal Frenchness in mentality and speech. Françoise is of peasant stock, though several generations removed from the land; Proust juxtaposes her with the duchess to emphasize that the authentic lineage of the French language is not a matter of nominal rank but of pure descent, which is found at either end of the social scale, but not in the middle. Both versions of the anecdote have aristocrats attempting to commune with their 'natural' inferiors, who are also their allies against the rootless, mobile, social-climbing middle classes. The comedy of their failure is a wounding reflection on the values which the aristocracy is supposed still to enshrine in the period, but it leaves untouched the linguistic authority which Mme de Guermantes embodies.

---

[6] Zeldin, II, 10–12. In Jacques Boulenger's *Un professeur de snobisme* (see Ch. 1, p. 25 n. 25), the narrator asks Sir Richard Fawcett 'À quoi tient la supériorité des Anglo-Saxons' [To what do the Anglo-Saxons owe their superiority?], and receives the reply: 'Principalement à la forme de leur tête' [Mainly to the shape of their heads] (p. 10). The French, apparently, have round heads on which hats look ridiculous.

This authority rests in the spoken, not the written word; it was a commonplace of philological theory that speech was a more conservative form of language than writing, more tenacious both of older forms of expression and of local or regional peculiarities; yet even speech can be undermined and corrupted, especially in cities; this is what eventually happens to Françoise's beautiful French, polluted by her daughter's Parisian slang. Paradoxically, it is by absorbing as a child Françoise's old-fashioned, peasant pronunciation of names such as 'Tarn' and 'Béarn' that the bourgeois Marcel can enter an aristocratic world where these forms are also preserved, without committing the solecisms which would expose his bourgeois ignorance. Although Marcel denies that Mme de Guermantes, in showing her aristocratic affinity with the peasantry, is cocking a snook at new money, his own scorn for Mme Bontemps does indeed draw a social line between those who are initiated—by birth or, in his own case, sensibility—and those who are not.

Marcel's appreciation of Mme de Guermantes's 'deliciously French' speech begins with a series of literary comparisons which reflect on Proust's own art. In each case the pair of writers signifies a contrast between pure and impure language, and in each case the impure is the greater writer. The *Pléiade* editors scrupulously unpick Proust's pairings, pointing out for example that Mérimée argued against the censoring of *Les Fleurs du mal* and that Stendhal admired Balzac with only a few reservations, but Proust's point stands up quite well if we think of the contrast as between styles of writing which spring from fundamentally opposed conceptions of art, one of which is conservative and sceptical, the other modern and experimental. From everything we know about Proust's critical judgement, both within *A la recherche* and in his other works, including his letters, it is clear where his own position in any such pairing would be. There are a number of candidates for the other, lesser writer against whom he might be measured, among them Anatole France and, more controversially, Flaubert, but no such pairing needs to be specified here. A still more significant contrast suggests itself between Proust and Marcel; on occasion the character has a greater belief in linguistic 'purity' than his author. When Françoise begins to adopt her daughter's Parisian slang, Marcel not only notices the phenomenon, but generalizes it: 'Ainsi perdent leur pureté toutes les langues par l'adjonction des termes nouveaux' [So it is that all languages lose their purity by the addition of new words], and he uses phrases which connote whole periods of history rather than the life-span of an individual:

Cette décadence du parler de Françoise, que j'avais connu à ses belles époques . . . La fille de Françoise . . . [avait] fait dégénérer jusqu'au plus bas jargon le langage classique de sa mère . . . elle se mit à parler avec sa fille un français qui devint bien vite celui des plus basses époques.

[This decadence of Françoise's speech, which I had known in its golden period . . . Françoise's daughter . . . [had] made her mother's classic language degenerate into the vilest slang . . . she took to conversing with her daughter in a French which rapidly became that of the most debased epochs.]

(III, 660–1; V, 169–70)

Marcel's lament is thoroughly conventional, and takes for granted the value-judgement which identifies 'le langage classique' as ancient and pure, and 'le plus bas jargon' as decadent and a product of 'les plus basses époques'. As so often in *A la recherche*, Marcel here echoes not the author of the novel but that author's earlier incarnation—the Proust who wrote a manifesto in 1896 called 'Contre l'obscurité', in which he praised

ces affinités anciennes et mystérieuses entre notre langage maternelle et notre sensibilité qui, au lieu d'un langage conventionnel comme sont les langues étrangères, en font une sorte de musique latente que le poète peut faire résonner en nous avec une douceur incomparable. Il rajeunit un mot en le prenant dans une vieille acception . . . à tout moment il nous fait respirer avec délices le parfum de la terre natale. Là est pour nous le charme natal du parler de France . . .

[those ancient and mysterious affinities between our mother tongue and our sensibility which make of it, instead of a conventional discourse as with foreign languages, a sort of latent music which the poet can cause to resonate in us with incomparable sweetness. He rejuvenates a word by taking it in an old sense . . . each moment he makes us breathe in with delight the scent of our native land. In that resides for us the native charm of the speech of France . . .][7]

Proust's language conforms—something that can rarely be said of it—to a set of received ideas about the intrinsic value of old-fashioned language;

---

[7] 'Contre l'obscurité', *La Revue blanche*, 15 July 1896, in *CSB* 393. Saint-Saëns has the same skill: 'Il sait rajeunir une formule en l'employant dans sa vieille acception, et prendre, pour ainsi dire, chaque phrase musicale, dans son sens étymologique' [He knows how to rejuvenate a motif by employing it according to its old usage, and to take each musical phrase, so to speak, in its etymological sense] ('Figures parisiennes: Camille Saint-Saëns', *Le Gaulois*, 14 Dec. 1895, in *CSB* 385).

both the ideas, and the ready-made expressions to which they gave rise, can be found in, for example, Émile Guénard's polemical preface to his study of a local dialect, *Le Patois de Courtisols*, published in 1905.[8] Guénard was a school-teacher in Chantilly, and a corresponding member of the Société d'Agriculture, Commerce, Sciences et Arts de la Marne; but he saw his local patriotism in a national context, placing a motto above his preface: *Pro Patria semper*. In addition to familiar attacks on *anglomanie*, Guénard insists on the importance of the conservation of local dialects not just for their own sake, but for what they represent:

Il importe de réagir contre une tendance fâcheuse et antifrançaise. Il faut faire connaître les richesses de notre patrimoine national . . . Il est nécessaire de remettre en honneur des expressions pittoresques, d'une saveur locale exquise . . . qui ont le grand mérite de nous rappeler la parlure de nos aïeux, la langue des chroniqueurs du moyen âge.

[It is incumbent on us to react against a harmful and anti-French tendency. We ought to make known the riches of our national heritage . . . It is necessary to restore the lustre of those picturesque expressions which have an exquisite local savour . . . which have the great merit of reminding us of the speech of our ancestors, the language of the chroniclers of the Middle Ages.][9]

But Proust's novel could not exist on these terms. On the contrary, the language of *A la recherche* springs from a recognition that the 'parfum de la terre natale' is all too charming, all too seductive. The 'patrimoine national' may actually be an impoverishing, not an enriching resource. '[Q]uand on était fatigué du composite et bigarré langage moderne,' Marcel remarks in *Le Côté de Guermantes II*, 'c'était, tout en sachant qu'elle exprimait bien moins de choses, un grand repos d'écouter la causerie de Mme de Guermantes' [when one was tired of the composite patchwork of modern speech, it was very restful to listen to Mme de

---

[8] *Le Patois de Courtisols; ses rapports avec les Patois marnais*, Châlons-sur-Marne: Imprimerie de l'Union Républicaine de la Marne, 1905. 'Patois' here means 'dialect'; it has positive connotations for Guénard, but can also be used disparagingly: an unimportant, 'provincial' language, or, referring to modern speech, 'jargon'; Remy de Gourmont has both these negative senses.

[9] Ferdinand Brunot was as sceptical of this position as he was of Remy de Gourmont's (see below, p. 179): 'L'amour-propre national ne fera point d'autres miracles que l'amour de Dieu, tant qu'angliciser sera considéré comme une élégance' [National self-love will not accomplish miracles any more than the love of God as long as anglicizing is seen as fashionable] (p. 812).

Guermantes's talk, even though one knew it could express far fewer things] (II, 785; III, 572). But writers cannot be lotus-eaters. 'Purity' is not only a restraining force on the imagination, but a sterilizing one; in another passage from *Le Côté de Guermantes II* in which Mme de Guermantes's authentic native speech is savoured, Marcel recognizes that 'la pureté même du langage de la duchesse était un signe de limitation . . . en elle l'intelligence et la sensibilité étaient restées fermées à toutes les nouveautés' [the very purity of the Duchess's language was a sign of limitation . . . in her, both intelligence and sensibility had remained closed against innovation] (II, 792; III, 581). When, therefore, he describes Mme de Guermantes's conversation as 'un vrai musée d'histoire de France', his admiring phrase is charged with ironic reservation. Proust did not see himself as the curator of such a museum. He loved the chroniclers of the Middle Ages—*A la recherche* is full of affectionate references to them—but he did not want to enlist as one of their number nine centuries late.

If we turn to the context in which the second version of Mme de Guermantes's anecdote is set, we can see this limitation of 'pure' French in theme as well as vocabulary. In Mme de Guermantes's speech, old titles of nobility such as 'prince des Laumes' have an authentic flavour, because they are in their proper place, complete with local colour, as the cathedral spire of Bourges 'belongs' in a Book of Hours, the literary museum of the age of faith. But the particular example of the 'des Laumes' title has other, less 'pure' associations. The story is set in motion by Gilberte's drawing attention to M. de Guermantes's luxuriant beard, a traditional sign of virility. Mme de Guermantes's mind goes back to the time when her husband did not wear a beard, and she adds—with what seems puzzling irrelevance—that in those days he went under the title of prince des Laumes. Gilberte is too ignorant to repress her curiosity, but the silent Marcel understands the reason for Mme de Guermantes's melancholy look as she explains that the title 'prince des Laumes' no longer exists. It is the title borne by the heir, in the male line, to the duchy of Guermantes, and Mme de Guermantes is childless. That is why she made the association between Basin's beardless state and his former title; as a young couple they might have expected to have children, but the prince des Laumes became in due course duc de Guermantes, and grew his beard, without fertilizing his wife, to whom he has been persistently unfaithful. Mme de Guermantes stays on this theme in thinking about her husband's friendship with Lady Israël, which represents a form of social cross-fertilization, and for which she uses the same word which, as we have seen, is used in horticulture, when she says to Basin 'Ça ne vous a pourtant pas si bien réussi ce genre de relations'.[10] Her own childlessness and Basin's unfruitful social relations are brought into contact; nor is it coincidence that this should happen in the aftermath of Gilberte's inane exclamation about the title 'des Laumes', 'Un si joli titre! Un des plus beaux titres français!' There is something truly French about the title which has been lost, yet Mme de Guermantes acidly notes that cultivating the un-French Jews with the English title and name has done her unfaithful husband no good.

The point of the anecdote for Mme de Guermantes may be to express some of her complex feelings about her marriage, but it is a different matter for Marcel. Let us remind ourselves of what M. de Guermantes is doing while his wife entertains their guests with her pure French conversation. He is reading an article by Marcel in *Le Figaro*, the first allusion in the novel to its narrator's literary vocation. Unlikely though it seems, Marcel insists that this article is no more than a reworking of the piece he wrote at Combray when he was little more than a child, on his way home in Doctor Percepied's carriage; it described three church towers whose dance of perspective, as they changed places according to the turns in the road, offered him a vision of the shifting, unstable nature of reality, and gave him his first taste of the delight of the artist who translates this vision into enduring form. This episode takes place towards the end of the 'Combray' section of *Du côté de chez Swann*; when he finishes writing, perched beside the driver in the doctor's carriage, on the seat where the poultry basket rests on market day, Marcel is overcome with pleasure: 'je me trouvai si heureux . . . que, comme si j'avais été moi-même une poule et si je venais de pondre un œuf, je me mis à chanter à tue-tête' [I was so filled with happiness . . . that, as though I myself were a hen and had just laid an egg, I began to sing at the top of my voice] (I, 180; I, 218). No wonder Mme de Guermantes's thoughts stray to her sterile youth, and to her unwilling husband, cock to any number of other hens, his attention entirely taken up by—metaphorically speaking—a fertilized egg.

---

[10] For this use of 'réussir', see Ch. 3, p. 149 n. 52.

Du pur vocabulaire

In the preface to his treatise, *Esthétique de la langue française*, Remy de Gourmont offers a definition which constitutes, at first sight, a challenge to the aesthetic foundations of *A la recherche*: 'Esthétique de la langue française, cela veut dire: examen des conditions dans lesquelles la langue française doit évoluer pour maintenir sa beauté, c'est-à-dire sa pureté originelle' [Aesthetic of the French language, that means: an examination of the conditions in which the French language must evolve in order to maintain its beauty, that is to say its original purity] (p. xiv). Whatever doubts Proust may have on the subject of the relations between 'beauty' and 'purity', Gourmont has none. The first chapter opens by dissociating aesthetic value from signification, and Gourmont finds this (let us say 'French') way of putting it: 'la signification d'un mot ni l'intelligence d'une femme n'ajoutent rien ni n'enlèvent rien à la pureté de leur forme. Pureté: voilà le déterminatif' [neither the signification of a word nor the intelligence of a woman add or subtract anything to the purity of their shape.

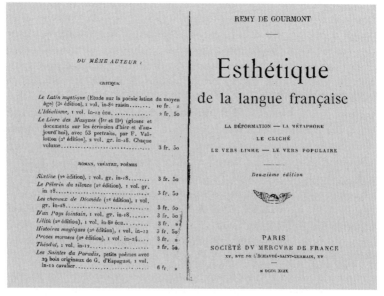

13. Title-page of Remy de Gourmont's *Esthétique de la langue française*, 1899.

Purity: that is the determining factor] (p. 1). The point is made again, more forcefully and with a wider scope, in the peroration to the essay:[11]

La beauté d'un mot est tout entière dans sa pureté, dans son originalité, dans sa race . . . nous avons cru que notre parler traditionnel devait accueillir tous les mots étrangers qu'on lui présente et nous avons pris pour un perpétuel enrichissement ce qui est le signe exact d'une indigence heureusement simulée. Il n'est pas possible qu'une langue littérairement aussi vivante ait perdu sa vieille puissance verbale; il suffira sans doute que l'on proscrive à l'avenir tout mot grec, tout mot anglais, toutes syllabes étrangères à l'idiome, pour que, convaincu par la nécessité, le français retrouve sa virilité, son orgueil et même son insolence. Il vaut mieux, à tout prendre, renoncer à l'expression d'une idée que de la formuler en patois. Il n'est pas nécessaire d'écrire; mais si l'on écrit il faut que cela soit en une langue véridique et de bonne couleur. (p. 68)

[The beauty of a word rests entirely in its purity, in its authentic origin, in its racial descent . . . we thought that our traditional speech should make welcome all the foreign words presented to it, and we mistook for a continuous process of enrichment what is in fact the sign of a cleverly disguised indigence. It is not possible that a language so literarily alive should have lost its old verbal potency; no doubt it will suffice to banish from our idiom in the future every Greek word, every English word, all foreign syllables, for French, driven by necessity, to recover its virility, its pride, and even its insolence. It is better, when all is said and done, to renounce the expression of an idea than to formulate it in jargon. It is not necessary to write; but if one does write, let it be in a language which is authentic and in a healthy state.]

Gourmont's rhetoric carries social, economic, and political meanings; the first edition of the essay was published in 1899, in the midst of the Dreyfus Affair; in *A la recherche* we find the word 'étrangers' applied to the Jews, even (or especially) when referring to naturalized or converted Jews like Swann and Bloch.[12] The idea that foreign imports are impoverishing the country, not enriching it, fits this analogy, as does that of an over-generous

---

[11] The volume containing *Esthétique de la langue française* opens with a ten-chapter essay bearing this title, followed by a series of separate pieces; this passage comes near the end of the tenth chapter.

[12] For example: ' "Vous n'avez pas tort, si vous voulez vous instruire, me dit M. de Charlus après m'avoir posé ces questions sur Bloch, d'avoir parmi vos amis quelques étrangers." Je répondis que Bloch était français. "Ah! dit M. de Charlus, j'avais cru qu'il était juif" ' ["It is not a bad idea, if you wish to learn about life," went on M. de Charlus when he had finished questioning me about Bloch, "to have a few foreigners among your friends." I replied that Bloch was French. "Indeed," said M. de Charlus, "I took him to be a Jew"] (II, 584; III, 330).

hospitality towards foreign words, followed by an absolute proscription: we can 'translate' such terms, for example, into the reaction against Lady Israël, whose acquaintance Robert de Saint-Loup's mother, Mme de Marsantes, decides to cut: 'Du reste, nous avons tous été trop confiants, trop hospitaliers. Je ne fréquenterai plus personne de cette nation. Pendant qu'on avait de vieux cousins de province du même sang, à qui on fermait sa porte, on l'ouvrait aux Juifs' [Besides, we have all been too trusting, too hospitable. I shall never go near anyone of that race again. While we closed our doors to old country cousins, people of our own flesh and blood, we threw them open to Jews] (II, 550; III, 289). By the same token, we can translate these 'vieux cousins de province du même sang' back into linguistic terms, to match the 'vocabulaire plus pur' which Marcel finds in certain writers, or in Mme de Guermantes's conversation, so evocative of 'native' Frenchness. And the same note recurs in the conversation of the two maids, the sisters Marie and Céleste, whom Marcel meets at the Grand Hotel in Balbec during his second visit.[13] Mme de Guermantes is herself from the provinces, and takes a pleasure in distinguishing one provincial accent from another which would be unknown to that heterodox creature, 'une Parisienne d'origine' (III, 546; V, 33). As for Marie and Céleste, they were born 'au pied des hautes montagnes du centre de la France, au bord de ruisseaux et de torrents' [at the foot of the high mountains in the centre of France, on the banks of rivulets and torrents] (III, 240; IV, 282); their provincial origin is central, defined by mountain and torrent, natural and mythic signs of sublime stability and life-giving motion. Their *parler* would delight Remy de Gourmont, as it delights Marcel, because it evinces an untutored native literary genius, entirely unaffected by outside influences; Gourmont would also approve of the fact that, although they are in the service of 'une dame étrangère', 'elles détestaient de confiance les Anglais, les Allemands, les Russes, les Italiens, la "vermine" des étrangers et n'aimaient, avec des exceptions, que les Français' [they heartily detested the English, the Germans, the Russians, the Italians, all foreign "vermin," and cared, with certain exceptions, for French people alone] (III, 243; IV, 285). But we should pause

---

[13] These characters were based on Proust's housekeeper Céleste Albaret and her sister Marie Gineste: see *Pléiade* note, III, 1476, and Céleste's memoir, *Monsieur Proust*, 115–16. Their native region, the Lozère, is further south than we would think 'central', though the French name for the south, 'le Midi', which also means 'noon', indicates where the country's centre of gravity is felt to be.

over what Marcel goes on to say about these untaught poets of French speech, for it tacitly reminds us, again, that *A la recherche* could not have been composed in such a language: 'Elles ne liront jamais de livres, mais n'en feront jamais non plus' [They will never read any books, but neither will they ever write any] (III, 243; IV, 286). Here too, in the very heart of France and of the French language, sterility threatens the writer.

Gourmont's rhetoric takes in hatred of foreign vermin, and he joins to this an anxiety about gender. Foreign words weaken the native potency of the language, threaten it with effeminacy and degeneration; these were all accusations levelled at the Jews during the Dreyfus Affair. A fantasy of rescue accompanies such anxieties: severe proscription will ensure that French recovers its virility and its insolence, the curled lip of a top dog. At the same time, Gourmont proposes to support this recovery with a self-denying ordinance, by which writers would choose *not to express* ideas rather than use adulterated language. It would be hard to imagine a greater heresy against Proust's artistic faith.

Gourmont toys with the notion of an aboriginally pure French language, unaffected even by Latin, which might have developed from the dialect of the Île-de-France.[14] Such a language would have had 'un caractère très original, très pur'; but though Latin may in the past have been a bad master, it is now a good servant:

peut-être faut-il regretter la longue tutelle qu'elle [la langue française] a subie au cours des siècles. Peut-être; à moins que la présence du latin n'ait été au contraire particulièrement bienfaisante; à moins que, comme un vigilant chien de garde, le latin, posté au seuil du palais verbal, n'ait eu pour mission d'étrangler au passage les mots étrangers et d'arrêter ainsi l'invasion qui, à l'heure actuelle, menace très sérieusement de déformer sans remède et d'humilier au rang de patois notre parler orgueilleux de sa noblesse et de sa beauté.

Je crois vraiment qu'en face de l'anglais et de l'allemand le latin est un chien de garde qu'il faut soigner, nourrir et caresser. (pp. 46–7)

---

[14] Mallarmé has a similar speculative thought about English: 'quelque savant pourrait-il, dans un mémoire curieux, poser ce doute: En supposant que l'Invasion Normande ne se fut pas effectuée . . . trouve-t-on, dans l'Anglo-Saxon d'alors, une vitalité et une force suffisantes, pour que ce langage, par des modifications dues à l'action du temps, produisît, à soi tout seul et sans levain étranger, quelque chose d'assimilable à l'Anglais d'aujourd'hui' [might not some scholar, in an intriguing essay, pose this question: Supposing the Norman Invasion had never occurred . . . can one detect, in the Anglo-Saxon of that time, sufficient vitality and strength for this language, evolving through time, to have produced, on its own and without the leaven of a foreign tongue, something resembling the English of today] (*Les Mots anglais*, 339–40).

[perhaps we should regret the long subservience which the French language has endured over the centuries. Perhaps; unless it be the case that the presence of Latin has been, on the contrary, particularly beneficial; unless it be the case that Latin, a vigilant guard-dog posted at the threshold of the verbal palace, has had the task of strangling foreign words as they came across, thus halting the invasion which, at the present time, seriously threatens to disfigure our speech beyond repair, and to bring it down, with all its pride of nobility and beauty, to the level of a provincial dialect.

Truly I think that, faced as we are with English and German, Latin is a guard-dog we must look after, feed, and cherish.]

Gourmont puns on the fact that 'palais' means 'palate' as well as 'palace'; it is as though Latin guards the physical threshold of speech.[15] The threat of foreign invasion is specifically assigned to France's two major European rivals at this period, and the violence of Gourmont's simile is an index of the anxiety he and others felt at the potential for the French nation, embodied in its language, to be reduced to an ignoble *patois*.

There were plenty of political extremists, then as now, who advocated the expulsion of foreigners from French soil; but Gourmont, to do him justice, questions the practicality, and even the benefit, of such policies in the linguistic domain. He believes in immigration control, but not in linguistic repatriation; on the other hand he is a fierce assimilationist, because his main concern, as he repeatedly emphasizes, is with the form of words. The conditions under which foreign words may settle in French are stringent: 'Un mot étranger ne peut devenir entièrement français que si rien ne rappelle plus son origine; on devra, autant que possible, en effacer toutes les traces' [A foreign word cannot become entirely French unless there is nothing left which recalls its origin; we must, as far as possible, erase all traces of that origin] (p. 38). Gourmont believes that the 'popular' assimilation of foreign words is powerful and effective in this respect, or at least has been so in the past; in a striking phrase he refers to 'le gosier populaire, ce terrible laminoir' [the throat of the people, that terrible rolling-mill] (p. 3). Words which have evaded the rolling-mill of common speech tend to come from learned or scientific sources, for which Gourmont has almost as great a scorn as he does for modern fashion; yet

---

[15] When Odette speaks in English to Gilberte, Marcel comments: 'une langue que nous ne savons pas est un palais clos' [a language which we do not know is a closed palace] (I, 572, my trans.; *Vintage* II, 182 has 'a fortress sealed').

he also concedes that the will to force newly arrived words through the 'rolling-mill' has weakened:

Nous avons de tout temps emprunté des mots aux divers peuples du monde, mais le français possédait alors une volonté d'assimilation qu'il a negligée en grande partie. Aujourd'hui, le mot étranger qui entre dans la langue, au lieu de se fondre dans la couleur générale, reste visible comme une tache. L'enseignement des langues étrangères nous a déjà inclinés au respect d'orthographes et de prononciations qui sont de vilains barbarismes pour nos yeux et nos oreilles. (p. 47)

[Since time immemorial we have borrowed words from the various peoples of the world, but French in the past possessed an assimilative willpower which it has largely neglected. Today, the foreign word which enters our language stands out like a stain instead of melting into the background. The teaching of foreign languages has already made us prone to respect spellings and pronunciations which are vile barbarisms for our eyes and ears.]

Education is to blame, as so often in arguments about the preservation of a national language; language teachers inculcate a misconceived respect for foreign words, which mustn't be bullied in the playground; but it is just this bullying which would knock the ugly newcomers into shape. As it is, they stick out amongst us, wearing their national dress and clinging to their strange ways; worse, they uglify their hosts. Gourmont's 'palais verbale' is also a city under siege: 'Il y a dans les langues une beauté visible que l'on diminue en introduisant dans la cité verbale des figures étrangères' [There is a visible beauty in languages which one diminishes by introducing foreign figures into the city of words] (p. 44). Viennet, in his *Épître à Boileau sur les mots nouveaux* (1855), makes a similar point, here specifically in relation to the 'termes nouveaux' introduced by the new technology of steam:

> La vapeur, renversant douanes et barrières,
> Les fait entrer sans droit par toutes nos frontières.
> On n'entend que des mots à déchirer le fer,
> Le *rail-way*, le *tunnel*, le *ballast*, le *tender*,
> *Express*, *trucks* et *wagons*. ... Une bouche française
> Semble broyer du verre et mâcher de la braise.
>   (pp. 165–70)

[Steam, overturning customs posts and barriers, brings them across all our frontiers without any authority. One hears nothing but words that screech like torn metal . . . For a French mouth it is like chewing glass and cinders.]

Viennet's hostility to these English words rests in part simply on their transgressive foreignness; though Gourmont is not unaffected by such feelings, he is mainly in sympathy with Viennet's distaste for the glass-chewing sensation brought about by trying to pronounce them. He has no objection in principle to foreign words, including English ones, which melt into the local population. Chapter IX of his essay begins with an anecdote about the 'birth' of a new word, the word *lirlie*:

J'entendais donc, à la campagne, appeler des pommes de terre roses hâtives, des *lirlies* roses: on ne put me donner aucune autre explication, et le mot m'étant inutile, je l'oubliai. Dix ans après, en feuilletant un catalogue de grainetier, je fus frappé par le nom d'*early rose* donné à une pomme de terre, et je compris les syllabes du jardinier. . . .
   Voilà un bon exemple et un mot agréable formé par l'heureuse ignorance d'un jardinier. C'est ainsi qu'il faut que la langue dévore tous les mots étrangers qui lui sont nécessaires, qu'elle les rende méconnaissables . . . (p. 58)

[I heard, then, in the country, early pink potatoes called *lirlies roses*: no one could give me any further explanation, and since the word was of no use to me I forgot it. Ten years later, leafing through a seed-merchant's catalogue, I was struck by the name *early rose* given to a potato, and I understood the gardener's syllables. . . .
   Here is a good example and a fine word coined by the happy ignorance of a gardener. This is how the language should devour all the foreign words it needs, and should make them unrecognizable . . .]

It should be stressed that the spelling *lirlie* was Gourmont's; he did not see the word written down, but only heard it spoken. Most words don't enter the language in this way; these call for more deliberate measures: 'Si le mot est venu par l'écriture seule, il faut le réformer et l'écrire comme le prononcerait un paysan ou un ouvrier tout à fait étranger à l'anglais ou à telle autre langue' [If the word has come from writing alone, it must be re-shaped and written as it would be pronounced by a peasant or a working man completely ignorant of English or whichever other language it might be] (p. 59). Gourmont goes on to give a list of words which, if they were subjected to this process of disfigurement, would become accept-able: among others *higuelife, fivocloque, groume, smoquine, yaute, snobe, metingue, clube* (pp. 59–61). In each case French pronunciation does necessary violence to English (*higuelife* in English would rhyme with 'feegleaf'); Gourmont knows that it is fashionable in *le high life* to single out English words such as *le five o'clock* with their 'correct' pronunciation; into the tumbril they go.

Gourmont's position is not entirely consistent. On the one hand he displays a list of words which are *not* being reshaped in the way he thinks should happen, including the word *starter* (at a horse race); but in a footnote to this word he gives a list of English horse-racing terms with what he claims is already their usual French pronunciation: *starteur, brocandeau, flieur, stiple, stayeur, didide, andicape, bêtin, ringue.* Some of these are guessable, but I don't think I would have got 'broken-down' or 'dead-heat'; Gourmont ought to be pleased about this, but his only comment is 'et tout cela est charivaresque!' [what a farce it all is!]. Perhaps the people who mispronounce these words believe that they are pronouncing them correctly; they are not lovers of pure French, merely ignorant and pretentious; but it shouldn't really matter to Gourmont how the desired result comes about as long as it conforms to his aesthetic standard. Ferdinand Brunot pointed out a more serious flaw in Gourmont's position: if *anglomanie* was responsible for people using English words, trying to change the form of the words themselves addressed the symptom, not the disease: 'en fait, la plupart du temps, les gens qui usent des mots anglais désirent . . . les laisser en saillie; quand *smoking-room* sera francisé, ils chercheront ailleurs. Ce n'est pas parce qu'il était utile qu'on l'a pris, puisque nous avions *fumoir*' [in fact, most of the time people who make use of English words want them . . . to stand out; when *smoking-room* is francisized they will look elsewhere. It it not because it was useful that it was taken up, since we already had *fumoir*] (p. 812, n. 2).

This kind of common sense made little difference to the debate; by 1912, when Albert Dauzat published *La Défense de la langue française*, '[la] crise du français' (which might itself be part of a 'crise de la culture française') was a well-established polemical issue. Dauzat is much less hostile to education than Gourmont—he makes the reasonable point that changes in the way people speak and write are part of a much more widespread social and linguistic phenomenon—but his analysis of 'la corruption générale du langage' is both more conventional and more strident:

L'argot, le jargon sportif, le parler populaire, que des évolutions fiévreuses et précipitées—on pourra en juger—ont tellement éloignés de la langue classique, ont acquis une prépondérance si impérieuse qu'ils menacent de rejeter dans les oubliettes le français traditionnel. . . . Une révolution totale menace de submerger la langue, qui double, triple les étapes avec une vitesse toujours plus rapide. (pp. vii–viii)

[Slang, sporting jargon, colloquial speech, which, in fevered and precipitous stages, have become, as anyone can tell, so far removed from the classic form of the language, have acquired so masterful a sway that they threaten to relegate traditional French to oblivion. . . . An all-embracing revolution threatens to engulf the language, one which doubles, triples its pace with ever-increasing speed.]

This is the orthodox position, but it is not quite Gourmont's. In all the examples he gives it is not the mere fact of linguistic change to which he objects, or even to its acceleration in modern times. A separate essay which follows the title-essay in *Esthétique de la langue française*, 'La Déformation', argues that the language has always been, and still is, in motion; the question is not the process of change itself, which is inevitable, but its provenance. 'Ce qui était déformation en 1850 est devenu aujourd'hui le principe d'une règle par quoi nous jugeons des déformations actuelles,' Gourmont states [That which was deformation in 1850 has today become the principle of a rule by which we judge current deformations]; in fact, 'L'histoire d'une langue n'est que l'histoire de déformations successives' [The history of a language is nothing more than the history of successive deformations] (p. 75). He has no difficulty in proving that each generation has lamented the degeneration of the language, and issued lists of banned words, idioms, and grammatical forms which are now taken for granted. Such attempts to control language use are doomed; those who think differently are snobs, and ignorant snobs at that. The philosopher and statesman Royer-Collard, for example, who declared that the verb *baser* should be banned from the dictionary as a useless synonym for *fonder*, 'ne savait pas que beaucoup des mots dont il protégeait l'aristocratisme contre cet intrus ingénu n'étaient eux-mêmes que des parvenus que le xviiᵉ siècle avait méprisés' [did not know that many of the words whose aristocratic status he was safeguarding from this artless intruder were themselves upstarts which the seventeenth century had despised] (p. 84).

The hit at Royer-Collard has a political edge, since he was the co-founder with Guizot of a moderate pro-royalist faction, 'Les Doctinaires', swept away in the revolution of 1848; but the combination of social, literary, and linguistic conservatism which he represents is equally evident in Viennet's *Épître à Boileau*. Viennet's devotion to Boileau, equivalent in mid-nineteenth-century France to making Pope your literary touchstone in Victorian England, marks out his position in the battle between the 'classic' and 'romantic' movements; the poem begins with a wholesale assault on the modern, 'progressive' spirit, represented by a degraded vocabulary, a 'mélange bizarre' of 'vingt jargons' (l. 5). The verb *baser* is singled out as Viennet sees his own position threatened:

> Je maudis ces auteurs dont le vocabulaire
> Nous encombre de mots dont nous n'avons que faire;
> Qui, sur de vains succès *basant* un fol orgueil,
> D'un œil ambitieux *fixent* notre fauteuil . . .
>
> (ll. 53–6)[16]

[I curse those authors whose vocabulary encumbers us with useless words; who, *basing* a foolish pride on a few hollow triumphs, *fix* their eyes on our seat in the Academy . . .]

Gourmont would have viewed with sardonic relish the list of words over which Viennet chokes: *bohèmes, fantaisistes, dégingander, lyrisme, entrain, utiliser, formulent, subjective, objective* (all of them to be found in Proust); in this part of the poem, at least, Viennet is aiming at the wrong target. Besides individual words, Gourmont defends the slippage of grammatical rules: the form of the possessive which consists in using 'à' rather than 'de' ('le cheval à mon père' instead of 'le cheval de mon père') may be a vulgar error, yet it descends, Gourmont takes pleasure in pointing out, from fifth-century Latin: 'Voilà un solécisme qui a de belles lettres de noblesse' [There's a solecism with fine patents of nobility] (p. 103).[17]

Not only does Gourmont defend the linguistic (and social) standing of 'deformation', he allows it a creative function, and he is willing to push this as far as it will go, moving from the statement that deformation is a kind of creativity, to the assertion that all art, and all science, works by deformation, to the logical conclusion that deformation is the principle of mental life itself, since each of us experiences the world through the 'deforming' prism of individual consciousness (pp. 75–6). Language, too, is stamped with the impress of each person's mind; and this process, Gourmont claims, is a source of pleasure:

l'homme spontané, peuple ou poète, a d'autres goûts que les grammairiens, et, en fait de langage, il use de tous les moyens pour atteindre à l'indispensable, à l'inconnu,

---

[16] There are forty seats, known as 'armchairs' ('fauteuils') in the Académie Française.

[17] The possessive 'à' encompasses the whole social scale of *A la recherche*: Mme de Guermantes, remember, uses the phrase '[le] frère à Robert' (see above, p. 161); replying to a question from Marcel's Aunt Léonie as to the identity of someone she has glimpsed in the street, the servant Françoise says: 'Mais ça sera la fille à M. Pupin' [But that must be M. Pupin's daughter] (I, 55; I, 65).

à l'expression non encore proférée, au mot vierge. L'homme éprouve une très grande jouissance à déformer son langage, c'est-à-dire à prendre de son langage une possession toujours plus intime et toujours plus personelle. L'imitation fait le reste: celui qui ne peut créer partage à demi, en imitant le créateur, les joies de la création. (p. 76)

[Spontaneous Man, whether embodied in a people or a poet, has different tastes from those of the grammarians, and, as regards language, uses every means to attain to the indispensable, the unknown, the expression not yet formed, the virgin word. Man experiences a very great delight in deforming his language, that is to say in taking an ever more intimate and personal possession of it. Imitation does the rest: he who cannot create acquires a half-share, by imitating the creator, in the joys of creation.]

The sexual meanings latent in Gourmont's vocabulary—*mot vierge*, *jouissance, prendre une possession toujours plus intime*—are all the more surprising because they appear to contradict his insistence, in the main essay which gives its title to *Esthétique de la langue française*, on purity and on linguistic continence. But the contradiction is lessened when we realize that Gourmont is describing a process in which language is 'naturally' modified by its (more or less creative) users, within a community whose identity persists through time. This is a version of a widely accepted philological doctrine in the nineteenth century, which corresponded to strongly held beliefs about the origins, destiny, and cohesion of both *la nation* and *la race françaises*. The younger Proust, as we have already seen, was not immune to such notions: in his article 'Contre l'obscurité' he describes true literary talent as amounting to more than 'l'originalité du tempérament'; it means 'le pouvoir de réduire un tempérament original aux lois générales de l'art, au génie permanent de la langue' [the power to make an original temperament submit to the general laws of art, to the enduring genius of the language] (*CSB* 390). The author of *A la recherche* would not give such hostages to fortune. For Gourmont, however, the existence of this 'génie permanent de la langue' is a given, and any evolution which takes place *within* it must, of necessity, be beneficial:

Un peuple qui ne connaît que sa propre langue et qui l'apprend de sa mère, et non des tristes pédagogues, ne peut pas la déformer, si l'on donne à ce mot un sens péjoratif. Il est porté constamment à la rendre différente; il ne peut la rendre mauvaise. (p. 77)

[A people which knows only its own language and which learns that language from its mothers, and not from dreary pedagogues, cannot deform it, if that word is taken in a pejorative sense. It tends constantly to make it different; it cannot spoil it.]

So far so good; but the problem comes with Gourmont's tacit recognition that this story has become a myth; it represents something which happened in the past, which *ought* to be happening still, but which is threatened by change *of a different kind*. Again, the culprit is education; the benign conditions under which French has evolved over time have been undermined by an oppressive system of public instruction in 'les prisons scolaires', where children 'perdent sous la peur de la grammaire cette liberté d'esprit qui faisait une part si agréable à la fantaisie dans l'évolution verbale' [lose, through fear of Grammar, that freedom of spirit which allowed fancy to play so attractive a part in the development of the language]. The natural growth of the French language is being artificially restricted (from *sa mère* to *la grammaire* is the defamiliarizing step); at the same time, as we have seen, the false respect which education inculcates for foreign languages means that they do not undergo the required 'deformation'. This explains how Gourmont is able to reconcile his praise for the *jouissance* of linguistic change with a policy which has all the *joie-de-vivre* of a Quaker orgy. Within a few pages he is able to return to the topic of 'purity' with renewed zeal and with a powerful metaphor of ethnic cleansing:

Quels que soient les changements et, si l'on veut, les déformations que l'usage lui impose, une langue reste belle tant qu'elle reste pure. Une langue est toujours pure quand elle s'est développée à l'abri des influences extérieures. C'est donc du dehors que sont venues nécessairement toutes les atteintes portées à la beauté et à l'integrité de la langue française. Elles sont venues de l'anglais: après avoir souillé notre vocabulaire usuel, il va, si l'on n'y prend garde, influencer la syntaxe, qui est comme l'épine dorsale du langage; du grec, manipulé si sottement par les pédants de la science, de la grammaire et de l'industrie; du grossier latin des codes que les avocats amenèrent avec eux dans la politique, dans le journalisme, et dans tout ce que l'on qualifie science sociale. Ces ruisseaux si lourdement chargés de sable et de bois mort ont encombré la langue française: il suffirait de les dessécher ou de les dériver pour rendre au large fleuve toute sa pureté, toute sa force et toute sa transparence. (p. 86)

[Whatever changes and, if you wish, deformations that usage imposes on a language, it remains beautiful as long as it remains pure. A language is always pure when its development has been shielded from external influences. It is therefore from outside that all the attacks against the beauty and integrity of the French language have come. They have come from English: after soiling our everyday vocabulary, it will, unless care is taken, influence syntax, which is like the spinal column of the language; from Greek, employed so stupidly by the pedants of science, grammar, and industry; from coarse law-Latin, which lawyers brought with them into politics, journalism, and everything which comes under the definition of social science. These streams, so thick with sand and dead wood, have clogged up the French language: it would suffice to dry them out or divert their course to restore to the great river all its purity, all its strength and all its clarity.]

However essential they may be to art, metaphors are a nuisance in formulating social and political thought. It is easy enough to envisage clearing a clogged stream, but how would this work in the domain of language use? Academies and dictionaries are no good, because they always lag behind the dynamic movement of the language; the official system of language teaching is part of the problem, not its solution; we are left with the sense that Gourmont's 'il suffirait' is a wish which has no social basis, hardly even a collective one unless it designates people like himself.

The same difficulty affects the uncompromising denunciation of refractory foreign words in the main essay of *Esthétique de la langue française*. 'Si le mot se refuse à la naturalisation, il faut l'abandonner résolument, le traduire ou lui chercher un équivalent' [If the word refuses to be naturalized, it must be resolutely abandoned, or translated, or replaced with an equivalent] (p. 64). Who does 'il faut' address, and what power are they assumed to possess? In the end Gourmont falls into the same trap as Royer-Collard and Viennet, and all those other ineffectual or misguided fulminators; he too has his form of linguistic snobbery, which carries with it, as Proust knew and remorselessly exposed, a corresponding aesthetic blindness. One of Gourmont's anathemas is pronounced against the word *steamer*, 'un doublet infiniment puéril de *vapeur*' [an infinitely puerile double] (p. 64).[18] Yet in Mallarmé's 'Brise marine', the fantasy of escape is unforgettably powered by this same puerile word:

> Je partirai! Steamer balançant ta mâture,
> Lève l'ancre pour une exotique nature![19]

What if Mallarmé had taken Gourmont's advice?

> Je partirai! Vapeur balançant ta mâture,
> Lève l'ancre pour une exotique nature!

[18] Le Robert dates *steamer* to 1829, only four years after its appearance in English.
[19] 'I shall leave! Steamer, swaying your masts, lift anchor for an exotic Nature'. It is impossible to translate Mallarmé; this is hopeless, but there is worse to come.

Or he might have adopted Viennet's suggestion of the proper, euphonious term to replace *steamer*:

> Je partirai! Pyroscaphe balançant ta mâture,
> Lève l'ancre pour une exotique nature![20]

I can think of nothing worse, except possibly to undertake a similar operation, but in reverse, for the next lines:

> Un Ennui, désolé par les cruels espoirs,
> Croit encore à l'adieu suprême des mouchoirs![21]

Why not replace this with an expression favoured by Odette?

> Un Ennui, désolé par les cruels espoirs,
> Croit encore au *good-bye* suprême des mouchoirs![22]

But Mallarmé was *ni Gourmont ni Odette*.

Qu'est-ce que l'Anglais?

The question is posed by Mallarmé at the outset of his philological treatise, *Les Mots anglais*, published in 1877. More fully:

Qu'est-ce que l'Anglais? Sérieuse et haute question: la trancher dans le sens où elle est faite ici, c'est-à-dire absolument, on ne le pourra qu'à la dernière de ces pages et tout analysé. Maintenant il sied de répondre, en tenant compte des caractères extérieurs et notoires de l'Anglais, que cet idiome est un de ceux du globe qu'un contemporain doit connaître. (p. 3)

[What is English? A question of high importance: to resolve it as here posed, that is absolutely, will not be possible until the last of these pages, and when all has

---

[20] *Épître à Boileau*, 196–200: 'Le grec nous façonnait un mot plein de douceur; | Mais ce mot, dont ma muse admirait l'euphonie, | A, pour venir à nous, passé par la Russie; | La guerre le repousse, et les coureurs de mers | Laissent le pyroscaphe et prennent les *steamers*' [Greek fashioned for us a most amenable word; but this word, whose euphony my muse admired, came to us via Russia; the war repulses it, and those who sail the seas abandon *le pyroscaphe* and take *les steamers*]. With due respect to Viennet, I do not think the Crimean War can be held responsible for the non-adoption of 'pyroscaphe'—a word which Gourmont would have loathed, since he objected to Greek imports as much as to English.

[21] 'A bored spirit, desolated by cruel hopes, still has faith in the supreme adieu of hand-kerchiefs'. Oh well . . .

[22] ' "Alors, vraiment, vous partez? Hé bien, *good bye*!" ' ["Really, must you go? Well then, *good-bye*!"] (I, 597; II, 212). Odette also uses *Good morning* (I, 626; II, 248) and *Good evening* (I, 613; II, 231, where however *Vintage* has another *Good-bye*).

been analysed. For the moment it behoves us to reply, taking into account the external and noteworthy features of English, that this is one of the world's languages which anyone now living ought to know.]

Mallarmé taught English in schools for over thirty years; Proust, as far as we know, never attended a single English lesson; nor is there any direct evidence that he read this particular work of Mallarmé's, though he admired him greatly and knew much of his poetry by heart, as does Marcel.[23] Nevertheless *Les Mots anglais* speaks powerfully to the English words of *A la recherche*. It does so, in part, because of a curious parallelism, or sympathy, between the structure of the two works. Like Proust, Mallarmé defers true understanding until the end, insisting that everything that bears on the question must be gone through: 'la dernière de ces pages et tout analysé'. When this end is reached, as we shall see, the English language looks uncannily like an emblem of Proust's art.

As its title suggests, *Les Mots anglais* has a restricted scope. It was to have been followed by a volume on grammar, which Mallarmé did not complete; as a result this is a book, like *A la recherche*, which is full of English words but has no English sentences. Mallarmé concentrates, with Proustian intensity, on the etymology of individual words and groups of words, and on the processes of phonetic and semantic change, but he deliberately refrains from applying any of his conclusions to English speech. He has no concept of linguistic purity, and though he uses terms such as 'barbare' and 'primitif' they carry quite different values from their appearance in Gourmont's *Esthétique de la langue française*. His discussion of the relations between French and English takes no account of Gourmont's 'aesthetic' principle, and there is every reason to believe he would have rejected it as hopelessly arbitrary—indeed, as being a form of the very provincialism, the dwindling of a language into a dialect, which Gourmont dreaded as the fate of French if it did not resist the foreign invader. Such resistance, Mallarmé observes, was put up by Scots, an example of 'le caractère taciturne et patriotique des

[23] For Proust's friendship with Mallarmé, see Pléiade note (IV, 1779, n. 5) and Tadié, 249–51. Marcel tells Albertine that he had intended to call the yacht he was going to offer her *Le Cygne*, and that it would have been engraved with lines from Mallarmé's sonnet of that name (IV, 39; V, 520). Brichot aims one of his ponderous witticisms at 'la chapelle mallarméenne' where Marcel worships (III 346; IV, 410) but he evidently knows nothing of Mallarmé's linguistic work. Jacques Michon discussess the biographical and intellectual contest, and Mallarmé's extensive adaptation of English philological sources, but does not mention Proust.

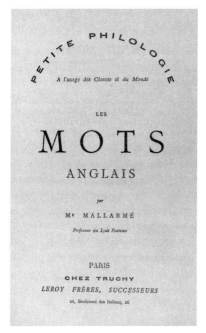

14. Title-page of Mallarmé's *Les Mots anglais*, 1877.

dialectes' [the taciturn and patriotic nature of dialects]; Burns and Walter Scott 'rajeunissent la vieille gloire de leur patois natal' [rejuvenate the ancient glory of their native dialect], Mallarmé concedes, but a less qualified praise is lavished on English writers:

Shakespeare, Milton, Shelley et Byron et tant de merveilleux prosateurs, voilà des génies qui se sont, à travers les siècles, transmis le trésor double du langage ici étudié; sans qu'aucun de ces maîtres n'ait tenté par un patriotisme mal entendu, de séparer dans la langue l'élément barbare de l'élément classique, c'est-à-dire français: tous tirant des effets très-beaux de l'indissoluble hymen qui a fait de l'Anglais le plus singulier et l'un des plus riches d'entre les idiomes modernes. (pp. 30–1)

[Shakespeare, Milton, Shelley and Byron and so many marvellous prose writers, these are the geniuses who, over the centuries, have passed on to each other the double treasure of the language here studied; without any of these masters having tried through misplaced patriotism to separate the "barbaric" element in their language from the "classical", that is to say French, element: all deriving very beautiful effects from the indissoluble marriage which has made English one of the most singular and richest of modern languages.]

The key word here is *double*. Mallarmé insists on this throughout his book: he sums it up in the phrase 'pas d'Anglais sans Français' (p. 32); strictly speaking, the English language as we know it today doesn't come into being before the marriage, or fusion, of Anglo-Saxon with Norman French. The metaphor which Mallarmé finds for this fusion is that of grafting, or cross-fertilization: English is not simply a double tongue, but a *mixed* one: 'La greffe seule peut offrir une image qui représente le phénomène nouveau: oui, du Français s'est enté sur de l'Anglais: et les deux plantes ont, toute hésitation passée, produit sur une même tige une fraternelle et magnifique végétation' [Grafting alone offers an image which represents the new phenomenon: yes, French has grafted itself on to English: and the two plants have, after an initial hesitation, produced on a single stem a fraternal and magnificent vegetation] (p. 31).

Mallarmé distinguishes this process from the binary mode of language formation which he describes in the opening pages of his book: on the one hand 'la formation *naturelle* ou *populaire*, mieux *instinctive*' [natural or popular formation, or rather instinctive], the slow work of time, and on the other hand the conscious manufacture of words by the educated class, 'Dérivation, toute *artificielle* que celle-là, et si l'on veut *savante*' [a form of derivation which is completely artificial, and you might say learnèd] (p. 8). These two processes correspond to those used by Gourmont, except that Mallarmé doesn't inflect the distinction with an aesthetic judgement; he nowhere suggests that the 'natural' mode of formation is superior to the artificial, and he lacks Gourmont's prejudice against either learned or foreign idioms. English, however, presents 'le troisième cas de formation linguistique, ni artificiel, ni naturel absolument . . . celui d'une langue quasi faite versée dans une langue presque faite, un mélange parfait s'opérant entre les deux' [the third case of linguistic formation, neither artificial nor completely natural . . . that of a language more or less fully formed poured into a language close to being fully formed, with a perfect mixture being accomplished between the two of them] (p. 31). The distinction between the language which is 'quasi faite', Norman French, and that which is 'presque faite', Anglo-Saxon, is so minimal as almost to constitute an equivalence. Mallarmé's phrasing closes up the tiny gap between them:—'quasi faite . . . presque faite . . . parfait'.

Inevitably, and perhaps without quite wishing to, Mallarmé raises the heretical question of whether the English language which resulted from this 'perfect mixture' might not be superior, in its subsequent development, to the French language; for of the two partners, one, Anglo-Saxon, lost its integrity (or as Gourmont might say, its purity), while the other did not. If metaphors of fertility attach themselves to the mixed, grafted language, might that not mean that the unmixed language is sterile, or at any rate less vigorous, less adaptable? Mallarmé is conscious of the world-reach of English—he talks of its spread to North America, to Australia, to South Africa, to India—and this process had occurred without the need of a special society (supported, let us say, by the Chief Rabbi and the Archbishop of Canterbury, by Mr Gladstone and Mr Disraeli) to promote the language abroad.[24] Though Mallarmé denies that English is superior as a literary resource to French, the denial comes as an after-thought in the sentence and feels like a gesture of obligation.[25] English has 'la vitalité issue d'un croisement classique' [the vitality which comes from cross-fertilization with a classical language] (p. 341) and Mallarmé notes its far greater facility in word-formation (p. 342).

The hint that English might be superior to French could only have occurred to a writer who, like Mallarmé, was not only steeped in the English language but was unaffected by the gross nationalism which flourished on both sides of the linguistic divide. The snort of French disdain for English is exemplified by Francis Wey, in a passage which fuses history with aesthetics:

Autrefois, l'Angleterre vassale de la France, recevait les lois de sa suzeraine qui lui imposait son langage. Le dialecte anglo-normand vivait alors humblement sous l'aile de la langue mère, de la langue française. Peu à peu l'influence saxonne, l'ignorance et le temps, achevèrent de corrompre ce jargon provincial, qui devenu pour nous inintelligible, forme un idiome particulier. . . . Ainsi fut constitué ce parler des Anglais, désagréable, dur, sifflant, hérissé d'épines et de ronces. (II, 59)

---

[24] See Ch. 1, p. 17.
[25] In support of his claim that no one can afford to ignore English, which I quoted above: 'Au point de vue des relations et politiques et commerciales, nul ne l'emporte sur lui par sa diffusion internationale; au point de vue littéraire ou des œuvres de l'esprit embrassant de la poésie à la science, lequel, par un éclat plus noble, le Français excepté?' [From the point of view of political and commercial relations, no language surpasses it for international diffusion; from the point of view of literature, or of works of the intellect ranging from poetry to science, what language outshines it with a nobler light, French excepted?] (pp. 3–4).

[In the old days, England, the vassal of France, received laws from her sovereign who imposed his language on her. The Anglo-Norman dialect at that time lived humbly under the wing of its maternal language, the French language. Little by little, the influence of the Saxons, combined with ignorance and the passage of time, succeeded in corrupting this provincial jargon, which, having become unintelligible to us, forms a separate idiom. . . . Thus was this English speech constituted, disagreeable, hard, whistling, bristling with thorns and brambles.]

Mallarmé disagreed with every part of this analysis, not least the idea that English has become 'inintelligible'. He dwells on the linguistic interest which English holds for French—the reason why a French writer, for example, ought to know something about English irrespective of the wish to order a cup of tea or read Shakespeare's Sonnets. In a chapter called 'Vieux Mots', Mallarmé presents English as a living museum of French, a repository of old words and forms which have disappeared from modern French but which English has preserved and which the scholar can unearth and recover. If an aesthetic charge is to be found anywhere in *Les Mots anglais* it is here, in Mallarmé's passion for such recuperations:

A quelque point de vue que se mette le linguiste français, et s'il s'enorgueillit plus de voir les mots de sa propre langue conquérir une place désormais indiscutable, dans l'Anglais, qu'il ne se chagrine de mainte détérioration par eux subie en cela; ou le contraire: une satisfaction presque exempte de mélange l'attend . . . Beaucoup de vieux et bons vocables, à jamais perdus ou si lointains que le parler actuel en ignore jusqu'au sens, se survivent dans l'idiome voisin: intacts, non; mais conservés à la faveur de Lois ou même déformés au gré de caprices entrevus tout-à-l'heure, ils sont d'aspect plus entier par le seul fait que la forme ne s'en étant point successivement modifiée chez nous pendant l'évolution de la langue, c'est souvent sans aucun point de comparaison demandé à notre parler moderne que nous y jetons les yeux. . . . Mille motifs de savoir l'Anglais . . . mais il n'en est point de plus cher que d'y reconnaître les mots français de jadis, si l'on a le patriotisme spécial du lettré à qui incombe le trésor passé et contemporain de sa langue. (p. 226)

[Whatever point of view the French linguist takes, and if he prides himself more on seeing the words of his own language conquer an unassailable place within English, than he is chagrined at the many deteriorations undergone by such words in the process; or vice-versa: a satisfaction almost without alloy awaits him . . . Many fine old words, lost for ever or so remote that the language of today doesn't even know their meaning, 'live on' in the neighbouring language:[26] not

---

[26] Mallarmé's phrase 'se survivent' implies that words which are dead in modern French are leading a kind of posthumous existence in English.

intact, no; but preserved by means of Laws, or even deformed according to the whims which we were looking at earlier, in either case they are in a better state of preservation for the sole reason that they did not change their form through the successive stages of the evolution of our language; as a result, we often contemplate them without seeking in our modern speech any point of comparison . . . There are a thousand motives for knowing English . . . but none so rewarding as to recognize the French words of former times, if one has the special patriotism of the scholar to whom is entrusted the past and present treasure of his language.]

An almost unmixed pleasure—'une satisfaction presque exempte de mélange'—rewards the contemplation of how mixed-up languages are; this is among the most Proustian observations in the book. Note that the current of this pleasure sets in the direction of French, not English; that is, *les mots anglais* are here a means to an end, and that end is to give pleasure to the custodian of the French language. Mallarmé locates the 'patriotisme spécial du lettré' in a place where Gourmont would not think of looking for it, at the very heart of the foreign language deemed the most hostile, the least assimilable of all.

Like Gourmont, Mallarmé acknowledges 'détérioration' and 'déformation' as processes of linguistic change, but his surprising turn in this passage is to think about the process differentially: words lost for ever in French are recoverable through the distortions they have undergone *in another language*. The irruption into *notre parler moderne* of a word from the past juxtaposes two time-frames with arbitrary power; English is like a metaphorical vehicle for French, or like a dream, whose distortions obey rigorous laws of mutation, whether linguistic or psychological; from an 'unconscious' English, images of aboriginal French rise to the surface, their appearance marked by that apparently *gratuitous* pleasure which is the signature of involuntary memory, of Proustian bliss. Indeed, English is in this special sense the involuntary memory of French.[27] No wonder Mallarmé speaks of 'une satisfaction presque exempte de mélange'—a *pure* joy, in other words—but not the purity which Gourmont so misconceivingly tries to name and preserve.

English is thus a double language in a double sense. When Mallarmé finally answers the question he posed at the outset—'Qu'est-ce-que

---

[27] Note the affinity of Mallarmé's phrase 'à jamais perdus' with Proust's 'Mort à jamais?' which introduces the episode of the 'madeleine' (I, 43; I, 50, where, however, the phrase is lifelessly rendered as 'Permanently dead?').

l'Anglais?'—he does so in five words, but they describe a complex phenomenon and are set in an intricate rhetorical design of their own:

CONCLUSION

et Résumé: Qu'est-ce-que l'Anglais; car cette interrogation, faite au début du tome, revient à la fin. Si l'on rappelle ses souvenirs autant que mille réflexions attendant, pour converger en l'esprit, que tout fût dit, cette réponse se présente comme la plus générale: l'Anglais est un idiome composite. (p. 335)

[CONCLUSION

and Summary: What is English; for this interrogation, made at the beginning of the volume, recurs at the end. If one recalls one's memories as well as a thousand thoughts which were waiting, to converge in one's mind, for everything to be said, this reply presents itself as the most general in scope: English is a composite idiom.]

Like *A la recherche*, *Les Mots anglais* has a circular form whose meaning can only be understood in an act of memory: the conditional phrase which introduces the answer to the question, 'Si l'on rappelle ses souvenirs autant que mille réflexions attendant, pour converger en l'esprit, que tout fût dit . . .' sounds remarkably akin to what Proust foresaw, from the beginning, as the necessary trajectory for each reader of his novel, as well as for its narrator. The mixed nature of English springs from the fusion of Anglo-Saxon with Norman French—that's to look at it from the point of view of English philology; from the French point of view, English is mixed because it 'remembers' French, resurrecting in its own impure, beautiful forms the lost time of language. This second, French aspect of the English language gives the concluding sentence of Mallarmé's book a peculiar interest for readers of Proust, because it speaks to the very principle of the novel's design, the conjunction of different times; all that is different in Mallarmé springs from the knowledge that language, unlike a work of art, is prospective and indefinite, a quality embodied in the very structure of *Les Mots anglais*, which announces itself as only part of an unfinished project:

Par sa Grammaire (dont il n'est question que dans l'autre tome de ce Traité) marche vers quelque point futur du Langage et se replonge aussi dans le passé, même très-ancien et mêlé aux débuts sacrés du Langage, l'Anglais: Langue Contemporaine peut-être par excellence, elle qui accuse le double caractère de l'époque, rétrospectif et avancé. (p. 348)

[By its Grammar (with which we are concerned only in the other volume of this Treatise) English strides towards some future state of the language, while simultaneously reimmersing itself in the past, even the very ancient past, one which blends into the sacred beginnings of Language: perhaps the epitome of a Modern Language, in that it matches the double nature of the epoch, both backward- and forward-looking.]

The verb *se replonge* makes an immediate bridge to the last sentence of *A la recherche*:

Aussi, si elle m'était laissée assez longtemps pour accomplir mon œuvre, ne manquerais-je pas d'abord d'y décrire les hommes, cela dût-il les faire ressembler à des êtres monstrueux, comme occupant une place si considérable, a côté de celle si restreinte qui leur est réservée dans l'espace, une place au contraire prolongée sans mesure puisqu'ils touchent simultanément, comme des géants plongés dans les années à des époques, vécues par eux si distantes, entre lesquelles tant de jours sont venus se placer—dans le Temps.

FIN

[So, if I were given long enough to accomplish my work, I should not fail, even if the effect were to make them resemble monsters, to describe men as occupying so considerable a place, compared with the restricted place which is reserved for them in space, a place on the contrary prolonged past measure, for simultaneously, like giants plunged into the years, they touch the distant epochs through which they have lived, between which so many days have come to range themselves—in Time.

THE END]

(IV, 625; VI, 451)[28]

There can be no 'FIN' to language; Mallarmé has it striding forwards even as it plunges back into the past; yet the work of art which Proust, in the act of accomplishing it, precariously announces, springs from an understanding of time with which Mallarmé is profoundly in sympathy. Mallarmé's English is an emblem of Proust's novel, whose double face makes it, too, 'contemporaine peut-être par excellence'.

[28] *Vintage* omits 'The End'; it is not helped by the fact that the final sentence comes exactly at the bottom of the page. However, earlier versions of the translation, which did not have this difficulty, also omitted 'The End'; it is rightly restored in the new Penguin translation by Ian Patterson (2002, p. 358), which, however, is blighted (in my view) by a more serious error, that of translating the title, *Le Temps retrouvé*, as *Finding Time Again*. *Time Regained* may be a touch too Miltonic (though Proustian in spirit: 'les vrais paradis sont les paradis qu'on a perdus' [the true paradises are the paradises we have lost], IV, 449; VI, 222) but it describes, as it should, a triumphant result.

Etymology and deformation

Marcel's fascination with etymology appears briefly in the 'Combray' section of *Du côté de chez Swann*, in an episode which, like many of those in the early part of the novel, is packed with meanings which don't reveal themselves until much later; and it reappears in full force during Marcel's second visit to Balbec, with Brichot's ponderously witty and long-winded discourses which enchant Marcel and bore everyone else. Etymology is one form of the passion for origins which preoccupies *A la recherche*; it connects, as we have seen, with issues of national and racial identity, and of the doubleness of time and memory; it also relates to the novel's interest in mutation and metamorphosis, both in the domain of art and of human sexuality. Deformation is at the origin of the words we use, none of which can claim to be of pure descent; the snobbery of language, one of the profoundest forms this vice takes in the novel, aligns the social value of aristocratic lineage and exclusivity with the philological value of 'purity', an alignment which is without justification or merit. That French descends from Latin can be made to sound very grand: 'c'est de l'idiome de Virgile et de Tacite ou de ses formes populaires que vient presque absolument ce vieux Français' [it is from the idiom of Virgil and Tacitus or from its popular forms that virtually the whole of this Old French comes], says Mallarmé in *Les Mots anglais*; but the Franks weren't Romans: six grammatical cases dwindled to two, 'à cause de la grande difficulté qu'éprouvèrent les barbares à manier habilement l'instrument, complexe et riche, aux six cas!' [because of the great difficulty which the barbarians experienced in handling with skill the rich and complex instrument, with its six cases!]. The result looks considerably less dignified: 'Du Latin comme détérioré aux lèvres de barbares; ainsi apparaît donc ce Français . . .' [Latin as deteriorated on the lips of barbarians; that, then, is what this French looks like] (p. 22). Proust has exactly the same thought; when Françoise makes a wounding remark about Albertine, Marcel retaliates by mocking her occasionally faulty pronunciation, and then rebukes himself,

car ces mots français que nous sommes si fiers de prononcer exactement ne sont eux-mêmes que des "cuirs" faits par des bouches gauloises qui prononçaient de travers le latin ou le saxon, notre langue n'étant que la prononçiation défectueuse de quelques autres. Le génie linguistique à l'état vivant, l'avenir et le passé du français, voilà ce qui eût dû m'intéresser dans les fautes de Françoise.

[for those French words which we are so proud of pronouncing accurately are themselves only "howlers" made by Gaulish lips which mispronounced Latin or Saxon, our language being merely a defective pronunciation of several others. The genius of language in its living state, the future and past of French, that is what ought to have interested me in Françoise's mistakes.]

(III, 134; II, 763)[29]

The last sentence shows that Proust, here also in agreement with Mallarmé, did not think of linguistic corruption in the context of general notions of cultural decline which had a wide circulation in *fin-de-siècle* Europe. In any event the support which etymology gives to theories of social or moral degeneration is limited by the awkward fact that the ancestral language is, indubitably, dead; attempts to revive or preserve old forms of speech, or to 'purify' the language as currently spoken, are even less likely to succeed than efforts to halt the decline in religious observance, put women in their place, or bring back absolute monarchy. On the other hand a language which forgets its past is one-dimensional, incapable of giving expression to a reality which is itself formed of layers of time, not always placed in sequence but juxtaposed according to laws which it is the business of Proust's novel to understand and to celebrate. 'Le génie linguistique à l'état vivant, l'avenir et le passé du français': in this formula the primitive has no more value in itself, whether linguistically or historically, than the contemporary; it is the *conjunction* of the two which is creative, liberating us from the prison of habit into the true, the poetic perception of reality.

Proust uses the term *couches* to describe the stratification of both historical periods and social classes; Mallarmé uses it in *Les Mots anglais* to describe language: 'Les mots, dans le dictionnaire, gisent, pareils ou de dates diverses, comme des stratifications: vite je parlerai de couches' [Words, in the dictionary, lie, similar or diverse in date, like (geological) layers; I reach for the word *strata*] (p. 7).[30] He goes on, in another of those

---

[29] 'Cuir' originally signified an incorrect liaison, for example pronouncing the final 't' in 'il a fait une erreur' (I owe this happy instance to *Harrap*).

[30] I have tried to translate Mallarmé's formula to bring into prominence the word which, in my view, is the equivalent of 'couches' here, namely 'strata'; but this means finding another word for 'stratifications'. The problem results from the fact that the Latinate 'stratifications' in French is less specific (for Mallarmé's purpose here) than the demotic 'couches', whereas in English 'strata' is more refined, more pointed, than 'layers'. Marcel says of Bloch: 'appartenant à une famille peu estimée [il] supportait comme au fond des mers les incalculables pressions que faisaient peser sur lui non seulement les chrétiens de la

passages which seem so close to the spirit of *A la recherche*, to speak of the organic, the material and bodily quality of words, sustaining themselves like all forms of life by continuous death and self-renewal:

A toute la nature apparenté et se rapprochant ainsi de l'organisme dépositaire de la vie, le Mot présente, dans ses voyelles et ses dipthongues, comme une chair; et dans ses consonnes, comme une ossature délicate à disséquer. Etc., etc. Si la vie s'alimente de son propre passé, ou d'une mort continuelle, la Science retrouvera ce fait dans le langage: lequel, distinguant l'homme du reste des choses, imitera encore celui-ci en tant que factice dans l'essence non moins que naturel; réfléchi, que fatal; volontaire, qu'aveugle.

[The Word, related to the whole of Nature and thus linked to the organism in which life is invested, displays something like flesh in its vowels and diphthongs; in its consonants it displays something like a fine bone structure for the purpose of dissection. Etc. etc. If life nourishes itself from its own past, or through a continuous process of dying, then Science will find this confirmed in language, which, as it distinguishes mankind from the rest of creation, so it will imitate mankind in being artificial in essence as much as natural; the product of reflection as much as necessity; self-willed as much as blind.][31]

The fusion of dual terms—life nourished by death, nature by artifice, the unconscious by the willed—is fundamental to Proust's artistic, and indeed moral, vision, seen at last in the joining of the two 'ways' at the end of the book, but adumbrated at every stage of the narrative and at every level, nowhere more powerfully or consistently than in the attention paid to the life of words.

Reflecting on his childhood visits to Combray, Marcel regrets not having spent more time talking to the local priest, 'car s'il n'entendait rien aux arts, il connaissait beaucoup d'étymologies' [for, even if he understood nothing about the arts, he knew a great many etymologies] (I, 101; I, 121).[32] But

surface, mais les couches superposées des castes juives supérieures à la sienne' [since he belonged to a family of little repute, (he) had to support, as on the floor of the ocean, the incalculable pressures imposed on him not only by the Christians at the surface but by all the intervening layers of Jewish castes superior to his own] (II, 103; II, 374). In *Le Temps retrouvé* the term designates not social hierarchy but the evolution of the social world itself: 'les nouvelles couches' are those who make up high society in post-war Paris, and to whom the duchesse de Guermantes is of little account (IV, 571; VI, 380).

[31] I think the last phrase means something like 'in control of his own destiny as much as driven by unconscious forces', but it is compressed even for Mallarmé.

[32] *Vintage* has 'cared nothing for the arts'.

this distinction between etymology and art belongs rather to Marcel as character than to Proust as author. True, the priest is a Philistine who regrets that his church is the only 'unrestored' (i.e. modernized) one in the district. But if Marcel were listening more closely he would hear more in the priest's conversation with his Aunt Léonie and her companion Eulalie. He might, for example, notice the fusion of opposites in the figure of Saint Hilaire, whom Aunt Léonie can't seem to 'place' in his stained-glass window:

—Mais je ne vois pas où est saint Hilaire?

—Mais si, dans le coin du vitrail vous n'avez jamais remarqué une dame en robe jaune? Hé bien! c'est saint Hilaire qu'on appelle aussi, vous le savez, dans certaines provinces saint Illiers, saint Hélier, et même, dans le Jura, saint Ylie. Ces diverses corruptions de *sanctus Hilarius* ne sont pas du reste les plus curieuses de celles qui se sont produites dans les noms des bienheureux. Ainsi votre patronne, ma bonne Eulalie, *sancta Eulalia*, savez-vous ce qu'elle est devenue en Bourgogne? *Saint Éloi* tout simplement: elle est devenue un saint. Voyez-vous, Eulalie, qu'après votre mort on fasse de vous un homme?

—M. le Curé a toujours le mot pour rigoler.

["But I don't see where Saint Hilaire comes in."

"Why yes, have you never noticed, in the corner of the window, a lady in a yellow robe? Well, that's Saint Hilaire, who is also known, you will remember, in certain parts of the country as Saint Illiers, Saint Hélier, and even, in the Jura, Saint Ylie. But these various corruptions of *Sanctus Hilarius* are by no means the most curious that have occurred in the names of the blessed. Take, for example, my good Eulalie, the case of your own patron, *Sancta Eulalia*; do you know what she has become in Burgundy? Saint Eloi, nothing more or less! The female saint has become a male.[33] Do you hear that, Eulalie—after you're dead they'll make a man of you!"

"His Reverence will always have his little joke."]

(I, 103–4; I, 124)

Marcel ought to remember this joke when he finds, in Elstir's studio, the portrait of Odette as 'Miss Sacripant' *en demi-travesti*; the transposition of gender is here also a matter of portraiture, *la dame en robe jaune* anticipating the mutations of *la dame en rose*. The linguistic 'corruptions diverses' by which male saints become female, and vice versa, has its counterpart in the physiological and moral 'corruptions' of human sexuality, and if we

---

[33] *Vintage* has 'The lady has become a gentleman.'

follow the logic of this analogy we will see that it is as futile to pass judgement on the different forms of human behaviour as it is to pass judgement on the legitimacy of words and names which have been shaped by the powerful collective action of generations of mis-speakers.

As well as anticipating the portrait of Miss Sacripant, the priest offers (without knowing it) a premonition of Elstir's 'metaphorical' technique as a painter; compare, for example, what he says about the view from the church tower at Combray with Elstir's method of suppressing the facts of topography in the interest of perceptual truth:

> Chaque fois que je suis allé à Jouy-le-Vicomte, j'ai bien vu un bout du canal, puis quand j'avais tourné une rue j'en voyais un autre, mais alors je ne voyais plus le précédent. J'avais beau les mettre ensemble par la pensée, cela ne me faisait pas grand effet. Du clocher de Saint-Hilaire c'est autre chose, c'est tout un réseau où la localité est prise. Seulement on ne distingue pas d'eau, on dirait de grandes fentes qui coupent si bien la ville en quartiers, qu'elle est comme une brioche dont les morceaux tiennent ensemble mais sont déjà découpés. Il faudrait pour bien faire être à la fois dans le clocher de Saint-Hilaire at à Jouy-le-Vicomte.

> ["Each time I've been to Jouy I've seen a bit of canal in one place, and then I've turned a corner and seen another, but when I saw the second I could no longer see the first. I tried to put them together in my mind's eye; it was no good. But from the top of Saint-Hilaire it's quite another matter—a regular network in which the place is enclosed. Only you can't see any water; it's as though there were great clefts slicing up the town so neatly that it looks like a loaf of bread which still holds together after it has been cut up. To get it all quite perfect you would have to be in both places at once; up at the top of the steeple of Saint-Hilaire and down there at Jouy-le-Vicomte."]

(I, 105; I, 125–6)

This game of spatial perspective operates also 'dans le Temps', where simultaneity is not a wish but a truth; involuntary memory allows you— indeed, compels you—to be in two places at once; from this 'vantage-point' you can grasp, in the curé's fine phrase, 'tout un réseau où la localité est prise'. Etymology is only less privileged as a form of time travel because it is a rational science; yet even this science, as we have already seen, has an 'unconscious' which can produce the phenomenon of involuntary memory within the life of a single word or name.

It is when we get to La Raspelière, the Verdurins' country house in Normandy, and begin to listen (if we can bear them) to Brichot's interminable explanations, that the full significance of this topic becomes clear.

Brichot's erudition is mainly displayed in the etymology of place-names. As with the words whose etymology Mallarmé elucidates, the origins of such names are almost always primitive, whether what is being brought to light belongs to history or to nature. Each place-name is, in this sense, 'un idiome composite', in which the older element is always the simpler, the more 'legible', but which has been subjected to deformation over time; the result is a modern word in which the original meaning is often disguised or travestied. Brichot gives numerous examples of this process: 'Montmartin' is not named after the Christian St Martin, but the older pagan god Mars (III, 283–4; IV, 334); the wood of Chantereine does not commemorate a queen of song, but a less lyric creature: 'reine n'est pas ici la femme d'un roi, mais la grenouille. C'est le nom qu'elle a gardé longtemps dans ce pays' [*reine*, in this instance, is not the wife of a king, but a frog. It is the name that the frog has long retained in this district] (III, 316; IV, 373–4); Pont-à-Couleuvre is devoid of snakes, because it was once Pont-à-Quileuvre, and before that 'Pons cui aperit' (III, 317; IV, 375). Brichot, like a scholarly Ovid, takes delight in metamorphosing members of the Académie Française or the diplomatic corps back into trees and plants: Houssaye to *houx* [holly], d'Ormesson to *l'orme* [elm], de La Boulaye to *le bouleau* [birch], d'Aunay to *l'aulne* [alder], Albaret to *l'aubier* [sapwood] (III, 322; IV, 381).[34] Such etymologies put evolution, or the hierarchies of science, into reverse, returning men to 'lower' forms; the same process is at work within human history, as a civilized façade opens to reveal a more 'savage' past. When, later in *Sodome et Gomorrhe*, Albertine catches Marcel's etymological bug, she asks Brichot about Marcouville-l'Orgueilleuse, saying how much she likes its proud-sounding name:

—Vous le trouveriez, répondit Brichot, plus fier encore si au lieu de sa forme française, ou même de basse latinité telle qu'on la trouve dans le cartulaire de l'évêque de Bayeux, *Marcovilla superba*, vous preniez la forme plus ancienne, plus voisine du normand, *Marculphivilla superba*, le village, le domaine de Merculph. Dans presque tous ces noms qui se terminent en *ville*, vous pourriez voir encore dressé sur cette côte, le fantôme des rudes envahisseurs normands.

["You would find it prouder still," Brichot replied, "if, instead of its French or even its low Latin form, as we find it in the cartulary of the Bishop of Bayeux,

---

[34] I haven't given all the names here, and Proust himself made a selection from the list he compiled in manuscript. One name, 'Albaret', is a grace-note: it is not that of an academician, but of Proust's housekeeper Céleste, and its etymology is fictive (*Pléiade* notes, pp. 1523, 1525).

Marcovilla superba, you were to take the older form, more akin to the Norman, *Marculphivilla superba*, the village, the domain of Merculph. In almost all these names which end in *ville*, you might see still marshalled upon this coast the ghosts of the rude Norman invaders . . . ."]

(III, 484; IV, 577–8)

Remy de Gourmont would approve of such discernment; it is not the old invaders he resents, but the new ones; time has softened the un-French syllable of *Merculph* to *Marcou*, but nothing has yet happened to make 'Birmingham' more euphonious. For Proust, however, the beauty of etymology lies precisely in its recovery of the past, in all its primitive concreteness, so that even Brichot's image of a ghost haunting the present may not be apt. Mallarmé is closer, perhaps, when he speaks in *Les Mots anglais* of the discovery of an ancient French word in English as a form of restitution: 'Trouvaille comme de titres anciens et oblitérés à restituer à des vivants' [A lucky find, like that of ancient and obliterated titles which are to be restored to their living heirs] (p. 227). The title of 'prince des Laumes' has gone for ever; only in the language of art can the loss of those 'beaux titres français' be made good.

Un arriviste digne de louange

The concept of linguistic purity, like so much else in *A la recherche*, is an ambivalent one. 'Pure' French, as Remy de Gourmont understands it, is threatened with adulteration from foreign words; but pure French turns out to have impure origins. Gourmont concedes that deformation is the principle of linguistic change; he wants to draw a line between 'natural' deformation (which is not degenerative) and invasive deformation; but the history of the language, and of society, exposes this as a fantasy, which would depend for its efficacy on an impracticable isolation. French cannot become the linguistic equivalent of the Galapagos islands. Languages, like nations, have borders; of mixed origins themselves, they trade with other languages. Mallarmé points to the bilingualism of all frontiers, and gives as a specific example the coexistence of French and English in the Channel ports (p. 25); but of course the border need not be geographical. Literary translation is one such liminal 'space'; but it, too, is only one of the points of contact between languages which allow each to permeate the other.

Despite its evident impossibility, the fantasy of a pure language, derived from authentic origins, carries enormous prestige and is associated with similar fantasies of race, nationality, and social status. Even Mallarmé, cannot resist the vocabulary, if not the concept, of aristocratic descent, though he applies it not to French but to English, or strictly speaking to Anglo-Saxon; speaking of the state of the language at the time of the Norman invasion, he emphasizes that it was already well set and did not, as it were, need French to civilize it:

> Maturité et presque perfection de son orthographe, régularité dans le maniement de ses formes: tout ce que demandent la traduction des auteurs latins et une application à l'éloquence et à la poésie, ce parler . . . l'avait en soi; outre une noblesse authentique de race.(p. 19)

[Considering the maturity and near-perfection of its orthography, and the regularity in its handling of grammatical forms, this language had in itself everything required for translating Latin authors and for the practice of eloquence and poetry; not to mention an authentically noble lineage.][35]

The value of this 'noblesse authentique de race' is continually affirmed by defenders both of the language and the aristocracy in this period; Mallarmé, like Gilberte ('Un des plus beaux titres français!'), utters a ready-made phrase as though by clockwork. But what is the actual value of 'noblesse authentique de race', whether in language or people? And what is the cost of preserving it?

In the course of *A la recherche*, Marcel discovers that the aristocracy of the *faubourg Saint-Germain*, which he thought a closed, stable, impenetrable society, is in fact continuously changing and renewing itself; social mobility is far more widespread than he realized; the immobility of any system is, so to speak, an optical illusion in time, which works because we are no more conscious of the passage of time than we are of the movement of the earth around the sun. Marcel had thought that his own penetration of the Guermantes circle was an exception, almost a unique event; by the time the novel ends, Gilberte has married Robert de Saint-Loup, Mme de Verdurin has become the princesse de Guermantes, and the Jewish *arriviste* Bloch (who now calls himself Jacques du Rozier) is a famous writer admitted to the most exclusive salons in Paris.

---

[35] Reshaping Mallarmé's syntax has meant eliminating the ellipsis in my quotation from the French text. I have rendered 'race' here as 'lineage', not 'race'; something like 'blood-line' is meant, I think, but the primary emphasis, from 'noblesse', is on noble ancestry. The first part of the sentence was adapted from an English philological treatise, but the phrase 'noblesse authentique de race' is Mallarmé's own (see Michon, 176).

The attraction of *noblesse authentique de race* is palpable in *A la recherche*. Marcel is affected by it both socially and linguistically; the pure lineage of Mme de Guermantes nourishes his first fantasies about her, and later on, after her descent from Geneviève de Brabant has ceased to stir his imagination, he enjoys the purity of her vocabulary. Yet the circle over which she presides, the 'esprit de Guermantes' which she incarnates, is sterile in every sense—physical, moral, intellectual, artistic. She is surrounded by men who have given up their careers to inhabit the closed world of her intimacy (II, 749; III, 529). Swann, of course, is chief among them, with his abortive study of Vermeer, his futile connoisseurship, his retreat from emotion. He can create nothing, except simulacra—the people he 'makes over' in the image of old paintings—in a reversal of the aesthetic principle espoused by Elstir. To remain within this circle would be death to Marcel as an artist, as it has been death to Swann. Nor could Marcel write his book in Mme de Guermantes's exquisite language. Only an impure language, the 'langue intermédiaire' to which he jokingly referred while dictating *Du côté de chez Swann* to an English typist, will taste of something true.[36]

It might be thought that there is one figure in *A la recherche* who inhabits two worlds, the *faubourg Saint-Germain* and the world of art, who is both an authentic Guermantes and a modern intellectual, Robert de Saint-Loup. But Saint-Loup's intellectualism is not a denial of his lineage, but an expression of it in a different mode, a 'deformation'. His physical and moral qualities are the flowering of a 'nobility' which can be traced, like the root of a word, through all its grammatical and semantic changes. This 'etymological' charm is what Marcel most responds to:

> par moments ma pensée démêlait en Saint-Loup un être plus général que lui-même, le "noble" . . . À retrouver toujours en lui cet être antérieur, séculaire, cet aristocrate que Robert aspirait justement à ne pas être, j'éprouvais une vive joie, mais d'intelligence, non d'amitié.

> [there were moments when my mind distinguished in Saint-Loup a personality more generalised than his own, that of the "nobleman" . . . The discovery in him of this pre-existent, this immemorial being, this aristocrat who was precisely what Robert aspired not to be, gave me intense joy, but a joy of the mind rather than the feelings.]

(II, 96; II, 365)

---

36 See the Introduction, p. 1.

Marcel sees this in the very shape of Saint-Loup's skull—though he doesn't claim that it is that of the ancient Celts:

je me rendais compte combien l'ossature énergique de son visage triangulaire devait être la même que celle de ses ancêtres . . . Sous la peau fine, la construction hardie, l'architecture féodale apparaissaient. Sa tête faisait penser à ces tours d'antique donjon dont les créneaux inutilisés restent visibles, mais qu'on a aménagées intérieurement en bibliothèque.

[I could see to what extent the vigorous bone structure of his triangular face must have been modelled on that of his ancestors . . . Beneath the delicate skin the bold construction, the feudal architecture were apparent. His head reminded one of those old castle keeps on which the disused battlements are still to be seen, although inside they have been converted into libraries.]

(II, 176; II, 460)

In the end Saint-Loup's lineage claims him: he becomes a warrior like his ancestors, dies on the field of battle in the Great War, and in death his identity is reduced, literally, to the sign of his family name:

Débarrassée de ses livres, la tourelle féodale était redevenue militaire. Et ce Guermantes était mort plus lui-même, ou plutôt plus de sa race, en laquelle il se fondait, en laquelle il n'était plus qu'un Guermantes, comme ce fut symboliquement visible à son enterrement dans l'église Saint-Hilaire de Combray, toute tendue de tentures noires où se détachait en rouge, sous la couronne fermée, sans initiales de prénoms ni titres, le G du Guermantes que par la mort il était redevenu.

[Freed from the books which encumbered it, the feudal turret had become military once more. And this Guermantes had died more himself than ever before, or rather more a member of his race, into which he dissolved, in which he was nothing more than a Guermantes, as was symbolically visible at his burial in the church of Saint-Hilaire at Combray, completely hung for the occasion with black draperies upon which stood out in red, beneath the closed circle of the coronet, without initials or Christian names or titles, the G of the Guermantes that he had again in death become.]

(IV, 429; VI, 197)[37]

---

[37] *Vintage* has 'into which slowly he dissolved until he became nothing more than a Guermantes'. Proust borrowed the image of the converted medieval tower, and the funeral pall with the single letter, from the article he published in *Le Figaro*, 6 Sept. 1903, 'Le Salon de la princesse Edmond de Polignac' (*CSB* 464–9) where they refer to the late prince, who died (peacefully) in 1901.

We should not forget the element of pleasure which accompanies such observations. Though he does not say so here, we know it gives Marcel an intellectual and aesthetic thrill to see Saint-Loup summed up in this way; he has told us before of the 'vive joie' he felt whenever he discerned Saint-Loup's ancestral identity. This joy is like that which Mallarmé finds in unmasking the English disguise of an old French word; it is also the counterpart of the delight which Gourmont says men feel when they 'deform' their language. We owe *A la recherche* to this pleasure, which is both self-seeking and procreative; and it tells us what position the artist, this pleasure-seeker, necessarily occupies in relation to his society and his language. He cannot himself belong to an aristocracy like Saint-Loup; he cannot be mastered by a salon, a religion, by friendship, by love; he cannot be single-minded, or single-gendered; he cannot commit himself to any destiny except that of art. In turn, this art cannot rest upon a concept of 'purity' which paradoxically, in its return to origins, is destructive of originality. Only in what is mixed, impure, composite, can art find the resources it needs to create the world anew, as Vinteuil's transcendent septet rises from a chaos of illegible scribbles abandoned at his death and reconstructed through the devotion of his daughter and her lesbian lover, whose immorality broke his heart while he was alive and who used to spit on his picture as part of the ritual of their love-making. The artist who gives supreme expression to this masterpiece is 'Charlie', the violinist Morel, who has none of Saint-Loup's 'nobility' but a different kind of medieval authenticity: 'Il ressemblait à un vieux livre du Moyen Âge, plein d'erreurs, de traditions absurdes, d'obscénités, il était extraordinairement composite' [He resembled an old book of the Middle Ages, full of mistakes, of absurd traditions, of obscenities; he was extraordinarily composite] (III, 420; IV, 499). All the images which Marcel assembles in the great final pages of *Le Temps retrouvé* to describe the novel which he is about to begin and which Proust is about to finish, from the Gothic cathedral to Françoise's *bœuf à la mode*, are 'composite' in one sense or another; none lays claim to a 'noblesse authentique de race' which is the sign of death-in-life.[38]

---

[38] Françoise's dish is presented at the dinner for M. de Norpois (I, 437, 449–50; II, 18, 33–4). See Proust's letter to Céline Cottin of 12 July 1909, at the outset of his composition of *A la recherche*: 'Je vous envoie vifs compliments pour le merveilleux bœuf mode[.] Je voudrais réussir aussi bien que vous ce que je vais faire cette nuit, que mon style soit aussi brillant, aussi clair, aussi solide que votre gelée—que mes idées soient aussi savoureueses

Comte Robert de Montesquiou, the principal model for M. de Charlus—who had *noblesse authentique de race* if anyone had, who was a sterile artist, and whose baffled, wounded response to Proust's fame was both odious and pitiable—described him as 'le fruit du croisement des races chrétiennes et israélites, qui, entre tous, produit l'arriviste' [the fruit obtained by crossing the Christian and Jewish races, which more than any other produces the social climber]. And he intended no more than a thin compliment when he added: 'Cependant, tout comme le mot *snob* peut avoir une acception louable, il y a des arrivistes dignes de louange' [Even so, just as the word *snob* can have a praiseworthy sense, so there are social climbers worthy of praise].[39] Proust would certainly have agreed with the comment on snobbery; he had said it first himself. What he would have thought of hearing himself described as an 'arriviste digne de louange' I do not know. I like to think of it as a consummate example of English understatement.

que vos carottes et aussi nourissantes et fraîches que votre viande' [Hearty congratulations on the splendid *bœuf à la mode*[.] I should like to accomplish as successfully as you what I am going to undertake tonight, so that my style might be as brilliant, as clear, as solid as your jelly—that my ideas might be as savoury as your carrots and as nutritious and fresh as your meat] (*Corr.* IX, 139). In *Le Temps retrouvé* he emphasizes the mixed nature of the dish: 'ne ferais-je pas mon livre de la façon que Françoise faisait ce bœuf mode, apprecié par M. de Norpois, et dont tant de morceaux de viande ajoutés et choisis enrichissaient la gelée?' [should I not make my book in the same way that Françoise made that *bœuf à la mode* which M. de Norpois so admired, whose jelly was enriched by the addition of so many selected cuts of meat?] (IV, 612, my translation; *Vintage* (VI, 434) turns the syntax a different way).

[39] *Les Pas effacés*, III, 289.

APPENDIX

The Location of English Words and Phrases in *À la recherche du temps perdu*

Nouns are identified as masculine or feminine by '*m*' or '*f*'. The first volume and page reference is to the Pléiade edition, followed by reference to the Vintage translation in brackets. A superscript number after the Pléiade reference indicates that the word occurs more than once on that page. An asterisk after the Vintage reference indicates that the translation is wrong or uses a different English word or idiom (e.g. 'picture-book' or 'visitors' book' for 'album'). In one instance ('liftier', II, 178) there is no translation at all, because the word occurs in the brief chapter heading to *Sodome et Gomorrhe* II, ii which is not reproduced in *Vintage*.

album (*m.*) (see also 'carte-album') II, 68 (II, 332); II, 246 (II, 546); II, 386 (III, 93)*; II, 475 (III, 199); II, 837 (III, 635)*; III, 565 (V, 55)
albums II, 386 (III, 93)*
antisnobisme (= anti-snobbery) III, 434 (IV, 515)
baby (*m.*) II, 60 (II, 322)
babys (= babies) I, 587 (II, 199)
bar (*m.*) (see also 'wagon-bar') II, 12^2 (II, 264); II, 694 (III, 462); IV, 407 (VI, 170); IV, 424 (VI, 191); IV, 496^2 (VI, 281)
bars, les IV, 186 (V, 695); IV, 388 (VI, 147)
bifteck (*m.*) (= beefsteak) I, 68 (I, 81); I, 109 (I, 130)
blackboulage (*m.*) (= blackballing) III, 802 (V, 338)
blackboulé (= blackballed) III, 91 (II, 107); III, 786 (V, 319)
bluff (*m.*) III, 856 (V, 404); III, 864 (V, 413); III, 865^2 (V, 414); IV, 17 (V, 594)
boston (*m.*) (= dance) I, 573 (II, 182); II, 233 (II, 530); III, 39 (IV, 45)
boxe (*f.*) (= boxing) II, 200 (II, 490); IV, 350 (VI, 100); IV, 373 (VI, 129)
boxeurs (*m.*) III, 23 (IV, 25); III, 710 (V, 229)
break (*m.*) (= carriage) II, 240 (II, 539); III, 417 (IV, 495)
bridge (*m.*) (= structure) III, 328 (IV, 389)
bridge (*m.*) (= card game) III, 137 (IV, 161); IV, 303 (VI, 42)
bristol (*m.*) (= pasteboard) I, 303 (I, 371); I, 534 (II, 136)
British (*m.*) (= abbr. of British Museum) II, 500 (III, 229)
budget (*m.*) I, 275 (I, 336); II, 24 (II, 278); III, 27 (IV, 30); III, 372 (IV, 442)
buggy (*m.*) I, 113 (I, 135); I, 145 (I, 176)

cab (*m.*) (see also 'hansom cab')   I, 214 (I, 261); I, 365² (I, 447)

cake (*m.*)   I, 498 (II, 92)

carte-album (*m.*) (= small-format photograph)   I, 478 (II, 68)*; II, 189 (II, 466)*; III, 708 (V, 226)

chester (*m.*) (= Cheshire cheese)   II, 250 (II, 551); II, 257 (II, 559)

Chippendale, un meuble de   II, 845 (III, 643)

Christmas (*m.*)   I, 517⁵ (II, 115)

cliff (*m.*)   III, 283 (IV, 333)

clown (*m.*)   II, 605 (III, 355)

club (*m.*) (see also 'Jockey-Club')   I, 624 (II, 245); I, 625 (II, 246)*; II, 122 (II, 397)*; II, 406 (III, 116); II, 523 (III, 257); III, 803 (V, 339)

clubman (*m.*)   II, 139 (II, 417); II, 867 (III, 670)

clubmen   I, 18 (I, 19)*

clubs, les (= associations)   II, 865 (III, 668); III, 33 (IV, 37); III, 548 (V, 36)

clubs, les (= golf clubs)   II, 146 (II, 426); II, 185 (II, 472); II, 186 (II, 473); III, 884 (V, 436)

cocktails (*m.*)   IV, 185 (V, 694); IV, 360 (VI, 113)

cold cream (*m.*)   III, 254 (IV, 299)

Cook (= Thomas Cook agency)   II, 27 (II, 282)

crack (= reputation)   I, 527 (II, 127)

cup (*m.*) (= champagne cup)   III 395 (IV, 469); III, 398 (IV, 473)

cup of tea, a   I, 77 (I, 92)

dandy (*m.*)   II, 268 (II, 571); III, 343 (IV, 406); IV, 518 (VI, 310)

darling   I, 240 (I, 266)

dominions (*m.*)   IV, 368 (VI, 123)

doper (= verb to dope, to drug)   I, 552 (II, 158)

dropiez (verb 'droper', to drop socially)   I, 629 (I, 689)

éditorial (*m.*)(= leading article)   IV, 216-17⁵ (V, 731-3)

englische, un (= Englishman)   III, 546 (V, 32)

English, un (= Englishman)   IV, 164 (V, 669)

express (train)   IV, 523 (VI, 315)

fair play (*m.*)   IV, 368 (VI, 123)

fast (= loose-living)   I, 503 (II, 98)

films (*m.*)   IV, 313 (VI, 54)

fishing for compliments   I, 188; I, 208)

five o'clock (*m.*) (= abbr. of 'five o'clock tea')   II, 452 (III, 172)*; IV, 170 (V, 676)*

five o'clock tea (*m.*)   I, 584 (II, 196)

flirt (*m.*) (= flirtation, casual affair)   I, 187 (I, 228)*; I, 332 (I, 407); III, 558 (V, 48); IV, 135 (V, 634); IV, 286 (VI, 22)

flirt (= flirtatious)   II, 242² (II, 541)

flirts (pl. of noun)   I, 192 (I, 234); III, 748 (V, 275)*

football (*m.*)   IV, 386 (VI, 144)
footing (*m.*) (= walking for exercise)   I, 605 (II, 222)*; I, 627 (II, 249)*
ford (*m.*)   III, 281 (IV, 331)
frac (= evening wear, 'tails')   I, 318 (I, 389); II, 342 (III, 40); II, 353 (III, 53)*;
    II, 563 (III, 305); II, 713 (III, 485); III, 52 (IV, 61); III, 481 (IV, 574)
garden-party (*f.*)   II, 42 (II, 301); II, 275 (II, 581); III, 69 (IV, 80); III, 71² (IV,
    83); III, 76 (IV, 89); III, 162 (IV, 191); III, 194 (IV, 228)
garden-parties   II, 288 (II, 596); III, 99 (IV, 117); III, 100 (IV, 117); III, 151
    (IV, 177)
gentleman (*m.*)   I, 77 (I, 92); I, 214 (I, 260); I, 242, (I, 296); I, 548 (II, 152);
    IV, 501 (VI, 288)
gin (*m.*)   II, 185 (II, 472)
globe-trotteur (*m.*)   II, 522 (III, 255)
goddam (= oath, 'God damn')   III, 801 (V, 336)
golf (*m.*)   I, 610 (II, 228); II, 89 (II, 357); II, 146 (II, 426); II, 185 (II, 472); II,
    186 (II, 472-3); II, 189 (II, 477); II, 201 (II, 491)*; II, 228 (II, 524); II, 231
    (II, 527-8); II, 232 (II, 528); II, 233 (II, 529); II, 234, (II, 531); II, 238 (II,
    535); II, 239 (II, 537); II, 242 (II, 541); II, 248² (II, 547); II, 282² (II, 589);
    II, 650 (III, 409); II, 651 (III, 410); III, 102 (IV, 120); III, 568 (V, 60); III, 650
    (V, 157)*; III, 884 (V, 436); III, 910³ (V, 467)*; III, 911 (V, 468); IV, 184 (V,
    693); IV, 186 (V, 695)*; IV, 187³ (V, 696)*; IV, 199 (V, 711)
golfs (= golf courses)   II, 235 (II, 533)
golfeuse (*f.*) (= female golfer)   IV, 51 (V, 535)
good bye   I, 597, (II, 212)
good evening   I, 613 (II, 231)*
good morning   I, 626 (II, 248)
great event   III, 704 (V, 222)
grog (*m.*)   II, 696 (III, 464)
groom (*m.*) (groom, page-boy, bell-hop)   I, 411 (I, 503); I, 417 (I, 510); II, 66
    (II, 329); II, 125⁵ (II, 400); II, 302 (II, 614); III, 380² (IV, 450-1)
grooms, les   I, 317 (I, 389); II, 82 (II, 349)
hall (*m.*)   I, 59 (I, 69); II, 23 (II, 277); II, 24 (II, 278); II, 43 (II, 301); II, 62
    (II, 324); II, 66 (II, 329); II, 83² (II, 350); II, 89 (II, 357); II, 156 (II, 437); II, 304
    (II, 615); II, 484 (III, 210); II, 747 (III, 526); III, 171 (IV, 201); III, 376 (IV, 446);
    III, 382 (IV, 453); III, 404 (IV, 479); III, 423 (IV, 502); IV, 426³ (VI, 192-3)
hansom cab (*m.*)   I, 536 (II, 138)
happy few   II, 558 (III, 299)
hay-fever (*m.*)   III, 208 (IV, 245)
home (*m.*)   I, 193 (I, 234); I, 588 (II, 200); II, 24 (II, 278)
iceberg (*m.*)   IV, 412 (VI, 176)
I do not speak french   III, 35 (IV, 40)

interview (*f.*)   II, 516 (III, 249)
jockey (*m.*)(= rider)   II, 251 (II, 552); III, 377 (IV, 447)
Jockey (= abbrev. of Jockey-Club)   I, 321 (I, 393); I, 413 (I, 505); I, 423 (II, 1);
   I, 461² (II, 47); I, 586 (II, 198); II, 109 (II, 380); II, 131 (II, 407); II, 378
   (III, 83); II, 392 (III, 100); II, 532² (III, 267-8); II, 534² (III, 271); II, 700
   (III, 470); II, 705 (III, 475); II, 786 (III, 573); II, 871 (III, 674-5); III, 4 (IV, 2);
   III, 76 (IV, 89); III, 91 (IV, 107); III, 307 (IV, 363); III, 432² (IV, 514); III,
   548 (V, 35); III, 549⁴ (V, 36-7); III, 812 (V, 350); IV, 467 (VI, 237); IV, 537
   (VI, 335)
Jockey-Club   I, 15 (I, 16); II, 352 (III, 52); III, 704 (V, 222)
John Bull   I, 449 (II, 32)
jury (*m.*) (= examining board)   II, 265 (II, 568); III, 421 (IV, 500)
jurys   III, 261 (IV, 307)*; III, 726 (V, 245)*
knickerbockers (*m.*)   II, 24 (II, 278)
lady-like   III, 300 (IV, 354)
leader article (*m.*)   I, 571 (II, 180)
liberty (= Liberty fabric or design)   I, 417 (I, 510); II, 373 (III, 78)
lift (*m.*) (= lift attendant, lift-boy)   II, 25 (II, 280); II, 26² (II, 281)*; II, 42 (II,
   300)*; II, 82 (II, 349); II, 97 ['laïft'] (II, 367); II, 99³ [incl. one 'laïft'] (II, 369);
   II, 157⁴ (II, 438-9); II, 158² (II, 439); II, 159 (II, 441); II, 284 (II, 591); III,
   160 (IV, 188); III, 170 (IV, 200); II, 184² (IV, 217); III, 186² (IV, 219); III,
   187 (IV, 220); III, 189² (IV, 222); III, 190 (IV, 223); III, 193 (IV, 227); III,
   200 (IV, 236); III, 219³ (IV, 258); III, 220⁴ (IV, 259-60); III, 221² (IV, 260-1);
   III, 222 (IV, 261); III, 226 (IV, 267); III, 249² (IV, 293); III, 251 (IV, 295); III,
   413² (IV, 490); III, 414³ (IV, 491); III, 502 (IV, 600); III, 509³ (IV, 608); III,
   510 (IV, 609); IV, 117 (V, 613); IV, 260 (V, 786); IV, 261 (V, 786); IV, 266²
   (V, 793); IV, 325 (VI, 69)*
liftier (*m.*) (= lift attendant, lift-boy)   II, 126 (II, 401); III, 152 (IV, 179); III,
   178 (no trans.); III, 187³ (IV, 220-1); III, 188 (IV, 221); III, 193 (IV, 227), III,
   221 (IV, 260)*; III, 369 (IV, 438); III, 576 (V, 69); IV, 209 (V, 723); IV, 259
   (V, 785); IV, 260² (V, 786); IV, 265 (V, 792); IV, 325 (VI, 69); IV, 326⁶
   (VI, 70); IV, 327 (VI, 70); IV, 360 (VI, 112)
liftiers   III, 220 (IV, 259)
liftman (*m.*) (= lift attendant)   II, 74 (II, 339)
loopings (*m.*)   II, 694 (III, 462); IV, 227 (V, 744)
lord (*m.*)   II, 99 (II, 369); II, 488 (III, 215)
lords   II, 99 (II, 369)
lunch (*m.*)   I, 516 (II, 114); II, 806 (III, 597-8)
magazine (*m.*)   II, 746 (III, 524)
manager (*m.*) (= impresario)   III, 303 (IV, 358)
match (*m.*) (= sporting occasion)   III, 654² (V, 161); IV, 373 (VI, 129)

médiumnimique II, 489 (III, 216)*; III, 396 (IV, 469); III, 398² (IV, 472)*

meeting (*m.*)   I, 516 (II, 114)

meetings (= race meetings)   II, 252 (II, 552)

mess (*m.*) (= officers' mess)   III, 486 (IV, 580)

Miss (= governess)   II 243² (II, 542-3)*

Miss Foster   II, 698 (III, 467)

Miss Sacripant   II, 205 (II, 495); II, 215 (II, 508); II, 563 (III, 305)

modern style (*m.*) (= Art Nouveau)   I, 376 (I, 461)*; II, 116 (II, 389); II, 839 (III, 637); III, 747 (V, 273); IV, 310 (VI, 50)

Mr   I, 536 (II, 138); I, 537² (II, 139)

muffins (*m.*)   I, 242 (I, 295)

music-halls (*m.*)   II, 238 (II, 536)

my dear   IV, 528 (VI, 323)

my love   I, 293 (I, 359)

nurse (*f.*)   I, 499² (II, 93)

paddock (*m.*)   II, 251 (II, 552)

palace (*m.*) (= luxury hotel)   III, 170 (IV, 200); III, 462 (IV, 550)

palaces   II, 43 (II, 301); III, 161 (IV, 189)

patronizing   I, 526 (II, 125)

pianola (*m.*)   III, 874 (V, 424); III, 883 (V, 436); III, 884² (V, 436), III, 885 (V, 437); IV, 13 (V, 490)

plaid (*m.*) (= plaid, travelling rug)   I, 151 (I, 184); I, 152 (I, 185)

plaids   III, 689 (V, 204)

plus-value (*f.*) (= increment, surplus value)   III, 788 (V 321)

poker (*m.*)   I, 192 (I, 212); II, 41 (II, 299); II, 492 (III, 220); III, 791 (V, 325)

polo (*m.*) (= game)   II, 89 (II, 357); III, 102 (IV, 120); IV, 184 (V, 693)

polo (*m.*) (= hat)   II, 151 (II, 431); II, 152 (II, 432); II, 185² (II, 472); II, 186 (II, 473); II, 199 (II, 489); II, 225 (II, 521); III, 403 (IV, 478); III, 576 (V, 69)*; III, 650 (V, 157)*; IV, 122 (V, 619)

porte revolver (*f.*) (= revolving door)   II, 695 (III, 463)

private (*m.*) (= soldier)   IV, 368 (VI, 123)

pudding (*m.*)   I, 457 (II, 43); I, 517 (II, 115)

pushing (= in social sense)   I, 525 (II, 124)

puzzle (*m.*) (= jigsaw puzzle)   I, 542 (II, 146); III, 597 (V, 94); IV, 532 (VI, 328)

pyjama (*m.*)   II, 233 (II, 530); II, 331 (III, 28); III, 22² (IV, 24); III, 528 (V, 11); IV, 338 (VI, 85)

raid (*m.*)   IV, 337² (VI, 83); IV, 380² (VI, 137); IV, 423 (VI, 189)

raids   IV, 330 (VI, 75); IV, 356 (VI, 108)

record (*m.*) (= sporting record)   II, 233 (II, 530)

redingote (*f.*) (= frock coat, tail coat)   I, 524 (II, 124); I, 537 (II, 139); I, 539² (II, 141, 142*); I, 583 (II, 194); II, 128 (II, 403); II, 302 (II, 614); II, 452 (III,

171); II, 475 (III, 199)*; II, 487 (III, 214); II, 488 (III, 215); II, 491 (III, 218); II, 563 (III, 305); II, 638² (III, 394); II, 866 (III, 669)

revolver (*m*.) (= weapon)   I, 470 (II, 59); I, 537 (II, 139); III, 26 (IV, 28); III, 468 (IV, 558); III, 563 (V, 53); III, 702 (V, 219); III, 804 (V, 341)

revolving door (*m*.)   II, 695 (III, 463)

right man in the right place, the   I, 571 (II, 180)

rocking (= rocking-chair)   II, 39 (II, 296)

rocking-chairs (*m*.)   II, 190 (II, 478)

Rolls Royce (*f*.)   IV, 5 (V, 480); IV, 39 (V, 520)

Rolls (abbrev. of prec.)   IV, 38 (V, 520); IV, 39 (V, 520)

rose-fever (*f*.)   III, 208 (IV, 245)

Royalties (*m*.) (= royal personages)   I, 510 (II, 106); IV, 538 (VI, 335)

Sam, l'oncle (= Uncle Sam)   I, 449 (II, 32)

sandwiches, sandwichs (*m*.)   II, 250 (II, 551); II, 251 (II, 551); II, 257 (II, 559); II, 302 (II, 613); II, 531 (III, 266); III, 62 (IV, 73)

scalp (*m*.)   I, 453 (II, 37)

season (*f*.)   II, 768 (III, 551); IV, 538 (VI, 336)

select (see also 'ultra-select')   III, 296 (IV, 349)

self-government (*m*.)   IV, 157 (V, 661)

shake-hand (*m*.) (= handshake)   II, 272, (II, 577); III, 291 (IV, 344)

schampooings (*m*.) (= shampooings)   II, 425 (III, 140)

shocking   IV, 305 (VI, 44)

skating (*m*.) (= skating-rink)   II, 459 (III, 180)*; II, 461 (III, 183)

sketches (*m*.) (= theatrical pieces)   IV, 184 (V, 693)

skunks (*m*.) (= furs)   I, 236 (I, 289)

smart (= chic, fashionable)   I, 193 (I, 235); I, 199 (I, 242)

smoking, le (= dinner-jacket, evening dress   II, 23 (II, 277), II, 42 (II, 300); II, 163 (II, 446); II, 233 (II, 530); II, 238 (II, 536); II, 771 (III, 555); III, 21 (IV, 23); III, 262 (IV, 309); III, 263 (IV, 309); III, 273 (IV, 321); III, 291 (IV, 344); III, 422 (IV, 502); III, 481 (IV, 574); IV, 186² (V, 695); IV, 408³ (VI, 171)

smokings   II, 98 (II, 368); III, 291 (IV, 344)

snob (*m*. and *f*.)   I, 127 (I, 153); I, 257 (I, 314); I, 547 (II, 151); I, 590 (II, 204); I, 596 (II, 210); II, 100 (II, 370); II, 102 (II, 373); II, 103 (II, 374); II, 293 (II, 602); II, 483 (III, 210); II, 607 (III, 357); II, 739 (III, 517); II, 743² (III, 521), II, 810² (III, 602); II, 858 (III, 660); III, 25 (IV, 27); III, 147 (IV, 173); III, 459 (IV, 547); III, 487 (IV, 580); III, 771 (V, 300)*; IV, 571 (VI, 380)*; IV, 584² (VI, 398)

snob (= snobbish)   I, 246 (I, 301); II, 104 (II, 375); II, 541 (III, 278)*; II, 758 (III, 539)*; II, 794 (III, 582); III, 145 (IV, 171)*; III, 286 (IV, 337); III, 360 (IV, 427); III, 768 (V, 298); IV, 241 (V, 762)*; IV, 242 (V, 764)*; IV, 541 (VI, 340); IV, 572 (VI, 381)*

snob (= chic, smart-looking)   I, 239 (I, 292)

snober (= snub)   II, 735 (III, 512)

snobait (imperfect of 'snober')   III, 323 (IV, 383)

snobinettes (*f.*) (= 'snoblings', technically female but applied by Proust to both genders)   II, 452 (III, 172); III, 269 (IV, 316)

snobisme (*m.*) (= snobbery, snobbishness)   I, 67 (I, 78); I, 127³ (I, 153-4); I, 128 (I, 154); I, 199 (I, 242); I, 263 (I, 321); I, 424 (II, 2); I, 461 (II, 48)*; I, 504 (II, 99); II, 100 (II, 370); II, 103 (II, 374); II, 106 (II, 378); II, 140 (II, 418); II, 201 (II, 490); II, 354 (III, 55); II, 470 (III, 193); II, 508 (III, 240); II, 526 (III, 261)*; II, 697² (III, 465); II, 720 (III, 493); II, 749 (III, 529); II, 771 (III, 555)*; II, 794 (III, 582); II, 803 (III, 594); II, 810² (III, 602-3); III, 100 (IV, 117); III, 105 (IV, 123); III, 143 (IV, 168); III, 147 (IV, 173); III, 150 (IV, 177); III, 209 (IV, 246); III, 278 (IV, 327); III, 305 (IV, 360); III, 315 (373); III, 434 (IV, 515); III, 435 (IV, 516); III, 461 (IV, 549); III, 524 (V, 7); III, 542 (V, 28); IV, 167 (V, 672); IV, 168 (V, 674); IV, 178 (V, 686); IV, 246 (V, 768); IV, 378 (VI, 135); IV, 409 (VI, 172); IV, 439³ (VI, 209); IV, 537 (VI, 335); IV, 571 (VI, 380); IV, 606 (VI, 426)

snobismes   IV, 409 (VI, 172)

snobs (pl. of *adj.*)   I, 322 (I, 394); II, 481 (III, 207); III, 723 (V, 241); IV, 582 (VI, 396)

snobs (pl. of *noun*)   I, 127² (I, 154); I, 511 (II, 108); II, 102 (II, 373); II, 109 (II, 382); II, 338 (III, 36)*; II, 484 (III, 211); II, 743 (III, 521); II, 794 (III, 582); III, 800 (V, 335); IV, 399 (VI, 160)

snow-boots (*m.*)   II, 835 (III, 632)

speech (*m.*)   I, 253 (I, 310)

spleen (*m.*)   III, 411 (IV, 487)*

sport (*m.*)   II, 149 (II, 428)*; II, 287 (II, 594)*; IV, 183 (V, 691)*; IV, 277 (VI, 11)

sportif, sportive (*adj.*)   II, 525 (III, 259); III, 102 (IV, 20); IV, 184 (V, 692)*; IV, 277 (VI, 11)*; IV, 324 (VI, 68)²

sportifs, sportives   IV, 201 (V, 713); IV, 309 (VI, 49)

sports   I, 557 (II, 164)*; II, 146 (II, 426); II, 295 (II, 604)*; III, 613 (V, 112)*; III, 654 (V, 161)*; IV, 50 (V, 534); IV, 110 (V, 605)*; IV, 310 (VI, 50)*

sportsman (*m.*)   II, 92 (II, 360)

square (*m.*) (= public square with enclosed garden)   I, 437 (II, 19)*; II, 344 (III, 43)*

steamer (*m.*)   II, 156 (II, 437)

stéréoscope (*m.*)   I, 72 (I, 86); II, 107⁴ (II, 379); II, 658 (III, 418); II, 837 (III, 634)

stock (*m.*) (= collection)   III, 459 (IV, 546)

Stones of Venäice, les (Bloch's mistaken pronunciation of Stones of Venice)   II, 99 (II, 369)

stopper (verb) (= stop, in naut. sense of vessels 'speaking' each other)   III, 381 (IV, 453)

struggle for lifer (= adherent of social Darwinism)   III, 269 (IV, 316)

sweaters (*m.*)   I, 610 (II, 228)

tea gown (*f.*) [used as a plural: 'mes tea gown'] (= elegant dress for indoor wear) III, 571 (V, 63)

tennis (*m.*)   II, 23^2 (II, 277); II, 35 (II, 292); II, 189 (II, 477); II, 222 (II, 517); II, 235 (II, 533); III, 73 (IV, 86); III, 75^2 (IV, 88); III, 102 (IV, 120); III, 170^2 (IV, 200); III, 246 (IV, 290); III, 425 (IV, 504); III, 859 (V, 408)

tilbury (*m.*)   II, 436 (III, 153)

Times, le   II, 583 (III, 329)

to meet (printed on invitation)   I, 536 (II, 138)

toast (*m.*) (= speech)   I, 451 (II, 35); I, 454^2 (II, 39); I, 455 (II, 40)

toasts (pl. of above)   I, 622 (II, 242)

toasts (*m.*) (= grilled bread)   I, 242 (I, 295); I, 499^2 (II, 93)

tommies (*m.*) (= British soldiers)   IV, 368 (VI, 123)

tory (= reactionary, old-school)   III, 825 (V, 366)

tract (*m.*) (= pamphlet)   I, 551 (II, 156)

tram (*m.*) (= nickname of local train at Balbec)   II, 231 (II, 528); III, 160 (IV, 188); III, 180 (IV, 212); III, 190 (IV, 224)*; III, 249 (IV, 292)*; III, 250^2 (IV, 294)*; III, 256 (IV, 301)*; III, 268 (IV, 316)*; III, 277^2 (IV, 326)*; III, 411 (IV, 488)*; III, 838 (V, 382)*; III, 840 (V, 384)*; III, 915 (V, 473)*

tram (= tramway)   II, 739 (III, 516)

tramway (*m.*)   II, 21 (II, 275); II, 190 (II, 477); II, 369 (III, 73); II, 396 (III, 105); II, 438 (III, 155); II, 813 (III, 606); II, 837^2 (III, 634-5); III, 12^3 (IV, 11-12); III; 264 (IV, 311); III, 519 (V, 1); III, 535 (V, 20); III, 642 (V, 147); III, 643^3 (V, 148); IV, 264 (V, 790)

tramways   II, 19 (II, 273); II, 374 (III, 79); II, 375^2 (III, 79-80); III, 180 (IV, 212); III, 911 (V, 468)

trust (*m.*) (in phrase 'faire le trust' = 'monopolize')   II, 590 (III, 337)

tub (*m.*)   I, 605 (II, 222)

ultra-select   III, 163 (IV, 192)

victoria (*f.*) (= carriage) I, 231 (I, 282); I, 232 (I, 284); I, 235 (I, 287); I, 267 (I, 327); I, 340 (I, 416); I, 358 (I, 439); I, 411 (I, 503); I, 417 (I, 510); I, 526 (II, 126); I, 627 (II, 249); II, 131 (II, 407); II, 552 (III, 292)

wagon (*m.*) (= railway carriage, compartment; in phrase 'en wagon' = in the train; the word 'wagon' itself never appears in trans.)   I, 157 (I, 190); I, 348 (I, 426); I, 371 (I, 455); I, 375 (I, 459)*; II, 8 (II, 259); II, 12 (II, 264); II, 13 (II, 265); II, 14 (II, 267); II, 21 (II, 275); II, 40 (II, 298); II, 161 (II, 443); II, 225 (II, 520); II, 310 (III, 2); II, 459 (III, 180); II, 529 (III, 264); II, 636 (III, 292); III, 181^2 (IV, 212-13); III, 251 (IV, 295); III, 252 (IV, 296); III, 254

List of Works Cited

Bibliographical references to works which are only mentioned once will also be found in the notes.

WORKS BY PROUST

À la recherche du temps perdu

À la recherche du temps perdu, gen. ed. Jean-Yves Tadié, Paris: Gallimard (Bibliothèque de la Pléiade), 1987–9, comprising: vol. I: *Du côté de chez Swann* (Combray; Un amour de Swann; Nom de pays: le pays); *A l'ombre des jeunes filles en fleurs I* (Autour de Mme Swann); vol. II: *A l'ombre des jeunes filles en fleurs II* (Nom de pays: le pays); *Le Côté de Guermantes I*; *Le Côté de Guermantes II*; vol. III: *Sodome et Gomorrhe*; *La Prisonnière*; vol. IV: *Albertine disparue**; *Le Temps retrouvé*.
In Search of Lost Time, trans. C. K. Scott Moncrieff and Terence Kilmartin, rev. D. J. Enright, London: Vintage, 2002, comprising: vol. I: *Swann's Way*; vol. II: *Within a Budding Grove*; vol. III: *The Guermantes Way*; vol. IV: *Sodom and Gomorrah*; vol. V: *The Captive* and *The Fugitive*; vol. VI: *Time Regained*.

Other works

Original works

Contre Sainte-Beuve, précédé de *Pastiches et mélanges*, et suivi de *Essais et articles*, ed. Pierre Clarac and Yves Sandre, Paris: Gallimard (Bibliothèque de la Pléiade), 1971.
Correspondance, ed. Philip Kolb, 21 vols., Paris: Librairie Plon, 1970–93.
Écrits sur l'art, ed. Jérôme Picon, Paris: Flammarion, 1999.
Jean Santeuil, précédé de *Les Plaisirs et les jours*, ed. Pierre Clarac and Yves Sandre, Paris: Gallimard (Bibliothèque de la Pléiade), 1971.
Les Plaisirs et les jours, suivi de *L'Indifférent*, ed. Thierry Laguet, Paris: Gallimard, 1993.

Translations of Ruskin

La Bible d'Amiens, Paris: Mercure de France, 1947 (first published 1904).
Sésame et les Lys, ed. Antoine Compagnon, Brussels: Éditions Complexe, 1987 (first published 1906).

* For this title see Note on Texts and Translations.

Marcel Proust: On Reading Ruskin: Prefaces to La Bible d'Amiens and Sésame et les Lys, trans. and ed. Jean Autret, William Burford, and Phillip J. Wolfe, New Haven and London: Yale University Press, 1987.

BIOGRAPHY, CRITICISM, REFERENCE WORKS

ALBARET, CÉLESTE, *Monsieur Proust*, trans. Barbara Bray, London: Collins & Harvill, 1976 (1st pub. in French, Paris: Éditions Robert Laffont, 1973).

BEAUCHAMP, LOUIS DE, *Marcel Proust et le Jockey Club*, Paris: Éditions Émile-Paul, 1973.

BLOCH, OSCAR, and WALTHER VON WARTBURG, *Dictionnaire étymologique de la langue française*, Paris: Presses Universitaires de France, 10th edn., 1994.

BONNAFFÉ, ÉDOUARD, *Dictionnaire étymologique et historique des anglicismes*, Paris: Librairie Delagrave, 1920.

BOULENGER, JACQUES, *Un professeur de snobisme*, Abbeville: Les Amis d'Édouard (No. 7), 1912.

BOURGET, PAUL, 'Gladys Harvey', in *Pastels (dix portraits de femmes)*, Paris: Alphonse Lemerre, 1889, 3–59.

BOURGET, PAUL, *Œuvres Complètes*, Paris: Librairie Plon, 1900: *Cruelle Énigme* in *Romans*, vol. I (1st pub. 1885); *L'Esthéticisme anglais*, in *Critique*, vol. II (1st pub. 1895); *Lettres de Londres* in *Critique*, vol. II (1st pub. 1885); *Outre-Mer*, in *Critique*, vol. II (1st pub. 1895); *Physiologie de l'amour moderne*, in *Romans*, vol. II (1st pub. 1890); *Un cœur de femme*, in *Romans*, vol. III (1st pub. 1890).

BRETSCHNEIDER, ÉMILE V., *History of European Botanical Discoveries in China*, London: Sampson Low, Marston & Co., 1898, repr. with an introduction by Kerrie L. MacPherson, London: Ganesha Publishing, 2002.

BRUNET, ÉTIENNE, *Le Vocabulaire de Proust: étude quantitative*, 3 vols., Geneva and Paris: Slatkine-Champion, 1983.

BRUNOT, FERDINAND, 'La Langue française de 1815 à nos jours', in vol. VIII (*Dix-neuvième siècle (période contemporaine)* of *Histoire de la langue at de la littérature française des origines à 1900*, gen. ed. Louis Petit de Julleville, 8 vols., Paris: A. Colin, 1896.

CARASSUS, ÉMILIEN, *Le Snobisme et les lettres françaises de Paul Bourget à Marcel Proust 1884–1914*, Paris: Librairie Armand Colin, 1966.

CASHMORE, T. H. R., *The Orléans Family in Twickenham 1800–1932*, Twickenham Local Historical Society, 1982.

DAUZAT, ALBERT, *La Défense de la langue française*, Paris: Librairie Armand Colin, 1912.

DUPONCHELLE, VALERIE, 'Le questionnaire de Proust aux enchères', *Le Figaro*, 21 May 2003.

EELLS, EMILY, *Proust's Cup of Tea: Homoeroticism and Victorian culture*, Aldershot: Ashgate, 2002.

Fitz-James, duchesse de, 'L'Anglomanie française', *La Nouvelle Revue*, Sept. – Oct. 1897, 591–609.

Goodell, Margaret Moore, *Three Satirists of Snobbery: Thackeray, Meredith, Proust. With an Introductory Chapter on the History of the Word Snob in England, France and Germany*, Hamburg: Friederichsen, de Gruyter & Co., 1939.

Gourmont, Remy de, *Esthétique de la langue française*, Paris: Mercure de France, 1955 (repr. of rev. edn., 1905; 1st pub. 1899).

Harrap, *Harrap's Standard French and English Dictionary*, gen. ed. J. E. Mansion, Part One: French – English, rev. edn., London: George G. Harrap, 1948 (1st pub. 1934).

Hatzfeld, Adolphe, and Arsène Darmesteter, *Dictionnaire Général de la langue française*, Paris: Librairie Delagrave, 1924.

Hayes, Jarrrod, 'Proust in the Tearoom', *PMLA* 110, no. 5 (Oct. 1995), 992–1005.

Howarth, Patrick, *When the Riviera was Ours*, London: Century, 1988 (1st pub. 1977).

Le Robert, *Dictionnaire historique de la langue française*, gen. ed. Alain Rey, Paris: Le Robert, 1993.

McGarry, Pascale, 'Proust et Wilde——"Mr W. H." et "Miss Sacripant": étude de deux portraits imaginaires', *Études irlandaises*, ns 12/2 (Dec. 1987), 45–64.

Mackenzie, Fraser, *Les Relations de l'Angleterre et de la France d'après le vocabulaire*: vol. I, *Les Infiltrations de la langue et de l'esprit anglais*, Paris: Librairie E. Droz, 1939.

Mallarmé, Stéphane, *La Dernière Mode*, ed. S. A. Rhodes, New York: Institute of French Studies, 1933.

—— *Les Mots anglais. Petite philologie à l'usage des Classes et du Monde*, Paris: Truchy, 1877.

Michon, Jacques, *Mallarmé et Les Mots anglais*, Montreal: Les Presses de l'Université de Montréal, 1978.

Montesquiou, Robert de, *Les Pas effacés. Mémoires*, 3 vols., Paris: Émile-Paul, 1923.

Nelson, Michael, *Queen Victoria and the Discovery of the Riviera*, London: I. B. Tauris, 2001.

Orchidophile, L'. Journal des amateurs d'orchidées. Publié avec la collaboration de M. le Comte du Buysson par la maison V.-F. Lebeuf, d'Argenteuil. A. Godefroy-Lebeuf, gendre et successeur, 1880–92.

Painter, George D., *Marcel Proust: a Biography*, 2 vols., new edn., London: Penguin, 1989 (1st pub. 1959–65).

Pechenard, Christian, *Proust à Cabourg*, Paris: Quai Voltaire, 1992

Reinikka, Merle A., *A History of the Orchid*, Coral Gables, Fl.: University of Miami Press, 1972.

SWANN, HARVEY J., *French Terminologies in the Making*, New York: Columbia University Press, 1918.

TADIÉ, JEAN-YVES, *Marcel Proust*, trans. Euan Cameron, London: Viking, 2000 (1st pub. in French, Paris: Gallimard, 1996).

THACKERAY, W. M., *The Book of Snobs*, London: Richard Edward King, 1895 (1st pub. 1848).

—— *Le Livre des snobs*, trans. Georges Guiffrey, Paris: Librairie de L. Hachette, 1857.

VALLÉE, CLAUDE, 'Proust et l'Angleterre', *Bulletin Marcel Proust*, no. 7 (1957), 410–13.

VIENNET, JEAN-PONS-GUILLAUME, *Épître à Boileau sur les mots nouveaux*, 1855.

WEY, FRANCIS, *Remarques sur la langue française au dix-neuvième siècle, sur le style et la composition littéraire*, 2 vols., Paris: Firmin Didot, 1845.

ZELDIN, THEODORE, *A History of French Passions*, 2 vols., Oxford: Oxford University Press, 1993 (1st pub. 1977).

Index

I English words and phrases

This list is selective; it includes only those words and phrases used by Proust which I discuss (rather than simply cite), and some which are used by other writers. It also includes translated expressions such as 'couper'.

II Characters in *À la recherche du temps perdu*

Entries for 'Marcel' are confined to instances involving his personal experience in the novel, as opposed to his narratorial function. Historical figures are marked with an asterisk.

III General index